THE PILGRIM
Messiah

A Novel Drawn from the Gospel of Mark

DR. RICHARD C. CHEATHAM

ISBN: 1461132770
ISBN 13: 9781461132776

ACKNOWLEDGEMENTS

One of the first books I encountered when I began my career as a professional clergyman in 1961 was William Barkley's *The Mind of Jesus*. It was refreshing and liberating at the same time. This brilliant New Testament scholar depicted Jesus as a genuine flesh and blood person, whose development as a human being essentially followed the same path as most people I know. I resonated to his thoughts! He allowed me to think of Jesus as a man.

At seminary, Dr. Albert Sundberg, my all-time favorite professor, gave me permission to think and reason for myself, and taught me to do so with scholastic integrity. He also showed me how to draw living people from the pages of Scripture. I shall forever be indebted to him for his brilliant, yet humble honesty of thought, and his folksy insights into Scripture and life-in-general.

Dr. Clarence Jordan, translator of *The Cotton Patch Versions* of Scripture, was the Preacher of the Quarter while I was at seminary. His treatment of Jesus further verified my developing understanding of Jesus. I am grateful to him for his down-to-earth vision of Jesus of Nazareth.

I owe a debt of gratitude to countless hundreds of parishioners who were open enough to think beyond their childhood Sunday School days to consider and accept my evolving understanding of the Man of Galilee we hailed as the Christ: God's Anointed One.

In the actual writing of this tale I must acknowledge the support and guidance of my friend, Jim Karlak. Jim is a spiritual pilgrim who lives out his constantly maturing faith. His responses and suggestions helped immeasurably in refining the manuscript. His enthusiasm for the project kept me going.

There are others who have contributed to this project. I thank the Rev. Dr. David Church for his sharp eye and early suggestions. So many others, who read one or both of my earlier books, gave enthusiastic support and encouragement which spurred me along the way.

I must thank my daughter, Dr. Cynthia Beamer. Her photographic artistry produced a photo far more flattering than the one on my passport.

My best friend, lover and wife, Diane ultimately deserves credit for anything I do of value. She believes in me far more than I do. Additionally, her sharp editorial eye picks up the details my mind never notices and adds whatever polish the work contains.

PREFACE

This is a book I have been preparing to write for half a century. It is the story of Jesus of Nazareth, fleshed out to make him understandable and real. The Gospels present snapshots of Jesus: "Here he is at his baptism." "Here he is being thrust into the wilderness." "Here he is at Capernaum." "Look! This one shows him performing a healing." "See! Here he is at Gethsemane," At best, one has the feeling of watching a drama lit only by strobe lighting. The characters jump from place to place with little or no understanding of their reasons for doing as they do.

There is no true narrative that carries a story line – that depicts Jesus and his followers as three dimensional people, living out their lives in a rational manner. As a result, far too many Christians have only a snap shot understanding of this Man of Galilee called forth by God to be His Christ. Consequently their impression of Jesus tends to be the blending of vaguely recalled Sunday School stories, bits and pieces of Scripture, a few Hollywood-style movies, and the images created by the preachers they have heard over the years.

Our creeds proclaim "Jesus Christ: Fully divine yet fully human." Yet I find that as a matter of actual practice the human dimension of Jesus is downplayed or completely overlooked. My doctoral specialty was Christology, in which I observed the gradual understanding that Jesus' humanity was being discarded until he eventually was understood as an essentially divine being in a human body. This is diametrically opposed to the view presented in the oldest Gospel account: *Mark*. I believe it also was to the detriment of our Christian faith. If Jesus is the Alpha and Omega, the starter and finisher, of our faith – our example and redeemer – *he must possess the same humanity as we* or he is merely someone we can admire and even worship, but his life cannot be our model - one we could hope to emulate.

Somewhere – early in our history - worshippers began to substitute adoration for obedience, saying, "Well Jesus may have done that, but after all . . . he was God in the flesh . . . or the son of God," thereby fulfilling his plaintive query, "Why do you call me Lord, Lord, and not do what I tell you?" (Luke 6:46). Too many Christians view themselves as passive, helpless sinners being saved by divine intervention rather than as children of God, made in His image and being called to service in Christ's name. They lose sight of the fact that Jesus was empowering us and calling us to continue his work.

The writers of Scripture merely gave us their words: Their recollections and understandings of the One we call The Christ. They did not tell us what to do with those words, or how to interpret them. Traditions and techniques have developed over the centuries that help the serious reader sort through those words to discover the person to whom those words pointed. Having used the various forms of scholarship, I still hungered for more. Thus this narrative in which I have blended research with life experiences over fifty years of ministry and a lifetime of living. Admittedly I created the minute by minute, day to day accounts from my own imagination and experience. The experience covers five decades of dealing with individuals in moments of crisis, sharing intimate thoughts with countless friends and strangers who opened their hearts to me, and in observing numerous persons as they dealt with life's unexpected dramas. It constitutes five decades of trying to serve this Anointed One of God, to understand his claim on my life and the manner in which he would be my lord and master.

At the onset of my ministry I was blessed with encountering some thinkers who helped to shape the basic form of my journey. One was Paul Tillich whose approach to the Christian faith immediately resonated within me. It combined a depth of intelligence blended with compassionate, affirming relevance to the human situation. Rather than beating the struggling pilgrim with a sense of sin, Tillich proclaimed "You are Accepted – by God and by life in general." To me, this was a vital part of the essence of Good News.

Another, equally important theological thinker was William Barkley. His book, *The Mind of Jesus,* also resonated deep within me. Although I had used the terms, Son of God and Word made Flesh, some part of me always had understood the man of Galilee as essentially a man. Anything else did not make sense. Barkley dealt with Jesus as a fully human boy-then-man. He utilized his knowledge to share how Jesus may have "grown in wisdom and stature." He removed the sense of Jesus following some preplanned script, or arriving on earth fully developed in mind, with a clear vision of precisely how he was to fulfill his messianic mission.

At Garrett Theological Seminary, Dr. Albert Sundberg, the professor of New Testament studies, supported this view and demonstrated its value in making the Christ's story relevant to life. He gave everyone of his students the right to follow his or her own instinctive interpretation of Jesus, as long as that interpretation could be defended intellectually. In doing so, he demonstrated a great belief in the essence of the faith to be able to override the individual differences in experience and thought that so many allow to divide and confuse us.

I had already embraced the Gospel of Mark with a passion. Mark viewed Jesus as a spirit-filled person. It is the oldest, and to me the most reliable, of the gospel accounts. The second century Bishop of Hieropolis named Papias, had written that Mark had served as the recorder for Simon Peter, recording in so far as he could recall, the words and actions of Jesus Christ, but not in chronological order, because Peter had not used the material in that fashion. This is the only statement that authenticates the authorship of any of the Gospel accounts. It also creates a strong case for accepting Mark as the oldest of the accounts. Since both Matthew and Luke follow Mark when ever the material is the same it seems reasonable to accept that Matthew and Luke must have had a copy of Mark, *who created the chronology used,* before them.

Another reason for accepting Mark as the oldest and most reliable account is this: We know more about Simon Peter than any of the other apostles. That is because Mark was Peter's story – his remembrances. He told it as he recalled it and he was in it

I have entitled this tale, *The Pilgrim Messiah* because this is my understanding of who Jesus was in Mark's account. As I read and reread Mark's account I became aware that there were small passages that simply were overlooked by preachers and teachers. Yet, when I paused to ponder them and to fill in the blanks I found them quite meaningful. For me they became clues to realizing the steady progression of Jesus' awareness of his messianic mission. Perhaps I drew rather heavily from my own experience of Christian ministry. I had no doubt that I had received a powerful, mystical call to preach. I was so convinced that I talked my loving wife, Diane, into selling our home and moving from a comfortable salary to near-poverty in a small village parsonage. However, although convinced of my calling, I had only a vague understanding of what it meant to be a minister. In my conversations with other preachers and many teachers I found they shared that experience. Our development to a mature awareness of our callings required decades. I see Jesus as having "got it" much earlier. Yet, because my Jesus also is *fully human*, I see him as searching and developing throughout his life's story . . . until, finally, he heads for Jerusalem.

I use the name Joshua, a transliteration of his actual Jewish name, rather than Jesus, the transliteration of the Greek. By doing so I hope the reader will rediscover the story afresh, rather than packing along all of the old impressions that are attached to the name Jesus.

Even though Mark is the oldest of the Gospels we do not possess a copy dating from the first or second centuries. Consequently there have been additions made by pious, well-intentioned copyists. The most glaring, perhaps, is found in the opening statement: "The beginning of the Good News of Jesus Christ, the Son of God." Footnotes will state that some ancient authorities omit "Son of God." Actually, it is the oldest manuscripts that omit this addition. Additionally, the translation is incorrect and any Greek scholar knows that. The statement in Greek reads *uiou theou*, which literally translates as *"a son of a god."* In order for it to read *The Son of God* or *God's Son* it would require the definite article *ho* before each noun: *Ho uiou ho theou.* The literal translation then would be *"The son of the god."* Capital letters were not used. Rather, the definite article identified deity as *"The One God."*

The various gospel accounts present contradictory images of Christ, ranging from Mark's spirit-filled man to John's Divine *Logos* (Word) made flesh. Terms such as Son of God and God-in-the-flesh are mutually exclusive terms on the surface. Yet, every writer and every theologian has been simply trying to say that in the person of Jesus Christ they experience both the human and the divine

I generally used the *New Revised Standard Version* or the *New English Bible* for the non-footnoted New Testament sayings. In a few instances I made my own translations from the Greek texts when I thought it appropriate,

I tend to dismiss most miracles listed in Mark as later, pious additions. I believe the healings are authentic. They are too numerous to be denied and are in keeping with the nature of Christ's mission. The others, however, serve no worthy purpose. Those who believe the miracle stories do so because they already believe Jesus is the Christ. If marvelous acts were required as proof of divinity then clever magicians would rule the churches. The same people who embrace the miracle stories of Jesus are the ones who dismiss the miracle stories found in other religions . . . which proves my point: Miracles are accepted because people first believe Jesus is God's Christ. They actually prove nothing.

In retirement I reflected upon this extraordinary journey of Christian ministry I have been on for half a century. I realized I had been guided by some of the best theological minds in the Christian tradition. I have experienced and witnessed innumerable deaths and resurrections, falls and redemptions, alienations and reconciliations . . . all the while aware of the soft voice within and the silent presence surrounding me. I decided I have arrived at a point where I have a rather clear understanding of hope and renewal we call Good News. It seemed the proper time to write this story. So with fear and trembling I began to flesh out the Gospel of Mark, writing what I first called, *An Unauthorized Biography*, but quickly realized I was writing a different story. In the course of writing a single chapter I often found the tale taking a different track than that which I had had envisioned as I started it. In some respects this story took on a life of its own. These unexpected turns usually gave me some fresh insight or caused me to wrestle with difficult issues

I would rather have ignored.

In the final analysis this is not Jesus' story. It is *my* story of *my* Jesus that I offer. I invite you now to share that story.

Richard Cheatham, May 28, 2011

CHAPTER ONE

THE PARTING

He arose early, before sunlight, as was his custom. He moved quietly so as not to disturb his brothers. He felt about for the tunic he had hung on the wall. Once found, he determined which side was the front and slipped into it, picked up his sandals and tiptoed to the doorway. He went through the larger, gathering room, stepped outside, braced himself against the wall and carefully slid the sandals onto his feet. He stretched himself, lifting his muscular arms over his head and swinging them in slow, large arcs. Then he began walking down the narrow street of Nazareth toward the edge of the village. Had a stranger been watching him pass he would have looked admiringly at him. Joshua was a half a head taller than the average Jew of his day. His hair was long, but neatly trimmed. He had a short beard, also neatly trimmed. His eyes were dark and bright, glowing with intelligence, yet sparkling with good humor. His predominant cheek bones made him appear to be wearing a constant, slight smile. He stood erect, without a hint of a slouch. Even when strolling he walked purposefully in long strides.

It was time to leave. He knew that although he did not yet fully understand what he was to do or where he was to go. Still, he had learned to trust that quiet voice that spoke within him. Also, with everything that had happened, he realized – somewhere deep within himself – that Nazareth could no longer be his home. As much as he loved his family - as much as he loved so many people who lived here – this village in which he was raised was not his home. This morning's walk through the streets was not his usual morning walk. It was a stroll of reminiscences - and silent farewells to those he had known as friends and neighbors.

Joshua knew the names of all who still lay sleeping in the houses he passed: *There lives Isaac the tailor; his wife, Rebecca; and their children, Benjamin, Mary and little Abigail. Isaac had worked for nearly fifteen years to save enough money to purchase a home and be able to support a wife.* Joseph and his father had built that house for them, he thought with a touch of pride as he paused to survey the workmanship. *The stones are even and well placed, unlike some of those that were constructed by builders far less skilled than my father and my father's father.* Then his thoughts turned again to the occupants. *Isaac is a little over thirty now (just about my age)* he winced slightly at this thought. *Rebecca is about sixteen. She passes my workshop every day on her way to the village's one well.* On his left lived David the tradesman. *He spends too much time away from his family but that is the only way he knows how to make a living.* In his mind he pictured the scene repeated ritualistically every first day of the week. David hitches up his donkey to the cart while his family gathers outside to bid him farewell for the next five days. Each one steps forward as on cue to give a hug and a kiss. Then David will begin walking along side the cart to Aaron's place, pick out some promising carvings, load them on the cart and descend to the valley below. There he will barter with the farmers for their produce and finally begin his route of the villages to peddle the food and try to sell some of the carvings. He and Aaron had developed a relationship of trust over the years. David keeps one third of whatever he sells, and he gives the remainder to Aaron. Whatever he says is the correct amount, Aaron will accept without question. There is no arguing.

They are both good men. Honest men, but they are poor men, as well. Nazareth is a good city, filled with good people, he thought. *They may be good,* but they *certainly are not reaping the rewards of their goodness which the Scripture seems to promise. David began his collection of psalms with the assertion:*

> *"Happy is the man who does not take the wicked for a guide, nor walk the road that sinners tread, or take his seat among the scornful; the law of the Lord is his delight, the law his meditation night and day. He is like a tree planted beside a watercourse, which yields its fruit in season and its leaf never withers; in all that he does he prospers."* [1]

Again, Joshua smiled wryly to himself. *I wish life worked that easily. The writer of Job knew it did not. This was his point, but people preferred the simple way of thinking: Find a formula that makes you feel secure. Forget the realities. Just stay with your delusions. "Righteous living brings prosperity; sin brings only misery." Well the sins of the citizens of Nazareth were that some forbearer was not a first son. Farmland could not be continually divided among the sons or eventually no one would have enough to survive. No, only the first son could inherit the land. The other sons needed to find some other means of earning a living. Joseph's father had been a second son, so he learned to become a builder. The people in the valleys thought of him as a carpenter; they had trees for building homes, beds and chairs and many of the niceties of life. Those on the barren mountains had to content themselves with stone houses, mats for beds . . . and chairs were a luxury few in the hills even dreamed of possessing.*

This philosophy of righteous riches troubled him greatly. He had witnessed it all his life. The Pharisees had developed their little formulae to feel righteous and secure. They were essentially good people but they had fallen into the trap of accepting the conventional wisdom passed along from generation to generation without ever examining it to see if it actually worked. They attributed all

---

[1] Psalm 1:1-3

failures, all illness, and all mishaps on bad behavior . . . and like Job, they could distance themselves from the suffering of others by laying the blame on them for their misery . . . that is unless - or *until* - they found themselves in Job's position. Still, by continually distancing themselves from those who suffered they developed emotional calluses that made them unfeeling – uncaring of those they considered "others."   They also had perpetuated an image of God as a judgmental, punishing heavenly being who, Joshua believed, actually was quite the opposite.

Joshua had observed that those considered unacceptable or ritualistically unclean, by the more pious crowd often tended to be more caring, more compassionate, than those who proudly claimed to be obeying the law of Moses. He pondered this as he continued to wend his way past the homes on the narrow streets, mentally imaging each family dwelling therein. *I shall miss them*, he thought as he quietly bade goodbye to each. Eventually he came to the place where the street ended and the land also seemed to end. He seated himself on a grassy mound at the edge of the precipice, and gazed at the scene unfolding beneath him as the first glints of soft morning light began to reveal the deep valley below. *Armageddon: The valley of Jezreel that holds Megiddo,* Joshua mused to himself. Then his eyes moved to his left and he surveyed the huge tel composed of the remains of more than two dozen fortress cities, each erected on the ruins of the previous occupant. He recalled exploring the tel two decades earlier when he returned from his first pilgrimage to Jerusalem. From a distance the tel resembled just one more of the many hills that crop up from the valley. However as they neared it they could see the scars, still uncovered by time, that told of the history of that mound. The ruins of many once-mighty fortress cities lay piled atop of one another: *David, Solomon, Nebuchadnezzar, Cyrus . . . the many fools who believed that might made right and they could rule by the sword,* he mused wryly. He recalled Joseph asking rhetorically as they climbed and crawled their way through the ruins: "When will people realize that those who live by the sword eventually die by that sword." Then his father had pointed toward the lush, verdant valley where the farmers were working in the fields. "These great rulers reigned for a while . . . then they disappeared, while those gentle people continue to dwell here, passing their land from generation to generation." Joshua smiled as he recalled Joseph's words: *It is these gentle folks – the meek ones - who inherit the earth,* he thought. For a while he just sat quietly contemplating the irony.

For a long moment his eyes rested on the rich valley beneath him where the wheat and barley, almost ready for harvest, had painted the valley a rich green blended with gold. *Wheat grows well in the valley,* he thought. *It does not do well here in the poor soil of the hillsides, so we eat barley bread. Wheat is a luxury most of us cannot afford.* Although he could not see them with his eyes, his mind's eyes lingered on the areas where the succulent melons and cucumbers were growing, and the fig trees were laden with fruit. *The land of milk and honey,* he mused: *Livestock and honey plus fruit for jams.* He breathed a soft sigh as he reflected on the difference in the quality of life between the valley and the hills.

Finally, reluctantly, as though bidding farewell to a beloved friend, Joshua arose and began his walk homeward. The silent streets were dusty and even though he walked softly the stirred up dust began to alter the color of his tunic. *I shall miss all this . . . even the dust,* he thought with a touch of wry humor. *It has been my home – my life – all these years. Still, I am certain it is time for me to go.*

He stood for a moment, looking at the house that had been the only home he had known. It was larger than the others. *A bonus for being a builder,* he thought. He recalled how Joseph had decided the women needed a room of their own, so he and his sons had made two additions: one for the sister and one for the brothers. That had left the original room as a place for him and Mary. He began a smile that quickly faded as he recalled how the family life had been radically changed when Joseph had died so suddenly.

As he entered the house the entire family was up and about their individual and collective business. James, Joseph, Simon and Judas were loading their tools into their pouches as they prepared to leave for Sepphoris, the nearby Hellenistic city where much building was taking place. *It is these Hellenistic towns that have caused me to have to learn to speak a third language. I even learned to read a bit from the signs. Greek is a strange language. It reads backward. You start at the left and move to the right. So different . . . but then, those people are also so different.* He smiled to himself at the thought. *So different, but yet so very much like us in many ways.* Joshua's sisters were making breakfast or assisting Mary in preparing the food which they would carry. There was no need to pack water. Sepphoris was nearby and had a much greater water supply than the single well in Nazareth provided.

They ceased their activities as they saw him enter. He had prepared them for this moment, and when they saw his face they realized this was the day — the moment — when he would leave them . . . perhaps never to return. Elizabeth turned away and began weeping silently. James stepped forward and embraced him warmly. Mary stood silently gazing directly at her eldest son. She had always known this moment would come, but she dreaded it. Joshua was different from any of her other children. He was good with his hands — a capable builder. Yet, it was his mind, and something which ran deeper than the mind which set him apart from the rest. There had always been this inner restlessness which caused him to appear to her as though he was merely going through the motions of being content with his lot in life. She had fervently prayed that whatever was slowly moving him from the family was good and worthy. Deep within her, however, was a fear that perhaps it was not.

"We will miss you, brother," Said James. "You have been the head of this family since Joseph died. We sense that you are resolute in your decision, but we really do not want you to leave us. Still, you have prepared us well. Simon is good with planning structures. Judas is skilled with carving pieces to fit snuggly. Joseph has an eye for worthy materials, and I . . . well I know how to give orders," he added this with a laugh, which served to ease the mood of the moment. Joanna stepped forth and silently hugged her older brother. He had been a father to her for most of her life. Something within Joshua stirred and for a moment he almost reconsidered his choice. Then he released her, kissing her lightly on her forehead. At this, Elizabeth placed herself before him, gave him a brief, disapproving look, then quickly smiled into his eyes and nodded as if in agreement. She was the next eldest in the family and the two of them shared a special bond. They were one another's confidents, so she had a greater sense of the inner force that was drawing him away from the family. For a moment they gazed deeply into one another's eyes. Then she stepped forward, hugged him fervently and warmly kissed him. Abruptly she sighed, stepped back and nodded to her brothers. Each stepped forward, almost reluctantly, and gave a kiss on the cheek followed by a more-than-perfunctory hug. "We will miss you, but we understand," was the sentiment each whispered. After Judas, the youngest, had given his hug and spoken his words, each left the room. Joshua and Mary needed to be alone for their final moment together.

"With everything that has happened here, Mother, I know it is time for me to leave Nazareth."

"I understand, son." She paused, wiped away the beginning of a tear, then she added: "I really do not understand . . . but in my heart . . . I suppose I do." She wanted to say more. She wanted to cry out her fear for him and her sorrow in losing him. But she just smiled and took a step nearer to him. Joshua recognized this as a signal that she was going to offer him some advice. Throughout the years, whenever she had wanted to counsel him, Mary had stepped forward physically just prior to stepping forward mentally or emotionally. "Your cousin, John, is near Jericho. You may want to talk with him as you search to understand what the Lord has in mind for you."

"Thank you, Mother." Joshua replied, although he already had intended to do that. "I also thought that would be a good first step."

For a long time they merely stood looking at each other. Myriads of memories rushed through their minds like a kaleidoscopic torrent of images: His first visit to the Temple when he was twelve. Joshua had been amazed at the magnificence of the structure, but dismayed at the blood-letting of the animals. It was at that moment they both had realized that his life was not destined to be lived out in the tiny village of Nazareth. They recalled the miniature doll and tiny house he had made for Elizabeth from leftovers Joseph had discarded. He had secretly carved them for her seventh birthday . . . and Elizabeth had them still. There was the time Mary was aching with fever and – though Joshua was little more than a child, he had laid his water-dripping hands on her brow and the fever seemed to subside. They smiled as they mentally thumbed through the many, many afternoon when they would work side by side in the little garden behind the house. The soil was poor and the water was scarce; still the seeds grew into plants capable of augmenting the family's meager diet. Then there were the many times he offered to make the long walk to the valley because the local merchant did not have some ingredient Mary needed for dinner. . . . and there was the night when Joseph suddenly became ill and died in his sleep. Mary had been Joshua's rock . . . and he had been hers as together they consoled the children and Joshua struggled to become the man of the family while still only sixteen. Oh, yes, Mary would miss him terribly. Of that she was certain.

Each moved toward the other, slowly, hesitantly, as though not really wanting to touch because the touch would become a final embrace and then they would be parted.

"Thank you, Mother. Thank you for believing in me over all these years. I love you dearly. I owe you much."

Mary smiled, and looked directly into his eyes: "You owe me nothing, son. It is I who has been blessed by the many years you have lived within these walls. You forsook taking a wife and raising your own family . . . and made us your family, instead." She paused, and then added: "You know your way here, son, and you know you are always welcome . . . always wanted." She added this with hesitation as though fearing it might sound like a plea for him to remain.

"I know that, Mother. I have always depended on your love." With that, Joshua leaned forward, kissed her lovingly, turned and departed.

CHAPTER TWO

THE JOURNEY BEGINS

Joshua followed the route of the Jordan River as he headed south toward Jericho. As the land ascended it began to resemble the hills of Galilee rather than the valley. The vegetation grew thin and the road became barren and dusty. If one followed the walking path along the river, however, the land remained rich and there were always some berries or roots one could munch on to take the edge off of any approaching hunger. There also was water, of course. Along the Jordan water was always at hand to quench his thirst. The first night Joshua camped with some travelers from Galilee who were making their way to Jerusalem. They all had carts filled with caged pigeons. Joshua recognized the routine. These men raised or captured pigeons; ate the ones with poor markings and took the flawless ones to sell at the Temple. Since he had some dried chicken and beans he was invited to share in the community stew. He also had some bread and a skin flask filled with red wine. After dining, as they sat waiting for the sun to disappear before retiring for the evening, they engaged in the chit chat strangers employ to fill the time. The Galileans came from the north end of the sea, so Joshua asked them if they knew his cousins James or John, fishermen who worked out of Capernaum. [*1]

[*1] The women recorded as witnessing Jesus' death and burial are the source of this information: Matthew 27:56 identifies them as "Mary Magdalene, and Mary the mother of James and Joseph, and the mother of the sons of Zebedee." Mark 15:40 identifies them as Mary Magdalene, Mary the mother of James the younger and of Joses, and Salome Luke fails to identify them by name.

"Met them, but don't really know them," was the response of one of the younger men.

"They have solid boats and equipment, and some good men working for them. James is strong and a natural leader." He smiled, shaking his head. "The younger one, John I think, looked more like he was cut out to be a scholar or poet or someone who worked with his head and not his hands."

"That's them!" Joshua responded, slapping his leg. "John should have been born five or six hundred years ago in Athens. He would have relished that." Joshua immediately sensed that none of the group had any idea what he was talking about, so he quietly withdrew, found a suitable sleeping place under some fruit trees, and closed his eyes.

He awoke before dawn, decided he would make better time alone, so he reached up and took a few figs from the tree that had served as his shelter, and quietly continued his solitary journey

---

John 19:25 identifies the women as "his mother, his (Jesus') mother's sister, Mary the wife of Clopas, and Mary Magdalene.'

John's addition of Mary the mother of Jesus is irrelevant to this issue. We may erase Mary Magdalene from the list because she is clearly identified and does not fit into the question.

This leaves Mary the mother of James and Joseph, Mary the mother of James the younger and of Joses, and Mary the wife of Clopas. I propose that these represent differing attributes of the same woman. Each bears the same name (Mary). Joses may well be another version of Joseph.

The remaining woman is Salome, who is identified as the sister of Jesus' mother Mary, and also as the woman identified as the mother of the sons of Zebedee (James and John). If we assume that these varied identities are of one person who – like the last Mary – also was identified in differing ways, then we have this: Salome who is the sister of Jesus' mother and the mother of the sons of Zebedee (James and John). This makes her Jesus' aunt in which case James and John would be cousins to Jesus.

southward. No matter how many people were gathered around him – no matter how much he might enjoy their company – Joshua had always felt a bit alone. He enjoyed the banter, the innocent gossip, the laughter and the good humor that tended to pervade the atmosphere wherever he went. Still, there was this deeper sense that all this surface jollity only masked whatever concerns, fears and pains that lay just beneath the surface of almost everyone. *Because we want others to think well of ourselves we shy away from sharing our struggles, our fears, sorrows and uncertainties. So we either brag about our successes or simply talk about nothing important, preferring to fail alone rather than suggest we are anything less that perfect. Life is good. Yes! But life also is difficult, and this rarely is acknowledged.*

We all are hypocrites to some extent, I suppose: Actors wearing happy masks in order to sneak through life with a good reputation and sense of our own worth.

The river side road to Jericho was well-traveled, by Jews, Samaritans and the Hellenists. It afforded shelter from the heat and an always handy supply of water. The road from Jericho into Jerusalem was another matter, however. Joshua remembered it well from the many pilgrimages he and his family had made over the years. The road curved, but the Jordan River continued running in a straight line to the Dead Sea where it became so thick with minerals that one could float on it for hours and never get his face wet. That last stretch of road into Jerusalem was without water – without the shade of trees which dotted the Jordan until it flowed so low that nothing would grow in the heat and ultimate barrenness of the land. The land also began to move more steadily upward, making the walk more of a steady climb. "Let us go up to Jerusalem," made more sense after one had made that assent.

Joshua recalled the first time he had journeyed that road to Jerusalem. He had just turned twelve and Joseph had announced that it was time for him to join him and Mary to make the Passover pilgrimage. The journey had been long and tiring, but when he saw the Temple reflecting the sun's early morning light his heart had leapt with excitement and he practically ran the final half mile to the city gates. The Temple shone like the sun itself, and seemed even more magnificent than any words could describe. Joseph had settled the business of where the family would stay even before they had entered the city. One of the men traveling with them had recommended that they set up their temporary quarters in a lovely garden just outside the city walls: Gethsemane, "Olive Press" was nestled in a grove of olive trees facing the town of Bethany. It was quiet and relatively unknown by all but the residents. A perfect place for pilgrims! Some of the men and women remained and began to set up the group camp site. Joseph had taken Joshua's hand, nodded to Mary and the three began the final climb to Jerusalem.

Within the city gates he had seen far more people moving through the narrow streets and milling about the market places than he had even imagined could live within a single city. The family had worked their way through the crowded streets until they stood at the entrance to the Temple. There they had encountered a line of fellow pilgrims, patiently waiting as the line inched its way forward. Most of them had young lambs in their arms. Joseph had placed Joshua and Mary in the line, insuring that those behind understood that he would return as soon as he had completed his business. He was gone for nearly an hour, during which time the line moved through the outer court of the Gentiles. Mary had explained that the non-Jews were allowed into this area, but not beyond. Each court moved up one step in the established cleanliness code. The next court was where the women could gather. Mary had told him not to worry, that Joseph was sure to return before they left that court. The next one was the men's court. Joshua was twelve now, so was welcome there. The court beyond that was reserved for the priests. "Is that the inner court, Mother?" Joshua had asked. Mary had paused for a moment; then she answered in a tone of hushed reverence: "No, my son. The inner court is the Holy of Holies. That is the Sanctuary of God, himself, where he resides. Only the high Priest, on the Day of Atonement may enter it to offer a sacrifice on behalf of all the people." Joshua had pondered that as the line slowly moved through the court of the women. It had seemed odd to him that God would want to be separated from his people.

Finally Joseph had arrived with a young, rather small lamb bearing a bronze band on its leg. As if in answer to the quizzical expression on his son's face he explained that only spotless sacrifices could be accepted and offered on behalf of the family. He had learned from experience that it was easier and safer to purchase the lamb from an approved merchant than to stand in another line for hours hoping the lamb, purchased from home at a much cheaper price would pass the priests' inspection. Joshua had not embarrassed Joseph by asking why the lamb was so small. He understood the family finances. Many was the night when he awoke to hear his father and mother quietly discussing which bills to pay and whom to ask for more time because business was slow.

Mary had left them as they entered the men's court. She would busy herself with some sewing she had brought along, or perhaps she would encounter someone with whom she could just chat and catch up on what was happening in Jerusalem.

When they reached the entrance to the Temple a priest stepped forward, inspected the tag, nodded to an aide, who lifted the lamb, slit its throat and began draining the blood into a silver basin as the frightened and dying lamb bleated mournfully. Joshua recalled how he had been shocked – sickened actually – at the sudden brutality. He had watched in horrified fascination as the basin was passed along from priest to priest and finally thrown on the altar. He was close enough to the entrance to smell the stench. It reminded him of the butcher's back room. Joseph had merely acknowledged the priest's return of the now-dead lamb, placed the carcass over his shoulder, taken Joshua's hand, and turned to find Mary in the women's court. As they walked he had muttered something about "Next time, I will have someone else do this for us."

The next day, the women began preparing the Passover Meal. Joshua had realized that the other two families traveling with them would act as a family and celebrate the Feast of the Unleavened Bread together. He then understood why James and the others had gone to stay with Isaac the merchant. They would be part of his family for the Passover meal. The men went into the city to do a bit of shopping for tools of their trade and to listen to the sages in the Sanhedrin who held their sessions in the open during this time.

Joshua had marveled and relished in the variety of food being offered in the markets and the vast array of merchandise he had seen in the booths. The aromas that had wafted their way to his nostrils from some of the open air stoves were absolutely delicious. His virginal olfactory senses knew nothing of such spices as thyme, sage, garlic or oregano. Mary's cooking was plain: A little salt, perhaps some pepper and whatever herbal plants might grow in the area. Eating was something one did – something one had to do to survive. He had never thought of it as delightful or even interesting. Silently, he had hoped that whoever was cooking their lamb had access to some of those wonderful spices.

As the youngest member of the assembled family Joshua had begun the ritual by asking "Why is this night different from any other night?" Then the story of Israel's miraculous exodus from Egypt was retold, as the meal was consumed in proper order. Joshua smiled to himself as he remembered that the biggest thrill for him that evening had not been celebrating the Festival of the Pascal Lamb in (or almost in) Jerusalem, but that the lamb had the wonderfully distinct odor of garlic.

There had been many families traveling together from Nazareth. By common consent they had subdivided themselves into families for the festival but they had committed themselves to journeying together as a group. It was safer that way. They also had agreed that they would remain in Jerusalem for two days after the Passover. Their children were being cared for, and there was no urgent business demanding their return. The women would spend their time shopping extravagantly – but purchasing sparingly – at the many vendor displays that filled the city at this time. The men would seat themselves near the Sanhedrin's open air forum. Both groups would be able to return as self-appointed experts on the fashions, luxuries and profundities of their magnificent capital city. It would be a brief but beneficial holiday for all.

Joshua smiled to himself as he remembered that the men soon became bored by the lengthy discussions and most of them drifted off to do their own shopping. Joseph had remained, primarily so that Joshua could listen to those learned men. He had long been aware that his son possessed an unusually keen intellect and he wished to foster it as much as possible. He had taken him to one of the rabbis in the village when Joshua was only five years old, and had asked him to teach his son to read. It had been obvious that the rabbi did not want to be bothered. However, he had called upon Joseph more than once to repair some portion of the synagogue or his own house. So reluctantly he had agreed to "give him the growing season in the fields to see if anything will take root."

Joshua had not known that portion of the story. It was later, when he was about fifteen that he had overheard his father bragging to some friends, that at the end of the growing season the rabbi had said, "I would like to keep him long enough to see the great harvest he will surely produce. The boy not only reads but he understands and remembers. I have never seen anyone who can recite the Scriptures as he does – and often after only one reading!" As Joshua recalled this he felt a surge of warmth within. *Joseph was a very special, very loving father. He gave so much of himself for each of his children.*

As the crowd around the Sanhedrin diminished, young Joshua found the opportunity to move closer. He was particularly impressed by a young man named Nicodemus, who seemed to be open to new ideas and was more in tune with the needs of the community. He had gathered his courage and spoke out to him:

"Nicodemus, sir. I have a question."

The young man had turned to him and saw he was the speaker. He had paused for just a moment to recover from the surprise of seeing one so young speak out so clearly.

"Yes, my young enquirer. What is your question?" he had said politely.

"Did not David say to the Lord: 'For you have no delight in sacrifice? Were I to give a burnt offering you would not be pleased. The sacrifice acceptable to God is a broken spirit. A broken and contrite heart, O Lord, you will not despise.'"

At this, Nicodemus had taken a step back warily as he considered his response. He sensed the young speaker was setting a trap for him. *This young lad is clever,* he thought. *The quote is from the 51st Psalm - word for word, as I recall. His question was straight forward, but I know he is setting me up. Still, I have to play his game – if only to see what he is up to.* Nicodemus took two steps toward Joshua to engage him directly. He smiled and replied, "Yes, he did, young man. Is that your question or only a preface?"

Joshua had smiled at this. Nicodemus was quick – quicker than the village rabbis in Nazareth. "Yes, this is the question:

Why then do the priests spend their time making sacrifices at the altar, rather than calling the people to repent and become more humble before one another as well as before God? The Prophet Amos had said that God did not want our sacrifices, but wanted justice to roll down like the waters and righteousness to be like an ever-flowing stream." He had paused, took a step toward Nicodemus, looked boldly into his eyes and then put forth the underlying question: "How can there be justice when we close the inner portions of the Temple to women and Gentiles?"

There had been a gasp from the crowd and many of the members of the Sanhedrin when he uttered those words. Nicodemus had raised his hand to calm the crowd. Then he stood silent with his head bowed for what had seemed to be an unusually long time – long enough for many to become uneasy. Some wondered if Nicodemus was confounded and unable to formulate a response. Others speculated that he was merely going to dismiss the young upstart as too immature to understand their customs.

Finally, Nicodemus raised his head, fixed his gaze directly at Joshua, and stepped forward to address him directly. At this point the two stood barely two feet apart from one another. Then he spoke: "Perhaps, young man, we still are in the process of learning what righteousness truly is. That is one of the reasons this group we call *Sanhedrin* meets. Moses gave us the Law, but we have yet to understand all the implications and gradations of that Law. Our current understanding tells us that Gentiles are people of worth and are welcome. However they are ritualistically unclean and do not belong in the inner part of the Temple. The women, of course belong in the Temple, but they are not equal to men in their minds or their bodies, so their place is just outside of where the men are permitted. The priests were specially chosen by God and therefore may occupy that part of the Temple next to where God himself resides."

Joshua had decided not to challenge him further. Nicodemus had acknowledged that there was still much to learn about the will of God. He had stated their present position, but had admitted ignorance. That was enough . . . for the moment. Still, he had determined to return and question them further on their policy of what was clean and what was unclean; and who was included and who was excluded. God had spoken through Isaiah, saying ""I will give you as a light to the nations that my salvation may reach to the ends of the earth." That meant everyone should have access to the inner Temple.

Suddenly Joshua was drawn from his reverie. The roof tops of Jericho loomed ahead. The time had passed so quickly as he relived that long-ago childhood adventure. He smiled at the recollection. It was then that he had first realized his mission in life was not merely to build things. It was more significant than that, but he had still to learn what it was. Now, he believed, he was on the path to discover just what his life's mission was meant to be. He hoped cousin John could help in some way.

CHAPTER THREE

THE DISCOVERY

John was nowhere to be found within the city limits of Jericho. "You'll find him somewhere out there," was the response Joshua got from anyone he asked. Each person just pointed out into the wilderness, waved their arms back and forth, shrugged and walked away.

Joshua was beginning to become discouraged. The wilderness was vast and unmarked. There was no way he could begin to search for his cousin there. Then – just as he was about to admit defeat – one person responded with, "Follow me. I am going out there, myself. I have been told by friends that I need to hear his message."

Relieved, Joshua followed his self-appointed guide. He realized that most of the people he had asked earlier had been pointing in the wrong direction. John was not in that stretch of wilderness that ran west of Jericho. Rather, he was camped east of town, in the small portion that sat just on the other side of the Jordan. Joshua breathed a sigh of relief as he understood where he would be spending the night. Water was just a short walk away. Food would not be that difficult to find. He knew he was on a mission. Yes, but . . . still . . . there was no need to suffer needlessly.

As they approached the area where John was staying, Joshua was surprised to see a veritable village camped in small groupings.

"There must be hundreds here." He whispered to his guide.

"I was told there was a crowd. Perhaps many of Jericho's finest know nothing of John. But his name is being spread throughout Judea. People are coming from everywhere to hear his message."

Joshua was not surprised by this. John always had a way of attracting a crowd. His clearest memories of John were when they both were in their early and mid twenties. John lived in Jerusalem. As the son of a priest he lived *quite well* in Jerusalem. Joshua had always enjoyed the time they spent together. John possessed a good mind, so they were able to discuss, and even debate, issues of Torah. He remembered that John still had his boyish good looks, and many young girls giggled and smiled as they walked by them on the streets. He also recalled that John appeared soft . . . even somewhat pudgy at the time. He wondered how he had ever found his way to this new life, and what it may have done to change him. With this thought, he quickened his pace.

As they passed small groups, Joshua heard pieces their conversations:

"John is right. Moses came to free us from bondage, but the Law he gave us has created a new bondage."

"He got me when he said we may be righteous by the Law, but we are not necessarily good people." Murmurs of agreement followed that one.

"How can one truly repent? "Old ways of thinking and acting do not die easily."

The conversations all had much more vitality than the intellectual discussions of the Sanhedrin, or the rather perfunctory discussions of the weekly kiddush. Joshua was becoming increasingly enthused about this reunion with his cousin.

The guide stopped and pointed at a man sitting quietly by the dying ashes of a small fire.

"There is your cousin. Perhaps I will see you tomorrow." Then he turned and departed into the gathering darkness.

Joshua's eyes followed the direction of the of his guide's arm. When he spied the figure indicated he almost gasped in surprise. *Is that really John? I would not have recognized him. Even his eyes seem to have changed. Gone are the fine clothes from Jerusalem. Gone is that lingering baby fat – and youthful appearance. I wonder what else has changed.*

As he drew nearer, John looked up. His sober face broke into a grin. "Joshua!" He rose quickly, but stood in his place until Joshua was within arms length. Then he stepped forward and embraced him with such zest that Joshua's feet were lifted off the ground. Joshua returned his hug with equal vitality. Then they both took a step backward and said in unison, "You have changed!"

"But you more than I," said Joshua. At this, they laughed and sat where they were.

For a long moment they sat quietly, each reliving shared memories that spanned the years:

The times they sat in the Temple courtyard watching the money changers working their scam. Only coins without images were acceptable as Temple offerings, so the merchants had scraped together a few foreign coins and then sold them at a huge markup to the worshippers. When they ran low, one of them would go to the back of the Temple where a priest would sell the coins back to them . . . for a small fee, of course. Then the process would repeat itself time and time again. The boys had tried to guess how much profit was made by whom off of each coin.

They had watched the sellers of pigeons and lambs hire a priest to approve their wares for Temple sacrifice. The priest would give an approval tag and then receive a small token of appreciation from the merchants. They had noticed that when the purity of some of the lambs and pigeons seemed to be disputed more coins were handed the priests for those approval tags. They had laughed over these things, but later they decided it was not at all laughable.

They had enjoyed watching pilgrims shopping in the narrow streets. The merchants could sense those who were seasoned travelers and those who were new to the process. For the new ones, the opening prices were always much higher. The experienced shoppers knew the values and were not deceived into believing they had made a good bargain by getting something at half price.

They remembered the girls – the pretty girls who smiled at them as they strolled past, trying their best to appear casual and manly.

Then there was the food. John's parents had both died and he had learned to cook quite well, using the assortment of spices and herbs to whip up delicacies for the palate.

"We had some good times, did we not, cousin?" John's eyes beamed as he spoke. Those days were forever gone, and only the memories would remain to gladden and comfort them in whatever future remained.

"That we did, John. Those days are behind us, though. Now tell me what happened to you to move you to this place in your life?"

John breathed a long sigh. When he spoke it seemed to be more to himself than to Joshua.

"We are living in a special era. It has been a thousand years since the time of David, Yahweh's first Anointed One. Many believe the Lord is going to give us a new anointed one – a new messiah – someone who will free us from the bondage of the Romans and again give us the great kingdom which David built."

"Do you believe that, John?"

"I can give you a 'yes' and a 'no' to that one, Joshua." I believe Yahweh is acting in a special way right now. I believe he is attempting to redeem Judea, but not necessarily from the Romans." He paused as though to ponder what to say next. "Perhaps he wishes to redeem us from ourselves – our sins or failures. Someone is always going to rule over us. What difference does it make, really, if it is Caesar or Herod? We have to serve somebody. At present we have them both, and neither is a prize. If we take an honest view of our history we see that Solomon was no prize either. He taxed us to death to indulge himself in women and luxuries. Sure, he built the Temple. We all know that and we cherish that – though we also ignore the fact that it contained many graven images. He spent eleven years building it. It was a major project for him. He also *spent thirteen years* building his own palace. We tend to forget that. Solomon paid for both by taxing us to death. It was he who set up the rebellion under his son, Rehoboam. If it had not been for his spendthrift ways, Jeroboam never would have been able to muster a successful rebellion."

"So where are you going with this, John?"

At this, John smiled guiltily. "Sorry. I got carried away. The 'yes' is that perhaps – just perhaps – Yahweh plans to reestablish David's kingdom. No one knows the mind of the Lord. The 'no' is that I doubt it. My understanding of Yahweh is that he is not so much interested in physical kingdoms as in a spiritual kingdom where all people may dwell in peace and harmony together. David's kingdom required constant battles to defend it. We are promised a time when there will be no more war. Only a spiritual kingdom that embraces all people can accomplish that." He paused, and looked around as if noticing his setting for the first time. "Let me get back to why I am here."

"Life has a far greater meaning than these few years we shall dwell on this land. The futility of Temple worship kept pounding into my head – my heart. I watched so many earnest pilgrims spend money that should have been used to feed their families or given to the poor. How did we ever get our minds so turned around that we think of God as some being who needs to be flattered and appeased? I lived well from it I admit that. Zechariah truly believed in what he was doing. He was a decent man – a simple man. He never questioned; he only obeyed the traditions and leaders." John shook his head and smiled ruefully. "Many were the times I wish I could have been like him. Life would have been much simpler." He seemed to mull this thought for a while. "It would have been pleasant to merely follow in his footsteps, marry a good woman, raise some children . . . and be content with serving in the Temple."

Here John paused for a considerable time, seemingly oblivious to Joshua's presence.

"That is not who I am – nor who you are, Joshua." John said, fixing his eyes steadily upon his cousin. "That is why I am here – and that is why *you* are here, as well." He leaned back, indicating he was finished, and it now was Joshua's time to speak.

"You're further along in this than I, John. I also sense that life has much more meaning than most men seem to realize. So many seem to be living by Ecclesiastes' advice that man 'should eat drink, and enjoy himself.'" [1] Their values are messed up. They use people and love things. They mindlessly obey the letter of the Law but appear not to understand the underlying spirit of that Law. They often are good by virtue of not being bad, but they seem uncaring of others. So many of the good people appear to be wearing masks – like actors. They hide behind smiles and solemn looks of piety. I see more honesty in the faces of those we were taught to think of as outcasts. Perhaps because they realize they have nothing left to hide. "

Joshua let these thoughts sit for a while. "I feel I should be doing something about these things. I just am not certain what it is." He smiled. "Maybe that's why I'm here speaking with you now. Do you have any suggestions?"

---

[1] Ecclesiastes 8:15

John leaned back and drew into himself for what seemed to Joshua like an eternity. "That's your decision, cousin. I have thought of you many times since I donned these camel hair garments. I have prayed for you, as well. As I reflect upon it now I believe I have always known that you and I were singled out to be servants of Yahweh, proclaiming His true message with our lives. That, my dear cousin, is why we were put together to share common experiences and to talk about them and to understand them. Yahweh has a plan for you. I am certain of that. I sense that your role is to be far greater than mine. It is as though I am only a forerunner of what you are to become. Spend the night here with me. Let us both pray about it. Then tomorrow – as I preach to the crowds – you listen for The Lord to speak to you."

Joshua nodded solemnly. Each lay back, closed his eyes in silent prayer . . . until sleep itself assured the eyes would remain shut for the night.

CHAPTER FOUR

THE AWAKENING

The long trek from Nazareth to Jericho had taken more from Joshua than he realized. Normally an early riser, he awoke to find much activity going on in the encampment. Some had already had their morning meal. Others were obviously long past the moment of shaking the remains of slumber from their heads. Self-consciously — almost sheepishly — Joshua had turned to discover that John was nowhere in sight. He rose quickly, smoothed his tunic. *For all the good that does*, he thought. He dipped into his dwindling cache of food, found a couple of figs and an olive, and began to munch on them as he gathered his thoughts and headed toward the river. If John was "The Baptizer" as people claimed, he certainly was going to be near the water.

If he had not deduced where John was, he had only to follow the crowd that was almost rushing toward the Jordan. There were some low lying hills so all could get a clear view of John, but they wanted to be certain that they could hear his every word. It was his message — not his strange appearance — that had drawn them to this remote area. Joshua ambled along with them. He intended to take John's advice and listen for the Word of the Lord while the others were listening for the Word of John.

"Repent! Change the way you have understood this world. The Lord's real kingdom is upon you. You have only to see it — to understand it as it is. Then you can enter into it. I cannot tell you how. I cannot tell you when. However, I can tell you with certainty that Yahweh will act boldly and decisively and you had better be ready when he does." At this, some Pharisees and Sadducees came wandering in. They began pushing themselves to the front of the crowd as though it was their right to be up front.

John stopped his proclamation, looked directly at the intruders, and shouted to them: "You brood of vipers. Who warned you to flee the wrath that is coming?"

The intruders stopped dead in their tracks. No one had ever spoken to them in that manner. Their impulse was to shout some insult in reply. One of them curled his lip in the beginning of a sneer. Just as quickly, however, the sneer became a smile as the face's owner realized the situation. This crowd belonged to John. It might be dangerous to confront him. He shrugged his shoulders and waved his hand as he apologized for the disturbance. "We just wanted to hear your message like all these others, he replied. He nodded to his companions and they sat where they were.

John paused for a moment, and then he continued. Joshua had been roused from his meditation by the ruckus. He observed the careful reactions of the Pharisees and Sadducees, the obvious power that John possessed which overflowed to everyone there. He turned his attention again to the Sadducee who had spoken. Now that he was seated and part of the crowd, the trace of a sneer appeared on his face as he looked about at the crowd. Joshua could read his thoughts. *He sees John as a threat - a danger to the established order, and he will warn both Herod and Pilate that they need to be rid of him.* A shiver ran through him as he realized this. Then he returned to within himself as John continued with his message.

Tell me, O Lord, what you would have me do. Show me the path you have chosen for me, and I will follow it . . . even if it means my death. Joshua was startled when he heard himself saying those words. He had thought in terms of living his life for the Lord. The idea of dying for Yahweh had not occurred to him. However he had just observed this Sadducee's fear and hatred of John and he realized that what he was to do would hold more danger than he had considered. With a new understanding and a stronger resolution he began to repeat this new-found phrase: *Wherever you lead; whatever you ask; I will be faithful. Make my way clear, is all I ask.* Time and time again he repeated this phrase until it became a mantra, drawing him deeper and deeper within himself. At this point, John had called the people to a new baptism. Joshua stood and slowly moved with the crowd that walked to the river almost in solemn procession. As each stepped to the water's edge he doffed his tunic. Waded into the middle, and began dipping himself and rubbing himself as if to rub off the old and allow that which was fresh to emerge. When there was room for Joshua to wade in and immerse himself, he also slipped out of his tunic and waded into the very center where the water was the deepest. The Jordan waters had their source in the snows of Mt. Hermon that towered above the landscape of the Assyrians. The sun had little time to warm the river before it arrived at Jericho. "Yet, Joshua did not begin to notice the chill. His thoughts were so totally focused on the mantra: *Wherever you lead; whatever you ask; I will be faithful. Make my way clear, is all I ask.*

He took a deep breath then dipped himself, intending to remain beneath the waters until he felt that some change had at least begun to take place within him.

Wherever you lead; whatever you ask; I will be faithful. Make my way clear, is all I ask.

Wherever you lead; whatever you ask; I will be faithful. Make my way clear, is all I ask.

Wherever you lead; whatever you ask; I will be faithful. Make my way clear, is all I ask.

In the waters he sensed warmth spreading though his body. Satisfied that some answer was awaiting him, he emerged into the sunlight and lifted his eyes to the sky as he took a welcomed breath. Suddenly there appeared to him a wondrous cloud – golden, shining as the sun – gently lowering itself to engulf him as a dove settling over its brood.

"You are my son, my beloved in whom I am well pleased." Joshua heard those words as clearly as he had heard the words of John - or Joseph – or any other person. The voice was different, however. It was powerful and gentle, soothing yet commanding, as if this declaration contained orders to be followed.

Joshua looked about him to see if others had heard this voice or seen this extraordinary cloud – *SPIRIT! That's what it was! – This spirit descending.*

Every person was going about his own business, oblivious to what was happening with or within those about him. The Pharisees and Sadducees remained seated where they had been confronted. Some were watching as if horrified by what they saw. Others were observing more closely. None acted as though they had witnessed anything out of the ordinary.

Joshua stood silent In the middle of the stream. Finally his gaze fell upon John, who was watching him intently. For a moment Joshua thought he saw what appeared to be a hint of a smile. Then John nodded at him and turned away to attend to those who were seeking his attention.

As he started to make his way to the shore, Joshua felt a thrusting at his back. He turned to see who this pushy fellow was and was momentarily taken back to discover that no one was there: No one at all. Yet the pressure remained. It abated long enough for him to regain his tunic, and then it began incessantly, insistently, to shove him toward the vast expanse of wilderness that lay west of Jericho. There was no opportunity to gather more food or even to fill his leather flask.

Joshua was being driven into the wilderness by this spirit. *1 Why, he did not know, but he was certain of this: He was going and he was going because Yahweh wanted him there.

Judea did not have desert. They had *wilderness*: rugged, arid land, devoid of life. The hills were precipitous, rising dramatically . . . or falling dramatically, steeply. When a person stood on the edge of one of the many hills he had the uneasy feeling of staring down into an endless pit. One careless step would become the last step taken. It was into this desolate land that the spirit was guiding him, thrusting him . . . deeper and deeper into a barren nothingness.

Finally the unseen but strongly felt force quit – abruptly – without a sign – without a sound. Joshua simply felt himself to be alone.

For a long time he merely stood in the spot where the spirit ceased to push at him. He stood, waiting to see if something else would occur to give him some clue as to why he was there.

After a while he decided to sit down. There was no need to look around. No one – no thing was anywhere near. He was certain of that.

So he sat . . . and he waited.

Nothing.

No sound.

No movement.

Nothing.

He was there . . . alone. And it was his task to figure out why, and what he was to do.

Night fell. He grew sleepy. So he slept.

Morning came quickly, reserving its slow dawn for other places, other occasions. One moment it was dark. The next moment the sun nearly blinded him with its direct rays beating down upon him.

He looked about for a place where he might escape the sun, but there was no shade to be seen.

He felt thirst . . . but there was no water.

He felt hunger . . . but there was no food.

Only silence: Absolute silence.

All day he waited. All day there was only silence: Silence and heat.

From time to time he roused himself to walk about the little space where he had settled. He stared out into the wilderness where there was nothing but barren waste. The hot air distorted even that view and caused the distant landscape to seem to become faded in and out of focus.

Eventually night would fall. There never were clouds to reflect the shades of light spreading orange and pink hues across the evening sky. In the arid air of the wilderness there was only the gradual shift from light to darkness Although he had napped on and off during the day, his body welcomed the respite from the heat, so he always embraced the darkness and slept . . . soundly.

His slumber was inevitably broken by the sudden burst of sunlight falling across his face.

What am I doing here? He mused. *Did I suffer some delusion while listening to John? Could that really have been the Lord's voice claming me as his son? Hold on there, Joshua, my friend. Maybe you're just suffering delusions of grandeur. If so, you're going to feel pretty foolish trying to explain to John why you disappeared without a word.*

At this he smiled. Now *you're talking to yourself. If my brothers could see me now they really would wonder if I was a little bit mad . . . or even slightly possessed.* With this thought, he grimaced. He had overheard James and Simon discussing him one day when he unexpectedly returned early from picking up supplies. Simon had just said something about his being beside himself when he walked through the doorway. Both had stopped what they were doing and looked guilty. Joshua had said nothing at the time. He knew he had been acting strangely by their standards. There was no need to defend himself. Still, it had stung him a bit to learn that his state of mind was the subject of family gossip.

The thirst began to occupy his thoughts. His mind raced back to the cool waters of the Jordan. He relived the moment of plunging himself beneath the surface and feeling the chill surge through his body. Though he had been almost oblivious to it at the time, there was enough memory of the moment to conjure up a feeling of pleasure and relief. *Cool water! We take it so for granted by the Jordan. Nothing good in life should be taken for granted.*

The hunger, too, was gnawing at him. He wished now that he had saved some of those figs and olives, instead of just gulping them down to fill his belly. The thought caused him to look around. Had there been any grass in the area he would have pulled it to chew on . . . There was none, however. He had known that. The quick look was merely a reaction to the incessant pangs of hunger.

To break the monotony, Joshua decided to roam the area, making sure to keep within a reasonable distance of where the spirit had led him. He walked to the edge of the high hill that had become his station, and he gazed down into the abyss below: Barren rock and baked-dry dirt that would grow nothing – nothing at all. The sun reflected off of the hard surfaces, creating an illusion of sparkling jewels. It was all worthless, however.

Then – slowly – yet clearly – Joshua realized that he was on the edge of a precipice that fell at least three hundred feet into the valley. Yet, he had no sensation of fear or concern. He remembered how he had responded the few times he stood at the edge of the hill in Nazareth and had stared into the valley of Jezreel. Queasy would be a mild way of expressing the sensation. He recalled feeling a tingling sensation that started in his legs, then ran upward until he became aware of some inner reaction that had caused him to quickly take a step backward.

This time, however, he felt no tingling – no sense of ill-ease. He was quite comfortable standing on the edge of this potentially lethal ledge. It was as though he was merely surveying his property, like some wealthy landowner gazing at his estate.

> *Though I walk through – or stand at the edge of – the shadow of the valley of death I shall fear no evil - - -for You are with me . . . !*

Something *had* happened to him in the Jordan. He was sure of that now. He needed to search inside himself a bit further. Perhaps the spirit had not abandoned him here in the wilderness. Perhaps that spirit which had descended upon him in the Jordan actually had *entered him and still was within him.*

He gazed straight downward for a moment, turned, walked back to the place where he first felt abandoned, sat down, closed his eyes, and began to recite again his new mantra:

> *Wherever you lead; whatever you ask; I will be faithful.*
> *Make my way clear, is all I ask.*
> *Wherever you lead; whatever you ask; I will be faithful.*
> *Make my way clear, is all I ask.*
> *Wherever you lead; whatever you ask; I will be faithful.*
> *Make my way clear, is all I ask.*

Lost within the inner recesses of his soul, he had been unaware of the darkness that settled onto the land. Later, when he reflected upon this moment, he could not discern where his meditation ended and sleep began. From that moment on, however, the thirst and the hunger . . . though real . . . no longer dominated his thoughts.

I am Yahweh's Son. The Lord actually had called to me and claimed me as his own!

Why? I have yet to discover.

Wherever you lead; whatever you ask; I will be faithful. Make my way clear, is all I ask.

CHAPTER FIVE

THE TESTING [1]

Joshua had lost all track of time. The first few days he had made a point of marking each sunrise. Now, however, he realized that time held no meaning. He was where he was for The Lord's purpose. He was on Yahweh's Time – not man's. What was to happen would happen – when it would happen and not before.

> *They who wait upon the Lord shall renew their strength.*
> *They shall mount up with wings as eagles.*
> *They shall run and not be weary.*
> *They shall walk and not faint.* [2]

Joshua reached for the Scriptures embedded in his mind, and began to feast upon the word of The Lord embedded therein. *Feeding the soul is more vital than feeding this mere body. Whatever my father has planned for – whenever He decides is the time to tell me . . . I can wait upon the Lord.*

With this thought, Joshua lay down, folded his hands behind his head . . . and allowed himself to drift deep within himself, to the place where he knew his father dwelt.

---

[1] The Greek word used for Test is the same used for Tempt *(perizomai)*. In the Book of Job, Satan was the Tester – not the Tempter. Over time, because of two major factors:

1. The introduction of dualism by the Persians.
2. To be tempted meant to be tested, the public thinking converted Satan from a Tester for God into one who tempted people away from God.

[2] Isaiah 40:31

In spite of this new attitude, Joshua was acutely aware that his body, now depleted of liquid and nourishment, was affecting his mind in some way. He seemed to hear voices – distant – but clear. He also saw images that he knew could not have substance to them.

Perhaps this is why I am here, without food . . . without water. I am being prepared for an encounter that is outside the ordinary. I shall have to see what my eyes cannot see and hear what my ears cannot hear.

He continued to wait in silence. An occasional image fluttered by, but was ignored and quickly faded. Joshua had moved inward beyond the need for a mantra – beyond the need for images.

Be still and know that I am God.

He sensed an understanding that no longer required words, nor symbols of any sort, to be absorbed into his being.

Quietness . . . Knowing beyond mere knowing about . . .

Eventually, gradually from the darkness within there came a rustling, much like the tiny whirlwinds one sees on a hot summer's day. Joshua watched it with a casual detachment as it appeared to gather in force and size. It slowly began to find a form, shadowy and vague, but a form nevertheless. Suddenly the whirling stopped and a dark, sinister figure emerged as if he either had stepped from the shadow or had been that shadow. Unafraid, Joshua waited for what would happen next. The figure strode around the hilltop, peering outward and downward. Then he turned and with a smile that was more foreboding than friendly, he whispered in a rasping voice:

"If you are the son of God command this stone to become bread. You can feed yourself and worry no more about what you are to do. Or you can feed the multitudes who struggle daily for bread. Think of it! No more hunger for anyone . . . that is . . . if you really are God's son and if you *really* have His power."

I know who you are now: Satan! The one who tested Job to see if he was worthy of God's admiration.(1) Feeding the hungry is worthy, but I have already determined that physical food is not as vital to our ultimate well-being as spiritual nurture.

"It is written that man shall not live by bread alone."

At this Satan gazed directly into Joshua's eyes and smiled – a smile more hideous than mirthful. He nodded slowly, as if sizing up his opponent. He retraced his steps around the edge of the hill, stopped, then turned and once again directed his gaze on Joshua.

"Come with me," he said as more of a command than an invitation (When Joshua reflected upon this later he recalled that it felt so real he could not – then or later – say whether this was a vision or a genuine transportation of his being). He was suddenly aloft, floating high above the earth. There, beneath him were spread all the great kingdoms he had heard of: Rome! Egypt! India! . . . and many he did not begin to recognize.

This time his voice was seductive and appealing: "All these can be yours. To you I will give all authority and their glory; for it has been delivered to me and I can give to whom I will." He paused to allow Joshua to survey the scene. "Just worship me and all this is yours."

Joshua considered the offer and its possibilities. If he were ruler he could create a massive kingdom on earth where justice and equality would reign. There would be no favorites receiving special benefits. He could eliminate hunger. He could open the prisons and let those who had been oppressed by unfair laws go free.

He could actually create God's Kingdom here on earth!

The catch, however, is that I would have to worship – to serve – this . . . creature.

"It is written, 'You shall worship the Lord and him only shall you serve.'"

Satan stood erect, scowling at him. For a full minute their eyes were engaged, neither backing down: Neither blinking.

"Satan reached out and grasped his hand. Joshua once again felt his feet leave the ground. Jericho passed underneath and he was suddenly in Jerusalem – hovering above the Temple.

The taunting, raspy voice returned. He pointed toward the pinnacle: "If you are the son of God throw yourself down from here. For it is written:

He will give his angels charge of you, and on their hands they will bear you up, lest you strike your foot against a stone.'"

The idea was absurd! He wasn't some kind of carnival performer. "Look at me! I can fly!" He had sensed a new power within himself, but that power was not to be used for personal exultation. His mission was not to point toward himself, but to point toward God.

He shouted out: "It is said, 'You shall not tempt the Lord your God!'"

With that, he abruptly found himself back on the hilltop in the Jericho wilderness. Satan was gone . . . if he ever actually had been there.

He lay gathering himself for a long time. This . . . experience had been profound. It seemed more real than anything he had undergone in his entire life. Yet, in that moment he was not at all certain that he had ever moved from the spot where he now found himself. "He glanced about to see whether there were any footprints – any traces of Satan ever having been there. *This Satan does not need to be physically present to play with your mind. All these thoughts represented far more than the mere images that appeared to me in that . . . encounter? . . . vision?*

It was then that Joshua understood the full implication of these temptations . . . these testings: Stones into bread. Ruler of kingdoms. Master magician. These represented roles he could play if he so chose. Charitable caregiver of the needy . . . or possibly self-indulgent, self-absorbed caregiver of self. Political ruler, using one's gifts to gain power and glory for himself. Miracle worker who could draw crowds by his tricks and gain as much power and wealth as anyone could ever want.

I do possess a new power. I am certain of that. I have not tried it yet, but I feel it surging inside, just waiting to erupt. I actuality am now choosing – have already chosen to some extent – the messianic role I shall play:

Not a mere helper of the helpless. That may be worthy, and it will be a part of what I do. However it is not to be primarily who I am to be: A feeder of the hungry – a healer of the sick. I shall do these things. I know that. But I am called to do much more than tend to physical needs.

Not a political ruler. He smiled wryly. *So much for being a new David! Kings and governors rule by force and coercion. This kingdom – that's it! Kingdom! This Kingdom which I am called to proclaim already exists, but it must be entered into voluntarily. I shall proclaim this Kingdom and invite anyone – everyone – to enter in . . . but I shall not compel them.*

Not a wonder worker, drawing people by spectacular performances. We have enough magicians roaming the countryside. Creation is a miracle. Life is a miracle. God does not need to prove himself by having me do tricks.

He paused here, as if at a loss. *I obviously have decided what I am not to be, but that is as far as I, or anyone, could go with Satan. We all can say no to him. We never can say yes . . .* Joshua paused with this thought . . . then he lifted his head skyward, extended his arms as if calling to be lifted up, and cried out in a plaintive voice that echoed across the wilderness: "What then, my father, am I to be?

CHAPTER SIX

THE SERVANT MESSIAH

As he settled himself back into the tiny area that had become his home in the wilderness, Joshua's mind began to scroll through the books of the Prophets. *The Prophets were the spokesmen for Yahweh. They seemed to possess special insight into his will – his plan for us. Perhaps they have something to say to me.*

*Amos made it clear that Yahweh is not one who desires that we spend our time praising and thanking him. Nor does he appreciate our offering sacrifices either for forgiveness or for favors: desired or received. [*1] Amos viewed God as a judge. I see him as a loving father – not only mine, but everyone's. Yet I totally agree with him as to God's will. Joseph never was one to want us to waste time or money thanking him or buying him gifts. What he wanted was for us to behave – to treat one another kindly and fairly.* (Joshua grinned at this thought: *That was never easy in a family with six brothers and sisters*). *Whatever I am to do- to become – it must involve a call to righteousness, which means not only doing right but setting right those things that are wrong. People need to seek this true righteousness with an insatiable hunger and a thirst that cannot be quenched until it is attained everywhere. Then, and then only, will Yahweh's Kingdom be as real on this earth as it is in heaven.*

Joshua rested with this thought, allowing it to flow over him and seep into his soul. His imagination envisioned a gigantic banquet hall overflowing with food, drink and laughter. Pharisees lay close to Publicans, who lay by paupers and prostitutes. Lepers were embraced by Scribes and even the Sadducees were laughing

---

[*1] Amos 5:21-24,

and sharing jokes with Gentiles. Hovering above them in an almost invisible, indistinct cloud-like shape was Yahweh, smiling and embracing the entire scene as a loving father drawing his children into his bosom.

In his mind he then scrolled down to Isaiah – a strange writing. It seemed to Joshua that it had been written by two different men at two different times. One part concerns itself with the struggles between Judah and Israel in the time when Israel was sent into exile by Assyria. The other speaks of the return of the exiles from Babylon into Judah. Both, however, saw the hand of Yahweh guiding the movement of history. Who he – or they – might have been was unimportant. It was their message that mattered.

"Behold my servant, whom I uphold, my chosen in whom my soul delights. I have put my spirit upon him. He will bring forth justice to the nations. He will not cry or lift his voice, or make it heard in the street. A bruised reed he will not break, and a dimly burning wick he will not quench. He will faithfully bring forth justice. He will not fail or be discouraged until he has established justice in the earth, and the coastlands wait for his law." [*2]

"How beautiful upon the mountains are the feet of him who brings good tidings, who publishes peace and who brings good tidings of good, who says to Zion, 'Your God reigns.'" [*3]

"It is too light a thing that you should be my servant to raise up the tribes of Jacob and to restore the preserved of Israel. I will give you as a light to the nations that my salvation may reach to the ends of the earth." (49:6). *That is what Yahweh had promised Israel would become.*

That was enough for the moment. He felt his mind had been guided to those passages, and something within him had resonated as the words moved through his mind. Now it was time to

---

[*2] Isaiah 42:1-4,
[*3] Isaiah 52:7,

let those words intermingle with whatever thoughts lay beneath the surface.

He lay back, stretched out and started to close his eyes in meditation. Then – abruptly – he arose. *No! This is something I must work with.* He looked about, as though searching for some item he could grasp to twist about, perhaps, as he would begin to mentally wrestle with the thoughts that now were thrashing about within him.

There was nothing. Not a stick. Not a twig. A few stones, but they offered no help.

He went to the edge of the hill and peered again into the valley below. *Perhaps I need to leave this high place and descend into the valley - - -with my body as well as my mind.*

With that thought Joshua began a slow but steady descent into the now darkening valley, as the sun continued its steady descent and the shadows below began to lengthen.

Satan caught me at one of my better moments. Although I would not admit it to him there is some part of me that would like to at least taste the feeling of being bowed to – catered to . . . esteemed and praised. When I was younger I had daydreams of suddenly becoming wealthy and magnanimously bestowing gifts and favors on the people in Nazareth. I'd been hurt and had become more than weary of hearing the rumors surrounding Joseph and Mary, that I was not quite legitimate. The thought of them bowing to me and begging forgiveness was tempting then . . . and perhaps has some residual appeal even now. That, I suppose, is why it was part of the test. Why good people should feel the need to disparage others is difficult to understand. I suppose we all want to feel superior in some way, and in Nazareth there are not many ways available. We are poor. All of us! We are considered second class because we have no land. I suppose some need to feel at least morally superior and the only way they can do that is to find fault and spread rumors.

Joshua shook his head sadly: *When will we learn that looking down on others only diminishes ourselves? It's when we can look up to others — or at least look them in the eyes as equals — that we grow in stature. When I have been in some of the larger, more prosperous towns I have seen and heard people shouting at their servants, venting their anger, pretending to be great by making others appear small.*

At this, Joshua looked out over the wilderness, wishing someone was there to speak with. But he saw only rocks — hard, dusty, dry rocks, incapable of absorbing anything — each one sitting where they had sat for hundreds of years. So he just shook his head again, and muttered to himself: *How totally backwards and foolish! It's when we can serve the needs of others, not because we have to, but because we choose to, that we stand tall. How can I get that idea across to those who need to learn?*

Joshua paused in his descent from the hill. He found a place to rest as he descended deeper within himself. Mentally he scrolled though the Scriptures to Jeremiah. He loved the raw humanity he found in his words. The man loved his people, but he was impatient with their shortsightedness. Joshua could relate to that. *They are like sheep without a shepherd. Good people but easily lead astray.* Jeremiah sensed the hand of Yahweh moving through their history, alternating between stern discipline and redemption. Joshua also could see that movement. Yahweh was like a loving parent, both demanding and forgiving . . . always loving. He recalled Jeremiah proclaiming Yahweh's promise to the people in exile:

"Behold the days are coming says the Lord when I will make a new covenant with the house of Israel and Judah, and they shall be my people, not like the covenant I made with their fathers when I took them by the hand to bring them out of the land of Egypt, my covenant which they broke, though I was their husband, says the Lord: I will put my law

*within them and I will write it upon their hearts, and they shall be my people." *⁴*

Joshua lay pondering those words. Suddenly his body twitched in sharp reaction to a startling insight. He leapt to his feet, looking about for someone to tell of this new understanding that seemed to refresh his now rather emaciated body with fresh energy.

He raised his hands and shouted to no one in particular and the world in general:

This New Covenant was never made!

*"I will give you as light unto the nations that my salvation may reach to the ends of the earth." *⁵*

Joshua almost began to race down the hill to reach the lowlands of the wilderness. His way was being made clear, he realized that. The pieces were there. They just needed to be put in their proper places.

Perhaps Yahweh is calling me – commissioning me – to be the source of the new covenant, promised by Jeremiah but never realized.

The enormity of this staggered him, and he leaned against the side of the hill to steady himself. Somewhere in the recesses of his mind he had imagined that Yahweh might possibly be calling him to be teacher or even to prophesy. Never had he even considered the possibility that he was to be ordained as the bearer of a new covenant.

Ezra had brought the returnees the Law. But he had misunderstood Yahweh's underlying intentions to be the light unto the nations. He had required that those with foreign wives either abandon their wives or leave Jerusalem. He had tried to put the Lord's light under a bushel, keeping

---

*⁴ Jeremiah 31: 31-33,
*⁵ Isaiah 49:6

it hidden rather than sharing it. He had written the law — not on the people's hearts, but in inflexible form: heartless in its demand!

Yahweh wishes to give all his people a way — not a law: A way to find their relationship to him as a loving child to a loving father. His spirit is available to all who open themselves to him. True obedience requires flexibility — not blind acceptance of written words. It demands justice and righteousness, to be sure. However, true justice has to consider factors that no general law can incorporate.

Yahweh's will should not — can not — be enforced by demands or coercion. Obedience must be voluntary: a loving response to one who genuinely is loved. Writing his law upon their hearts is listening to his silent words — living in his presence — treasuring his will instead of fearing his wrath.

The messenger must be a servant — not a master. He must be one who himself is totally obedient to Yahweh - - - and all the demands of Yahweh's love.

Joshua stopped abruptly. He stared about him. The barren stones sat silently, unseeing. Timeless dust covered the landscape. The sky overhead stretched into a pale blue opaque nothingness. Towering above him was the hill where he had spent so many days and nights pondering his fate. The echo of his mantra-like plea resounded in his soul:

Wherever you lead; whatever you ask; I will be faithful. Make my way clear, is all I ask.

Joshua fell to his knees, almost assuming a fetal position. He remained motionless, except for the heaving of his chest as he emitted great sobs — not of sorrow — but of overwhelming emotion — wonder — amazement — love. *That quiet voice I have been hearing all my life — that voice which has guided me in times of confusion, comforted me in times of sorrow, and encouraged me when I have been sliding into despair: This was Yahweh, my father . . . with me all the while.*

Yahweh actually is calling me — ME! - to become those feet upon the mountain that proclaim Good News.

Joshua composed himself. He straightened his body. Still on his knees, he gazed about at the barren, lifeless landscape. Then he slowly turned his head in the direction of Jerusalem. A new bearing emerged from within him. Calm and controlled, he arose, surveying the land as a ruler. A smile began to form on his face. He looked down at his feet, dirty and bruised. Then he looked up at the hill he had abandoned, raised his arms heavenward and shouted:

Get ready, mountains: Beautiful or not: Here these feet come!

CHAPTER SEVEN

THE REENTRY

Going into the wilderness, Joshua had not noticed the sharp division in the land. Perhaps he had been so absorbed by the baptism experience that he simply failed to notice the abruptness of the transition. One moment he had been in wilderness – not a sign of life anywhere. The next moment he was immersed in greenery. The landscape was lush with grass, trees and crawling objects.

Water does make a difference! It turns brown into green – death into life. I imagine it is the same with the spirit. Scripture tells us Yahweh breathed his spirit into clay and it became humanity: death – nothingness – into life and being.

Joshua had determined to return to John's camp prior to embarking on whatever mission awaited him. He needed to allow his body to recover from its extended fast. More importantly, he needed to speak with John, to tell him of his experience and decision . . . and to seek his advice.

From his first visit he had learned that John would be found where the most people were gathered. Although they respected his privacy they seemed to find some comfort by being near him. With this as his guide he quickly worked his way through the little groupings of spiritual pilgrims to the center, where John sat silently, absentmindedly chewing some indiscernible herb.

As Joshua approached him, John slowly tilted his head and lifted his gaze to watch him as he took the final few steps and then stood silently as though waiting for an invitation. John observed the sunken cheeks, the sunburned face and the parched lips. Just as quickly he also saw the depth in his eyes – eyes that always glowed with intelligence, but now – something new, deeper . . . much more powerful. For a moment he sat, surveying this new Joshua that had returned from the wilderness. Then he nodded – a nod that conveyed both approval and an invitation to sit beside him.

Joshua lowered himself to sit directly in front of his cousin, and for a long moment they merely sat, as though affirming the other.

John spoke first: "It appears that your fast has changed you." Joshua nodded but said nothing, so John continued: "You saw Him? You spoke with Him?"

"I felt Him. He spoke to me?"

"He has called you." Not a question, but a statement of fact.

Joshua nodded. "He has called me."

John noticed a slight tremble in Joshua's response. He continued: "You are the One?"

"I think so."

"Think so is not enough. Do you *know* so?"

Joshua hesitated. Yes, he *knew* so. Still, it seemed so arrogant to make that claim. The Messiah was a long-believed promise. People believed it. They wanted to believe it. They *needed* to believe it. They just never expected it to happen in their lifetime. Oh yes, there had been more than thirty false messiahs in their history. Each one had claimed to be the promised son of David who would lift the sword, sound the battle cry, drive out the hated invaders, and restore Israel to its earlier glory. Each one of these "messiahs" had caused the deaths of hundreds – even thousands – of loyal believers. Joshua wanted no part of that. For him the long-awaited Promised One would be the Servant spoken of by Isaiah: Not a warrior king but a Prince of Peace. Yet, for him to make that claim seemed preposterously arrogant and self-serving.

John observed the inner wrestling of his cousin. Some part of him wanted to help. Still, the better part knew this was a matter that had to be settled alone, from within. Only then could Joshua be equipped to serve the role Yahweh had chosen for him.

In his mind, Joshua retraced his path down the wilderness hill. *That voice I heard was Yahweh's. It really was. I know it! I suppose I always knew it. Now I am certain of it. Whenever my desires or fears do not agree with this silent voice I must listen to and obey that voice.* It had been one thing for him to think it. It would be quite another for him to speak it aloud. Once spoken, the words could not be recalled. It was a risk. He gazed deeply into John's eyes, looking beneath the surface as though peering into his soul. He really was not certain if John was encouraging him, or if he was baiting him. John could be like that in his attempt to awaken the dreamer with a cold bucket of reality water. He realized this was not a matter of trusting John, however. It was a matter of trusting Yahweh, his heavenly father. He took a deep breath. He spoke slowly and decisively:

"Yes, John. I *know* it to be so. Yahweh has proclaimed me to be his son, the Anointed One, and he has given me the mission of proclaiming the good news of his unequivocal, redeeming love."

John smiled. "I was certain he would."

Joshua smiled a sigh of relief and also embarrassment. His next question was going to take the aura off of his previous, bold proclamation: "The difficulty now, John, is that I do not have the slightest idea of how to go about being this messenger."

"So you now are a pilgrim messiah, my cousin? You are called to proclaim a message that at this moment you do not fully understand, in a manner you have yet to figure out . . . in places you have never been?" He smiled: "I wish you well."

With this both laughed so loudly that they drew the attention of the nearby pilgrims. They turned their heads toward the sound of the joviality and you could see the questions on some of their faces: "Have they been drinking?"

Observing this, John and Joshua laughed all the harder with such a contagious abandonment that one – then another – of the pilgrims joined in, until the laughter had spread throughout the encampment. Even those who had no idea as to the source were wiping tears from their eyes and slapping one another on their backsides. While their outburst spread, both John's and Joshua's laughter subsided and they sat, alternately observing the spread of mirth and alternately, then staring quietly into one another's eyes in tacit harmony of spirit.

"It has already begun," said John. "The good news of Yahweh's love should be greeted with joy."

CHAPTER EIGHT

THE PLAN

"Before you can proclaim good news, my cousin, you need to understand the present bad news. So what is it?" John asked this, knowing full well that Joshua would have garnered a great understanding of this. He recalled Joshua's keen insights into human nature even when they were too young to be invited into the Temple.

"There are many aspects to this, John. I will try to put them into some systematic order as I explain them, but I can assure you of this: They are far more in number and in complexity than I will be able to identify here and now."

"Agreed, cousin. Proceed."

We are so limited in our view of the world. We see it only from our little circle of self-concern. Just listen to our language. We speak of the Jews and of "The Others." That is how we distinguish people: Us and Them. We automatically believe that *Us* is better than *Them*, no matter who the individual is. This attitude puts us at odds with everyone not Jewish."

John nodded: "Good start. Keep on."

"Most of the sins – the failures – we commit are not intentional acts against others. They are the result of our lack of awareness or concern for those around us. We act from our own narrow self-awareness, never even considering the effect on others. We do not try to be bad; we just fail to act responsibly to others."

"Because we do not consider them."

"That's correct, John. It is as though others, particularly those we do not know, were invisible. We say things we would not say if we were aware how they would affect the one who hears. I often hear parents talking about their children in negative ways while the children are in the room. They are oblivious to the effect of those words or they never would intentionally hurt their children. A woman reaches for something at the market and a neighbor snatches it up, totally unaware that she may have offended her friend. A man may make a joke at his friend's expense and not stop to think that his words may have done more damage than a punch in the face. A person steals without ever thinking of the pain his action will inflict. He steals without a thought of the victim, because the victim is unimportant to him as a person. Self-centeredness is the root cause of all our sins."

John nodded tacit agreement. "Keep going, cousin."

"We have totally perverted the way of life that Moses offered us on Sinai. Moses had to write it in stone because that was all that was available to him. However, the way he showed us must remain flexible to deal with the realities of the times and to recognize the individuality of persons. Somewhere along the way we lost sight of that and set his words in stone in our minds and our hearts. People have substituted piety for spirituality. They have come to believe that obedience to a set of written rules is more important than a living relationship with Yahweh. Jeremiah said the law must be written in our hearts. I believe he was expressing the need for a living relationship rather than a dead set of rules. What we live with today are a set of laws that have been shaped to make those in control feel good about themselves. Rather than obedience to the spirit of the rules set forth by Moses, we make sacrifices to atone for our failures and we live in fear that Yahweh will punish us. We have created a hierarchy of unnecessary priests (forgive me for that John)." John nodded his understanding and agreement. "All we need are teachers who will serve as guides for us. Our reason for obedience to Yahweh's rules should be love – not fear."

"Why could we as a people have done this? I mean, how could anyone turn simple rules for living into a set of inflexible laws?"

Joshua paused and withdrew within himself. What he had stated was an intuitive grasp of the situation. He knew it to be true, but it was not easy to explain. He had envisioned it as a whole, much as he had been able to envision the wilderness as an entire entity as he stood gazing at it from atop his tiny hill. To break it down and explain it piece by piece in a way that would allow a linear thinker to understand it would not be easy.

He looked again at John, shrugged his shoulders, and thought, *I'm going to have to try this sometime or everyone will think me some kind of a madman:*

"Most people seem to believe that the words Moses wrote were eternal truths. I believe they were symbols meant to express an idea that needed to be understood in the time and place Moses wrote them." He saw the troubled look on John's face, and raised his hand: "Stay with me until I finish. Then state your mind." John nodded. "Some, of course conveyed truths that are eternal." John relaxed. "Some did not." He smiled at John. "The trick is in deciding which are which."

"You have to remember what was happening with the people in the wilderness. There were a series of blood feuds being carried on between various tribes. These were destroying the sense of unity Moses needed to build if he was to create a new nation out of those motley tribes. When he gave the commandment of 'an eye for an eye, and a tooth for a tooth,' he was not telling the people to seek revenge. He was calling for peace." A confused look spread across John's face, but Joshua raised his hand to quell any question at the time. "Until he gave that commandment, one injury started an endless series of vengeful acts. Once he gave this order, a proportionate response settled the matter. Yahweh never wanted bloodshed. However he knew too well that where the Israelites were in their spiritual growth at that time, simple retribution was the best he could hope for. What he really wants is for people merely to turn their other cheek and let it go. Grow up and stop acting like little children!" Joshua said this with emotion, allowing his impatience to show. "Those who cannot understand this – either because they cannot or they do not wish to – believe Yahweh blesses our desire for revenge. Yet, 'Vengeance is mine,'[1] is what Yahweh said. By this he meant it was his right – not ours."

Joshua paused to gather his thoughts.

John just sat quietly. He had expected – even hoped for - this from Joshua and he was not being disappointed.

"It is always easier to follow rules than to have to think about what is proper. Lazy minds – simple minds – prefer rules, so they read the words, accept them as truths and simply follow the rules. One of the great commandments says, 'You shall have no other gods before me.'[2] John, you and I - and hopefully anybody with good sense – knows there are no other gods.'[3] Isaiah said it well. So how could we have other gods? The answer is this: We cannot, but the Israelites in the wilderness could. They had not progressed to the point where we have been since Isaiah's time. The golden cow, Hathor[4] was thought to be real. Today, we reword

---

[1] Leviticus 19:18,

[2] Exodus 20:3,

[3] Isaiah 46:9,

[4] The so-called Golden Calf probably was the Egyptian Cow goddess Hathor. The language betrays the attempt to present her as a calf: "*These* are your *gods*, O Israel," Both *These* and *gods* are plural terms. *Calf* is singular. Hathor's consort, Ba'al was the other deity represented. He would have been presented as a phallic symbol or wooden pole. Archeologists concur that the "calf: was not molten. This would have required a cast and smelting equipment. In the Cairo museum there are carved wooden cows bearing traces of the gold from the thin gold sheets that once had covered them.

that in our minds to say 'You shall not have *false* gods before you.' In other words we should not create our own gods."

Joshua gave a look of exasperation and exclaimed: "And would you look at what we have done to the Sabbath! It was meant to be a day of rest: A simple day of rest where everyone could refrain from toiling and spend time with family and friends, to enjoy this life Yahweh has given us, and to reflect upon his love and his plan for us. Now it is a day when we live in fear of violating one of its ordinances for fear of being put to death if we do so." He shook his head in despair. "What constitutes work? How far can we walk before it is work? How much can we carry before it is work? Is cooking work? Is lifting a friend who has fallen work? Why can we not simply understand the spirit of the law, enjoy the gift Yahweh has given us, and not try to make it something it was not meant to be?"

John grinned in appreciation for his cousin's insight and frankness of expression.

"Where you and I may differ, John is that I do not see people as sinners. Sin merely means to fall short or to miss the target. Sin is not something we are. It is something we do. Even with that it suggests that we are at least attempting to do the right thing." At this, John started to speak, but Joshua raised his hand and continued: "You cannot miss a target unless you are aiming at it." He said this, slowly with a sly smile, watching John's reaction as he grasped the truth underlying Joshua's statement. Then he paused to allow John to absorb the thought and react.

"You have a point, cousin. Failing or falling short does suggest that we are at least attempting. It is like children learning to speak or to walk. They do it poorly at first, so we could say they are sinning in their attempt. Instead, we praise them for what they can do, and encourage them to improve." Having said this, John leaned back and drew deeper within himself. What Joshua was saying was an oversimplification, he knew this — and he understood that Joshua also was aware of it. He remembered that Joshua used this technique whenever he was attempting to break through someone's set way of thinking. He would make a radical statement that was difficult to deny, then he would amplify and clarify once he got the listener's interest. Still, this was a radically different way of perceiving sin. It was not bad or evil. It was inadequate or misdirected. That is why he said we needed teachers to guide and correct us, not priests to seek our forgiveness and restore our relationship to Yahweh.

Joshua saw that John had settled his inner debate, so he pressed on:

"What everyone seems to be missing is that Yahweh is not residing in the Jerusalem Temple, waiting to be served. Yahweh is where he has always been: Here, in the midst of his people. His Kingdom is not some vague future hope. It is forever available to anyone. All that is required for entrance is radical repentance - -"

"A total rethinking of the way we perceive Yahweh, Creation, and our role in it." John bursts in as he began to grasp where Joshua was leading him.

"That's as good a definition of repentance as I've heard for this, John. Technically repentance just means to transform the way your mind works around a subject — after due consideration, of course." *5

"But you hit it head on. The repentance I'm talking about smacks conventional wisdom squarely in the face. So much of what people have come to call *good* is not worthy at all. So much

---

*5 The term we translate as repent is from the Greek *metanoia*. *Meta* means to radically change or transform, as in metamorphosis. *Noia* refers to the function of the mind. Therefore *metanoia* = transformation of the mind. The common usage implied "after careful consideration."

of what they have been trained to think of as *bad* is not bad – and even, in some cases, may be good."

John shook his head – half in admiration – half in despair. "But how can you get people to radically change their way of thinking, and –more importantly – their way of acting? Tell me, cousin, how do you plan to accomplish that?"

The question apparently caught Joshua by surprise. He leaned back and rested on his elbows . . . his head tilted toward the large, fluffy clouds that were drifting slowly by.

For a moment, John thought he had fallen asleep. *Probably worn out from that ordeal in the wilderness,* he thought.

Suddenly, as though jarred into wakefulness, Joshua sat up and looked at John. A smile flashed across his face.

"I shall tell them stories."

"Stories?"

"Yes, John: Stories. Do you recall how the rabbis taught us wisdom when we were children? They told us stories. We were too young to have enough life experiences to accumulate wisdom on our own."

"So the rabbis told us stories to give us those experiences. I remember. Yes!"

"They drew us into their tales and we felt what the people in the stories felt, so we could understand the wisdom they gleaned . . . at least in part. That is what I shall do, John. Thank you for asking. I will tell them of ordinary people and ordinary experiences and show them the presence of the divine or the value they thought value-less. Again, thank you for making me think this through. In the ordinary, the people will find the extraordinary that is the miracle of Yahweh's power and love. And More! Much more. There is no limit to what can be taught by stories."

"We've probably explored this facet as far as we can right now?" It was phrased as a question, but by saying it John had acknowledged that Joshua need not tell him more. He knew his cousin was weary – exhausted, really. He needed some light nourishment and a long rest on something more comfortable than the rocks of the wilderness.

Still, one question lingered in his mind that he at least wanted Joshua to think about.

"What title are you going to take for yourself, Joshua? You realize, of course, that the Romans will be looking for any signs of a new messiah arising. Since you come from Galilee they will be particularly watchful. That has been the hotbed of most of the messianic insurrections. Also, you can be certain that the Pharisees will not welcome your radical approach that is sure to disrupt the social structure which gives them such comfort. Remember in the Book of Deuteronomy Moses warns the people that false prophets will come and try to lead the people astray to false gods. He said these people should be put to death." [*6]

"It's even more than that, John. I understand their fear of rule-breakers, and that is what I shall be. They've taken very seriously Jeremiah's admonition that we were sent into exile because we had broken the covenant. If we break the covenant, we lose the land. That is why they are the keepers of the covenant. They even built in safeguards to be certain that one does not accidentally cross the boundaries of the law. They are good people who mean well. I just believe they have been led terribly astray over the years. Yes, I know I shall have to watch my back with them."

"So what title will you use that will allow the people to know who you are, but not get you in trouble with either the Romans or the Pharisees – and don't forget the Sadducees? They, too, will have something at stake in your social revolution."

[*6] Deuteronomy 13 ff

Joshua smiled. "Thanks for the reminder, cousin. Who is left that might be on my side? The poor and the outcast probably sum it up. Well, good enough then. They are the ones most likely to listen and to understand. Everyone else will be too absorbed in themselves – too complacent with what they believe they have – to pay much attention."

"You know you will not be welcomed with open arms. People who are satisfied do not appreciate change – even if it is their best interest. So - pick a title."

"'Messiah' won't work. We know that. Besides, it still does not feel right to me: Too grandiose. 'Son of God' would do me in . . . even though I now believe it to be true. 'Rabbi' is too common. No shine to it."

They both grinned at one another as Joshua continued to work his way through a variety of possibilities. It was as though they both recalled the younger days when they sneaked into the priests' dressing room and tried on the various garbs they found hanging on the walls. They had almost been caught then, and it was one of those delicious secrets they had shared and recounted through the years.

Suddenly Joshua stood up as though his name had been called and he had to respond:

"Son of Man! Yes! That's it!" He repeated it slowly and with a touch of reverence: "Son of Man. That really is who I am called to be."

John smiled a smile of appreciation as he began to grasp the full meaning of the term:

"What is man that you are mindful of him and the son of man that you should visit him?" *7

---

*7 Psalm 8:4

Joshua nodded: "Precisely, John. I am a man – just a man after all is said and done. But more – much more as I go about my father's work."

"Adam really only means mankind or humanity. Our tradition tells us that Yahweh knew Adam was going to disobey his orders and fall from grace, so he created a second Adam – a Son of Man – who would be obedient . . . even to the death (You had better watch for that one, cousin). In doing so he would undo the damage of the First Man."

Joshua nodded, "As time went on the tradition expanded to believe the Son of Man would be the forerunner of the time when Yahweh would reclaim and redeem this earth and all that was on it. I believe that is my mission: To be the one proclaiming the ever-present Kingdom of God!"

He shook his head in disbelief. "I don't even know what that means, John. The words just jumped out of my mouth."

John stared at Joshua with admiration that bordered on awe. "I think you will work that out, Joshua." He no longer could call him *cousin*. The gap between them had suddenly widened and *cousin* was too familiar a term. "In reflection, I believe it is you who should have baptized me."

Abruptly, John's look of admiration disappeared. In its place a brooding look of concern emerged. He stared deeply into Joshua's eyes as though seeking to gaze into his soul.

"It will not all be good news for you. You know that, don't you, Joshua? What you will be proclaiming is a threat to all those who now hold some power in our society. "

Joshua was taken aback by this sudden change in mood. He had not yet begun to consider the consequences of his message upon the rich and powerful. His focus had been entirely upon those who would be recipients of the good news he was to proclaim. He leaned toward John with a questioning look that required no words for John to continue.

"This entire social system is based upon clean and unclean, those who are accepted and respected and those who are outcasts. It is based on guilt and innocence, reward and punishment, sin and forgiveness. The priests make their living by offering sacrifices to a god of wrath and punishment. Your God of love, acceptance and forgiveness will threaten their very livelihood if believed. The Pharisees who find their sense of righteousness and self-respect will be intimidated by the demands placed upon them by a god of justice and mercy. At best they will view you as a radical who encourages people to violate the law which gives them such comfort and security. The Romans will see you as a threat to the status quo – a revolutionary. Our society is organized to favor the powerful and exploit the powerless. Your message will contradict that and will not be well-accepted." He paused to let these ideas settle in Joshua's mind.

"In Galilee, the Hellenistic cities pose a real threat to the Law of Moses. I have seen that. The people in the Decapolis have no restrictions put upon them. There are no Sabbath observances, no dietary do's and don'ts, no dress codes. From the hillsides we can see them dancing and playing during our Sabbath times. Many of our young people are drawn to their ways. I know the Pharisees are concerned for fear that we as a people might break the covenant and be sent into exile again – away from the land – away from the Temple."

John nodded. "This will be a constant problem for you, Joshua. For what they believe is a valid reason, many will oppose you and may even wish you . . . to simply disappear." He added this with an ominous tone in his voice, gazing even more deeply into Joshua's eyes. For a long moment they sat, quietly staring at one another. The camp had grown silent as each little cluster of pilgrims settled themselves for a night's rest.

John offered Joshua his remaining food. Joshua gratefully took half and began to chew on it. Words seemed superfluous. They ate in silence, neither even glancing at the other.

CHAPTER NINE

THE EMERGING MESSIAH

When Joshua awoke the encampment was deserted. There was not a sound to be heard – not a soul to be seen. Joshua looked up at the cloudless sky. The sun was shining brightly almost directly overhead.

It must be almost the sixth hour. For a moment he felt embarrassed. He whose practice was to awaken and be about his business before sunup had let half the day elapse while he slumbered. Then, remembering where he was and why, he lay back and relaxed. He smiled at the absurdity of what he was thinking. *I suppose I needed the rest. It's not every day that one endures a fast in the wilderness and wrestles with Satan.* He looked about to see if there was any food someone may have left. Then he saw, lying at his feet, a bowl filled with figs, dates and a few dried locusts. *Good old cousin John, he smiled. I hope the locusts taste better than they look.* With that, he lifted one to eye level, took a deep breath and plunged it into his mouth. *I suppose if one is hungry enough dead rats might appear to be a delicacy.* However, he quickly stuffed in a fig to sweeten the taste.

Finally, refreshed and alert, he arose. He hesitated for a moment, deciding whether to go to the river to bid farewell to John. Then deciding there was no need for that closing formality he turned and headed for the road which would lead him back from Jericho to Galilee. He and John had said all that needed to be said between them.

He encountered no one on the road back, which was all the better for him. There was much to think about, and people would be a distraction at this time. *Where to begin? Where to stay?* He knew he would need some base to which he could return to rest and consider his strategy. *Galilee is so lovely. Surely I could be renewed just by walking the shores of the sea, or sitting on one of the hillsides and gazing at the rich lushness of the land.* He felt a warm glow of comfort at the thought and set his course for beyond Nazareth to Capernaum, the tiny village at the northern edge of the sea.

A more important issue was the content of his message. He felt compelled to proclaim good news of Yahweh's unconditional acceptance of his children. That, however, required some elaboration in order not to sound as though everything would turn out well for us, no matter what we did. That was not the case – not at all. What people did mattered greatly to Yahweh, and to their future. From his contacts with the Hellenists Joshua had learned of the very significant differences they had in understanding what constitutes a person.

For us it is simple: Yahweh created us by shaping a body and breathing his spirit into it. Body plus spirit makes a living soul. The Hellenists, however, see us as more complex: A person is composed of a body that is activated by a spirit, and contains an eternal soul and a mind that interacts with the soul. The body is covered with a specific type of flesh which gives its characteristics of being able to fly as a bird or swim like a fish. When the body dies, the soul is freed to return to its source. Some believe the soul is corrupted by its affiliation with the body, but the mind can guide it back. It will be much more difficult to explain Yahweh's message to them . . . but it might also be easier in a way. The Hellenists understand the idea of a soul that bears the characteristics of underlying goodness – or evil. They have a basis for seeing that essential quality of being as capable of change over time. How can I speak to the Jews about a soul when they understand it to mean the living person – body and spirit?

Joshua continued to tread along the well-worn path leading from Jericho to Galilee, pondering this problem.

He felt that an important part of his message must be to proclaim that God's Kingdom was not some future idea, but a present possibility. People had only to change their perception of reality, affirm Yahweh as the ruler of their lives, and they would find themselves living at least partially within his kingdom. He realized this had political ramifications and he would have to be careful how he said it, or he could find himself accused of treason. As he played with the possibilities contained in the term Kingdom, the pieces fell together in his mind:

I can tell stories about the Kingdom so that people will come to see that it is more than a place. They can come to see it as a new relationship with God. It is a radically new state of mind, a symbol of what the Hellenists are trying to express by their term, "soul." With this thought, Joshua turned to see if there was someone he could share this with. The idea excited him. It would challenge his mind to find ways to express this concept of the kingdom until everyone who truly paid attention would grasp his meaning.

I will use agricultural models. The soul grows slowly. It heals slowly. Like seeds sown in the spring they require tending if they are to flourish. Yes! Agricultural models should convey the meaning I want to express.

He quickened his pace. The excitement within was growing and he was eager to begin. After four days he approached the village of Magdala, another town at the northern tip of the sea. Joshua decided to stop there to speak with Mary, the widow who ran a most successful trading business. She had married when she was fourteen, and it soon became apparent that she was not to bear any children for her husband. Isaac had recognized her shrewdness of mind when they were wed, so had brought her into the trading business with him. Together, they seemed to have made quite a team. The business expanded, and soon tales of their wealth began to spread through the region. It was not great wealth of course, but anyone that looked prosperous in that area was considered to be rich. Mary's husband had died some years ago. Then and only then did the people begin to understand and appreciate that it was not the team of Isaac and Mary that was so successful. It was Mary alone who had developed the business into its present prosperous status.

As a widow she had turned her house over to her nephew and technically moved in with him to allow him to care for her. Silas was competent. Mary had trained him to manage most of the business, but it was a bit of a joke to the people of Magdala that anyone had to watch over Mary Magdala. Joshua found himself smiling at the absurdity of the thought. Still she had changed since Isaac's death. Sometimes he found her quietly staring at a blank wall, smoldering slowly inside. Other times he could hear her ranting at one of her servants as he approached her home. This was unlike her. *Perhaps,* he thought, *Silas does provide some calming influence.*

Mary looked up to see Joshua striding toward the large structure which served as both business and home. Even from a distance she could recognize him. No matter how long he had been walking he carried himself with a degree of nobility as though the land over which he traveled was his and his alone. She had always admired this quality, even while thinking it strange that one so low-born could convey a sense of majesty by the simple act of walking.

"Hello there, man of Nazareth. What brings you this way, except your feet, of course?"

She rose and pulled the cushion from across her table to where it sat closer to her. "Come, sit here, and I will have my maid servant wash your dirty feet." She rang a small bell that sat on the table. Sada looked out the window, sized up the situation and quickly disappeared.

"And hello to you, Mary Magdala." He replied with a friendly grin. "I see you still believe your services are required to keep your business and fleet of ships afloat."

They enjoyed this exchange. Both were quick of mind and a bit of friendly banter lifted both of their spirits. Joshua sat on the cushion as Mary's maid reappeared with a bowl of water and a towel. Joshua felt a shiver of delight as the maid began soothingly washing and massaging his weary feet. *Aaah, where were you when I needed you in the wilderness,* he thought.

"You are on your way to visit your cousins?"

"Not this time, Mary. This is far more important than a family visit."

She leaned forward and affected a confidential tone: "And what might that be, my intriguing friend?"

Mary had known Joshua from the time she married Isaac when she was a mere fourteen years of age. Joshua was about twelve then. During all the years while Isaac was alive they had been friends – no more. Now that she was widowed she had sensed some long-delayed attraction, but Joshua had never indicated an interest in being other than a friend, so Mary contented herself with an occasional mildly flirtatious remark. She thought this "just as well." Joshua had delayed marrying because he felt an obligation to care for Mary and his younger siblings. When he finally did marry he would want children. Every man did. He knew she was barren. He would not want her. Still . . . he always made a point of seeing her when he was in the area, so she privately nursed a few innocent dreams.

Joshua either missed her mood or chose to ignore it. "Mary, Yahweh has given me a message to proclaim to the people." He said this, then he waited for her response. He had selected her to be his first test case. Mary was sensible. She was intelligent. She was a trusted friend. Her response was critical to him in suggesting how he and his message would be received.

Joshua's statement had caught Mary by surprise. She sensed that her response would be particularly important to him. *That is why he dropped by this time. He sees me as a friend. Nothing more. He respects my judgment. I know that.* She agonized at the thought that her reaction may in some way interfere with what he obviously perceived to be a God-given mission.

"Joshua, why do you believe it is Yahweh who has given you this mission?" The simple, obvious question seemed to be a safe response. She waited now to hear what Joshua would say.

"Mary, I know this must sound presumptuous, but this is what I believe happened." He then went on to relate his baptism experience, the spirit actually shoving him into the wilderness, the testing by Satan, and his own search of Scripture to understand the mission and message. During this time he watched Mary closely, but she listened impassively, without any sense of judging his words.

When he had finished, he leaned back in his seat to hear Mary's reaction. He sat for a long moment while Mary collected her thoughts.

"Joshua, I believe you.. I have known you for almost twenty years. Throughout all those years I believed there was something special about you. I did not know what it was. It was difficult to even begin to define. Your bearing; the way you walked. The manner in which you spoke; the ideas you expressed. You were different. That was evident. Now I believe I understand why you were – and are so obviously different from other men. Yahweh must have chosen you long ago. All of your living until now has been preparation."

"I am still struggling to know what is expected of me."

"You have been led to this. You will be led to understand." She spoke that simply and with conviction. It gave Joshua a sense of confidence just to hear those words.

"Thank you, Mary, for your faith in me. I hope others will be as certain — as open to believe."

"You cannot return to Nazareth. Where will you be staying?" She asked this without a trace of self-consciousness. She was beginning to understand her long-time attraction to this man. *Admiration — not romance. Romance had never felt quite right. I admired this unique man-of-God. It is so easy to confuse feelings that have never been named — never been experienced. I wanted only to be near him, to listen to him, to serve him.*

"If you wish to stay here, I shall move in with my brother and you can stay at this house."

"Thank you, Mary. I do not believe I shall have a home to call my own . . . until . . . ." He left the thought unfinished. He looked up at her with a suddenly sad and weary expression. "Let's just say my work will keep me moving."

She did not understand why, but she felt she was about to cry.

"If I can help in any way . . . . ."

"Thank you, Mary. You are a true friend." With that, he stood, took a step toward her and gave her a kiss which felt more like a blessing than a kiss."

"Goodbye for now, my friend." He turned and strode out into the yard and out of the village. He had appreciated this time with Mary. She was a troubled woman. Still, she was intelligent and insightful.

CHAPTER TEN

TESTING THE CALL

On his way to Capernaum Joshua climbed the steadily rising path that led him to a glorious mountainside view of the Sea of Galilee. Where he stood actually was below sea level. But the Galilean Sea lay 650 feet below that line. Since temperatures are directly influenced by elevation this caused the area to remain temperate all year. As a result the land was lush, teeming with trees bearing fruits, nuts and olives. The vineyards were drooping from the weight of grapes hanging from them. This was a favorite spot for him. It was one he never failed to visit on his trip to the area. This day, however, his purpose was more than esthetic. He needed time to pray, to prepare himself for the work ahead.

Joshua walked over to one of the many boulders that had been thrown to the surface by some long-forgotten cataclysm. He perched himself on one, closed his eyes, and began to repeat what had become his mantra:

Wherever you lead; whatever you ask; I will be faithful. Make my way clear, is all I ask.

Wherever you lead; whatever you ask; I will be faithful. Make my way clear, is all I ask.

In the silence, Joshua began to sense a presence which had become increasingly familiar to him. It was one that he had instantly recognized as a life-long presence, but always had taken it for granted as one is apt to ignore, as common, his own family.

The time passed quickly. The shadows were lengthening, stretching into distorted geometric shapes that covered the landscape. He knew he must speak with James and John before night-fall. Reluctantly, as one does when leaving a dear friend, he arose and continued his trek. He could see the roofs of Capernaum below his feet as he followed the curving path.

He descended to the lake where the fishermen were drying their nets and storing the supplies in nearby sheds. Spontaneously, Joshua decided to begin his proclamation to these men as they prepared to end their day's work. He sat down on one of the boulders that spotted the shore line, and began drawing a pattern in the hard sand. After a few moments some of the men noticed him. They recognized him from his many visits. He was always interesting – always challenging in a useful manner. Their curiosity whetted, they wandered over to see what he was drawing. It was a fish. Just an ordinary fish. He was taking great pains, however, to see that it was properly drawn. Eventually a crowd had gathered and he began to speak.

"Some people spend their days fishing. They rise early in the morning; go to their boats, load their equipment, board their boats, and spend their day casting nets, pulling them in, hoping they bear enough fish to make the day worthwhile. They grunt and they gasp at the effort. As their day moves on the nets seem to get heavier, the fish – smellier. They finish their day as you did just now: weary and hungry enough to devour their entire catch. Others buy the fish and spend their days preparing the fish for eating. They scour the market places and hillsides, searching for the right ingredients to make their offering acceptable. They grind the spices and slice or peel the vegetables, working to make them tasty and attractive. Finally there are those who simply eat the fishes caught by you fishermen and prepared by the women. They do so without much thought of the work that was given to make their meal. They eat the fish. Look around as though to ask if that is all there is. Then they leave the table and go about their business – often without so much as a thank you."

The fishermen nodded in agreement. Joshua could see the looks of dissatisfaction appearing on their faces as they realized the thanklessness of their labors.

"No one ever asks who made the fishes and put them in the sea, so that you have a means of earning a livelihood, or have something to serve for dinner – or something with which to fill your belly."

This sudden turn caught everyone by surprise. The looks on the fishermen rapidly turned from self-pity to embarrassment.

"Your heavenly father does not ask for or need your gratitude any more than the women who spent their day preparing the meal. It would be nice if someone gave them thanks, of course, but it is enough for them to be able to show their love by serving. So it is with God. So it can be with you. You can work only for yourselves and forever be dissatisfied with what you receive. You can work to feed others and feel the satisfaction of serving your community. When you do that you are doing the work of your heavenly father. The choice always is yours."

As he spoke he saw the looks of discomfort slowly change into looks of understanding and appreciation. *Stories do work,* he thought. He also observed the hunger in the eyes of Simon and his brother Andrew. *I shall try to satisfy that hunger for you,* he thought.

When he had concluded his lesson James and John rushed forward to greet him. James stood back while his younger brother embraced his beloved cousin. James was the family's oldest at twenty seven. John was the baby, thirteen years younger. They had been separated by three sisters and a few who died at or near their births. As the only two boys, they had developed a special bond over the years. Their father, Zebedee, had brought them into the family fishing business at an early age. Now, because of his health he had essentially retired and James managed their many boats and the crews.

Joshua measured John as they hugged: Fourteen, full of life, slender but muscular. His infectious smile spread across his face as they embraced one another.

"You have grown, cousin!" Last time I saw you, you barely came up to my chin. Now I can hardly see over the top of your head."

"John beamed even more. Next time we will be looking eye to eye. James has placed me in charge of the second boat now." This was spoken with a mixture of pride and masculinity.

At this, James stepped forward and embraced Joshua with his powerful arms. Years of rowing and hauling in nets had given him a formidable body. He stood slightly taller than Joshua, had a craggy but attractive face which the young ladies of the village seemed to admire. Unofficially he was the wrestling champion of the village.

"James, your body feels as strong as ever, but your eyes appear to be a bit weary. So I ask, wanting more than your customary answer, 'Fine:' How are you?"

James relaxed his embrace, taken back by Joshua's candor. He paused for a moment to find the words. An honest question deserved an honest reply, but he wanted to frame his words so that they would neither be misleading nor too revealing.

"The body works well and has no pains. The fishing is good. The nights are peaceful. But, you are right, cousin. There is a sameness that has crept into my life that seems to make one day just like another."

"We shall talk about that tonight, after we have dined on some of your day's catch."

"I shall look forward to it. Now what is it that brings you this way, during what should be a busy time for builders?"

"That, too, will wait until we talk. Agreed?"

"Agreed!" With that settled, Joshua put his arms around both their shoulders and they walked together to the house of Zebedee.

The house was spacious by Galilean standards. Zebedee had prospered early as a fisherman. He seemed to have a special sense of where the fish would be gathered depending upon the temperature of the air and the clarity of the sky. He had done well, and to celebrate (and probably demonstrate) his success he had Joseph build him a two story house complete with an overhanging cloth to cover the doorway.

James ducked his head, more by habit than necessity, as he lead the way into the house. Joshua saw Aunt Salome tending to the meal preparation with her two yet-unmarried daughters. Uncle Zebedee was still at the synagogue discussing the Scriptures with some of the elders of the village. When Salome saw Joshua, she gave a gasp of delight, quickly placed her bowl on a table and rushed over to greet him. Joshua had always been the favorite nephew. She may have tried to hide it, but the sparkle in her eyes whenever she looked at him betrayed her attempt at impartiality.

"Joshua! What a delightful surprise! You will stay for dinner, won't you?" She asked this as though there were an alternative. They both knew there was none, but an invitation made her welcome more hospitable.

"Of course, dear aunt. Of course." This younger sister of his mother was such a delight: Outgoing and spontaneous in her expressions of affection. She was someone he wanted to see every time he visited Capernaum. It was never just a dutiful call on a relative. It was a necessity of the heart. For a moment they simply stood facing one another in a light embrace. As they did so Joshua read the lines in her face. She was about forty two years of age, and the lines traced the history of the joys and trials she had experienced in those years. Without a word he began to kiss those lines, and to stroke them with his fingers. Salome sensed what he was doing, so she stood silently reliving some of those moments. Her mind eventually arrived at the moment of her sister's announced pregnancy and Joshua's birth. She recalled holding this strong, skilled builder in her arms, marveling at the miracle of Yahweh's loving, re-creative power.

She smiled tenderly up at him. Joshua seemed to sense where her thoughts had traveled. They looked into one another's eyes as though seeing a long-ago drama acted out in pantomime. Suddenly Salome turned and walked back to her bowl.

"You have had a long walk. We will need a few extra fish. I hope you brought some, James."

James had been watching this mini drama unfold. He was grateful that his mother and Joshua had this special bond . . . still . . . there was always a sense of being an outsider as they communicated so deeply without words.

"I saw him coming, Mother. He looked like he had lost some weight and I knew you would want to fatten him up a bit." He patted his own stomach as he said that, emphasizing how his mother loved to feed her men. "I picked out two extras before I went over to hear him tell his story to the men."

Salome, gave a quick glance at Joshua, then returned to whatever it was she had in her bowl. "So now you are a story teller? Does that pay better than building?" She said this in a joking manner, but Joshua sensed that she was on to the fact that something new was happening in his life.

"Not yet, Aunt Salome." He paused, weighing whether he should use this opportunity to announce his mission. Then, deciding to be honest, but to temper it in order to reduce the emotional reaction, he added, "But I am hoping it can provide enough to keep body and spirit together." He leaned back on the mat and let that lay before them.

James was the first to respond: "So that's what brings you here – and away from the building business in Nazareth? You want to be a story teller! You've always been good at story telling. Tell me, is it as an entertainer or rabbi?"

Joshua looked directly at James: "I am not an entertainer, cousin. My life has to have more meaning than that.

He had spoken those words kindly, but James felt the light sting of his words. "I apologize, Joshua. You know I respect you and would never intentionally offend you. You have no credentials, though. The rabbis who have taught you have no reputation to pass along to you. Who will come to listen to you?"

"I will go to them," Joshua replied quickly and calmly.

James liked his answer but wanted to push the issue of credentials further. "That is fine, but why should they want to listen?"

"People like stories. They will listen."

"But will they accept what you teach?" James was not willing to let this go easily. He admired his cousin. However he felt compelled to make him think his way into the reality of what he would encounter in this new career.

With a confidence that he was unaware he possessed until he spoke, Joshua responded with slow, measured words: "They will believe because it will ring true in their hearts."

James looked at Joshua in awe. This cousin of his looked the same as always, but there was something different – something new and somehow more powerful within him.

"I hope . . . I believe . . . yes, *believe* . . . they just might listen to what you have to say."

Silence filled the room. A hushed silence that crept into the corners and ran across the floor encircling everyone where they stood or sat. No one even felt as though they had words which might be appropriate for the moment.

James just lowered his head and seemed to draw within himself.

John sat quietly gazing in admiration at his cousin. He had always admired Joshua, but had never seen him so composed – so certain ... so ... His smile slowly broadened and his eyes glowed in warm admiration.

The two sisters stood frozen where they were. Their faces suggested they had just been told some profound truth.

Salome sat impassively staring at the ceiling. Her mind was racing to make sense of what she had just experienced. Somewhere along life's way little Joshua had become big Joshua. She had seen that and had rejoiced in it. Now, however, he suddenly appeared even bigger ... in some way she could not quite grasp. She remembered again his birth and the first time she had held him in her arms. Now it was as though he had become large enough to cradle her.

At this point Zebedee entered into the room. He immediately was caught in the silence, even as his eyes darted about and saw Joshua. Their eyes met and they nodded. Then Zebedee turned and seated himself at the short platform that served as the dining table.

"When's diner?" He asked, breaking the bond of silence that had held them.

Chapter Eleven

Announcement and Invitation

After dinner and enough pleasant banter to have fulfilled the courtesies required, Joshua rose, nodded to James and stepped out into the early dusk. Night came quickly in the valley. The sun slipped behind one of the ridges and suddenly the evening colors of pinks, yellow, reds and orange disappeared into darkness. As James was making his exit Joshua looked about to take a last look at the glorious landscape of that Galilean valley before it faded into the night.. The sea lay calm, as though it, too, had completed its day's work. Overhead, a fingernail moon was resting on a wisp of cloud. To the north there was the snow-capped peak of Mt. Hermon still glistening in the fading light.. *Sometimes I wish Joseph had found his way here and become a fisherman. It is pleasant to end the day wrapped in such beauty.* James appearance interrupted his reverie.

"Well, cousin, I think you shared your news, so let's just talk about me," said James. Joshua smiled at his words. He realized he had been the center of attention for most of the evening, and this had to ruffle a few feathers not matter how warm the bond between them.

"Yes, James. Enough about me. Even I tired of it. Tell me of this unrest you are feeling." With that Joshua began to stroll along the shore, realizing that the upcoming conversation might flow better if they walked side by side.

"It's not that I am unhappy . . . It's just that something seems to be missing from my life that I had never noticed before."

Joshua took a quick sidelong glance at James. *Nearing his thirtieth birthday. That's about the time I began to feel the unrest – the vague dissatisfaction – that led me to the Jordan.* "So, James, can you name this missing something?

"I wish I could. Then at least I would have some idea of what I am looking for."

"Tell me, James, could it be some item or some activity that you feel would fill the void?"

At this, James drew into himself and the walked in silence. Joshua turned his attention to the sea on his right. He observed that the reflection of the moon's light appeared to come directly to them and to follow them as they walked along the shore. *Isn't that interesting . . . I've noticed that happening whenever I've been here by the sea. No matter where I am on the shore, the moon's light comes directly to me . . . I suppose it does that for everyone, no matter where they are standing . . . something like Yahweh's love, shining down on everyone . . . all from one source . . .* His thought was interrupted as James broke the silence.

"It's not either of those, Joshua. It is something I feel that is missing inside of me. There is some inner yearning or craving that I cannot identify. It's as though something deep inside of me has suddenly awakened to what I am doing and who I really am apart from the fishing, the wrestling, and the things I do to fill the days. I sense there is so much more to me – to life – and I hunger for it."

He looked sheepishly at Joshua: "Forgive me if I sound as if I am trying to be a philosopher. I have no ambitions to do that. I know I do not have the kind of mind that you have . . . or that John has. That also is some cause for my unrest or dissatisfaction – or whatever you may call it. John is different from most of the people here. Oh, he's a good enough fisherman. The men like and respect him. The women love him, and many of the young girls of the village (and their mothers) already have set their sights on him.

But just as you did not belong in Nazareth, John does not belong in Capernaum. His mind should be trained. You have not seen or heard him as I have. He sees things most people do not see, and he seems to understand things in a different way . . . a way that makes sense – a different kind of sense than our way of thinking . . . just as you do, my cousin. I worry that he will waste these gifts as a fisherman."

Having said this, James settled back into an embarrassed silence. He was not sure that Joshua would understand or even take him seriously. He had tried to express some of these thoughts to some of his friends, but had always stopped short when he sensed that they either did not begin to understand or that they really were not interested. Wine and wrestling was what they shared in common. Nothing more. On occasion that had caused James to feel alone even in the midst of a roaring, laughing crowd.

"Perhaps John should travel with me," Joshua offered in a quiet, steady voice. "You, too, may find whatever it is you are looking for where I am going." He let this sit, without elaboration. Not quite an invitation, but an opening of a door if James wished to enter.

They continued to tread slowly along the shore. The stars had begun to appear as a glistening canopy over their heads. The lights from the villages rose up on the hillsides to greet them and join them in creating an illusion of being surrounded by thousands of tiny lamps lighting the night and signaling that all was well and the evening was safe..

"I shall think about that . . . and I shall speak to John."

As if by common consent they turned and began a slow trek back to Capernaum. Though they continued to walk side by side, each man was on his separate journey.

When they arrived home, James spoke with John and the two of them stepped outside. Joshua turned his attention to the two girls, Martha and Elizabeth. He had essentially ignored them when he first arrived. They had been busy with their chores and his attention was focused upon Salome and James. He cared deeply for both girls. In many ways they reminded him of his sisters. Both were bright and perceptive. Both had accepted that their lot in life was to become wives and mothers, but both also had longings just beneath the surface that wanted to experience life far more fully than their role as women would allow. He invited them to sit outside with him, gaze at the stars, and listen to him as he explained the Scriptures and told them stories that opened their hearts and their minds to more than what their meager lives would offer.

Both Martha and Elizabeth adored their older cousin for the respect he showed them and the wonders he opened up to them. He always managed to give them a feeling of worth and a storehouse of wonders they could hold in their minds and use to fill the tedium of their days.

As Joshua was giving each girl a good night hug he looked up to see James and John returning from their moonlight stroll. James stood fully a head taller than his brother, and his hand rested on John's shoulder as they walked. He noticed that John seemed to be nodding agreement to whatever it was that James was saying.

He assessed the situation, nodded quietly to himself, entered the house, and found the mat that Salome always saved and laid out especially for him. Then he sat himself down, removed his sandals, lay down, stretched out, closed his eyes and awaited the arrival of restful slumber.

Just as he was dozing off he heard James and John as they entered the house and found their ways to their mats. Their whispering continued for a few moments then faded into silence.

The house of Zebedee was at rest.

CHAPTER TWELVE

CALLING THE DISCIPLES

It did not seem to matter where he slept: The hills of Megiddo, the streets of Jerusalem, the valley of Galilee. Some inner sense always awoke him just before the morning light began to break the darkness. Joshua's eyes opened - not with the bleariness of still - clinging sleep – but with clarity and anticipation as though they wished to see what the world was preparing to lay out for the morning.

Joshua turned, sat up, crossed his legs, and rose straight up from that position. His legs had become powerful through years of scaling the hillsides and they were enough to let him stand without even the need of steadying himself against the wall. He bent over, lifted his sandals, went to the entrance and stepped into the slowly emerging dawn of a Galilean morning. The air was fresh and he breathed it in deeply as he stretched his body and began to observe the breaking of the day. He could dimly see a few sea birds floating on the air a few feet above the small waves as they searched for their breakfasts. Occasionally one would swoop down and there would be a splash followed by the sight of a beak filled with a flopping fish about to be devoured. *God's natural fisherman*, he thought with a glow of admiration. Then he turned his attention to the north and gazed up at Mt. Hermon. It still was mostly hidden by the shadows, but its snow-capped peak had been seen and lighted by the first rays of the sun as they began their task of melting the snows that would flow southward to become the Jordan River.

He walked up a beaten pathway to the hillside where he had prayed before his arrival. There was a citrus grove in the area. He could smell its spicy aroma before his eyes were able to locate it. For a moment he stood still and just breathed in the entire richness of the unfolding morning. As he did so the first rays of the sun flashed across the surface of the sea below him, and in that moment he felt himself in complete harmony – complete unity – with the entirety of Creation.

My Father! My Father! How I thank you for the beauty – the goodness - you have created that is so readily available to all who would see. With this thought, he quickly seated himself upon one of the large rocks, intentionally slowed his breathing and began to settle himself into a deeper part within him as he repeated his mantra:

Wherever you lead; whatever you ask; I will be faithful. Make my way clear, is all I ask.

Wherever you lead; whatever you ask; I will be faithful. Make my way clear, is all I ask.

Wherever you lead; whatever you ask; I will be faithful. Make my way clear, is all I ask.

The dim inner recess where he had begun to settle himself began to glow with a soft iridescent light. The sense of unity flowed through him and engulfed him in a gentle blending of assurance and love which transcended the ability of any words to describe.

This was not a time for words. There was no need for words in this morning meditation. He already knew what he was to do and where he was headed that day. It was enough to be embraced by the underlying wholeness – the oneness – of Creation.

Eventually he opened his eyes and saw a few boats beginning to move across the water. He could hear the voices of the villagers wafting across the fields. It was time – past time, perhaps – to join the house of Zebedee for their morning meal. Reluctantly he rose from the comfort of his rocky perch and walked the path back to the village.

When he arrived inside the house, the family was just gathering around the large plank of driftwood that served as the family table. The table was laden with hunks of goat cheese, smoked fish, rich, dark bread, dates, figs, grapes, and a few nuts. Lunch and supper were light meals. Breakfast was the time to stoke up for the day's work.

"Come join us, Joshua, Zebedee offered. "We were just about the give thanks to God for the new day."

Joshua paused where he was as his uncle gave thanks and asked the blessings for the day. Then he found a place around the table and lowered himself to the floor. He rested on his left elbow and reached for the loaf of bread, tore off a large hunk, and began to munch on it. James was busy slicing pieces of cheese and passing them along. Elizabeth and Martha smiled shyly at him and he returned the smile with a nod to each. As he did so, he made a quick appraisal of each in the morning light. Zebedee had already denied the requests of two suitors for Martha. She was attractive in a pleasant way. About average height, with an ever-present smile and sparkling eyes which suggested both intelligence and spirit. *I think Uncle Zeb has higher goals for Martha, perhaps the rabbi's son. He soon should be looking for a bride. Elizabeth now is another issue. She is a nice person but she was not blessed with much of a body – a bit dumpy I believe. Her nose is a tad oversized and her eyes are squinty. She is sweet and intelligent, but most young men do not see much beyond the face and body. What a shame. Someone is missing a good bet and will live his life alone . . . or with an attractive shrew.* He reached for some cheese and stretched a bit farther to select some figs.

"Well, Joshua," Salome said almost laughingly, "When are you going to begin telling your stories?"

Joshua paused for a moment as he struggled to chew down the large hunk of cheese he had just placed in his mouth. Salome and John grinned as they watched his discomfort. The others had either ignored or not heard the question and continued to munch their morsels in silence.

"Today is the day, dear aunt." Joshua replied in a slow, steady voice that caused the others to tune in. "I shall launch my new career here, in Capernaum."

James reacted automatically: "Everyone is working, Joshua. They have no time for stories."

"Not everyone, James. Some of (he glanced quickly at Zebedee) the elders and most of the children have some free time. I shall begin with them. Then we shall see whose curiosity calls them to join in."

"Children!" Zebedee shouted indignantly. "You are going to waste your time telling stories to children? Why do you think we elders would be interested in children's stories?"

Everyone at the table froze. Zebedee's reaction was unexpected. Their eyes all focused on Joshua to see how he would respond.

Joshua looked directly into his uncle's eyes. He smiled pleasantly. Then calmly, with measured words he said, "There is a child in every one of us, uncle. We grow older and hopefully wiser as we age, but there remains that child that we were who still wants to laugh and play freely, who still looks at the world in wonder, and — yes - who still wants to be held and to feel secure and loved by someone who truly cares for – and watches over him."

Zebedee's face softened. Joshua's words had resonated in some near-forgotten place that lay deep within him. He nodded, almost meekly as though he had just lost a game of dice. After a long silence, he spoke: "I want to hear your stories, my wise nephew. I shall invite some of my friends to join me."

Salome eyes moved back and forth between her husband and her nephew. She knew she had just witnessed a memorable moment. Her husband, who never lost an argument or gave an inch, and enjoyed talking with the rabbi and the other wise men of the village, was obviously impressed by the wisdom of his relatively young nephew. *Perhaps, Joshua can make his living as a story teller.* She lowered her head and reached for some nuts.

After they had eaten their fill each rose and began to prepare for the day's work. James and John stepped outside and strode toward the shore where the fishermen already were beginning to assemble. Elizabeth and Martha picked up the scraps and cleared away the remaining food. Salome had decided it was the day for her to mend some of the family's garments, so she gathered them up, selected some needles and thread and took them outside into the light. Zebedee stretched himself out on his mat. He was at the point in life where a brief after-breakfast nap was a pleasant luxury he occasionally allowed himself.

Joshua strolled toward a point on the shore that was vacant. Once there, he knelt and began to mold the wet sand into geometric forms. He worked with painstaking care, carefully shaping each item with great detail. In a matter of hours he had constructed what appeared to be a palatial mansion, complete with a flat roof containing mats made of seaweed. He seemed totally absorbed in the process and appeared not to notice the crowd of young children, and some of their mothers, who had come to watch. By this time, Zebedee had wakened from his nap and had invited some of his friends to come to the shore to watch . . . and to listen.

As though suddenly aware of his audience, Joshua began his story:

"There was a man, a very wealthy man, who had lived his life and made his fortune in Jerusalem. All the while he was working, earning huge sums of money in the noisy, busy city he had dreamed of owning a home by the sea. He pictured himself here by the sea, rising early in the morning and watching the sun rise, sending its rays glistening across the waters. He imagined how it would be to step out a few feet from his doorway and walk along the beach, allowing the gentle waves to wash his feet. He would have a sail boat. Yes, a large sailboat with a crew of men to handle the oars and manage the sails while he and his wife reclined on pillows and enjoyed the passing landscape. His home would be complete – with every thing a person needed or desired."

At this, Joshua began to point toward sections of the house.

"Here was a master bedroom, with a large window facing the sea. The bed had a thick mattress made of sheep's wool which the servants fluffed every evening before bedtime." The children (and some of the mothers) gave murmurs of delight at this. He then pointed to another part of the house. "Here is where they dined (rich people dine, they do not just eat,)" he said with a laugh – which caused all to chuckle. "The kitchen is here next to it, with an outside kitchen covered by this little shelter. Over here are the children's rooms complete with a fenced in play area. On the roof is an outside bedroom for those warm nights when the entire family chooses to sleep under the stars in the quietness of this Galilean valley. It is also a more than suitable place to construct a booth for Succoth." He said this with a nod to the rabbi who also had accepted Zebedee's invitation. By this time, many of the women and even some of the elders are displaying dreamy eyes as they envision such a home for themselves. Joshua smiled. He had them snared as surely as if he had used a net. He continued: "There is the walled shower. The water supply is kept full by the servants who use this large goat skin bag to carry the water from the sea." At this Joshua lifted a large skin bag, went to the shore's edge and dipped the bag into the water. He returned to the sand mansion, suddenly lifted the bag and threw its contents on it, causing it to instantly melt and disappear, but for a few lumps of shapeless sand. The crowd gasped in horror and disbelief. *How could anyone do that to such a thing of beauty!* Joshua waited for their emotions to quiet, though a few of the young ones still clung to their mothers, and stared at him with shocked eyes.

He looked at the crowd, allowing his eyes to pause for a moment as he focused on each person there: "The man was a fool. Rich, yes! Clever, yes! Still he was a fool." He paused to let this thought settle. "He had built his house – this beautiful mansion – on sand. Every one of you knows better than that, do you not? We know that even the more serene of seas can suddenly become a stormy torrent of water. In the same way, our quiet secure lives may suddenly be filled with dangerous storms." He walked over a few feet to where the smooth tip of a nearly-buried rock jutted just above the sands. "Here is where he needed to build his home. Here on rock that does not shift beneath him or melt away in the storms of life." He nodded to the rabbi, who was listening attentively and appreciatively. "This man is one who knows about that rock." With that, Joshua sat, rested his arm on the rock, and gazed out toward the fishing boats where some of the crews were drawing in their nets, apparently with a goodly catch, as well.

It looks as though they may be returning soon, he thought. He smiled and began to scoop up some of the dry sand behind him. He sifted it into a small pile, scooped up another and another and added to the pile until it became a noticeable mound. Then he stretched himself, lay back with his head nestled on the mound, closed his eyes and whispered to himself: *I think I shall do a bit more fishing.*

He began pondering how to explain himself to those who would become his student followers, his disciples. *If I make a claim at being the messiah I may lose them. They might think me mad – or another one of those false messiahs that have overrun our history with their wild claims and even wilder actions. A lot of people – mostly Jews – were slain in vain efforts at revolt.* His mind began to recount the innumerable uprisings in Galilee. Each had been led by some deranged or overly ambitious person claiming to be the long-awaited Son-of-David who would drive out the new Philistines and rebuild the kingdom to the glory days of old. *I wonder how glorious those glory days actually were,* he mused. *No, I shall simply pass myself off as a teacher of wisdom – a new wisdom. Hopefully they will figure it out for themselves.* He shook his head and grinned: *If they do not . . . well, then perhaps I am just another one of the false messiahs. However, this time no one will know, but me.*

In less than an hour the first boats began to arrive. Joshua had been right in his estimate. Fishing had been exceptionally good. There was a limited number of fish that could be cleaned and sold each day, and this number had been reached quite early.

Joshua observed that many of the boats were part of the large fishing fleet owned by Andrew and Simon's father. They clustered together at the shore to work together as one large crew. He looked at the sky to estimate the hour. The sun straight up was six: the half-way mark. *The seventh hour. A good sign.* He began a casual, but purposeful stroll along the shore toward Andrew and Simon.

Both Andrew and Simon were totally engaged in their work. This was a short fishing day, which gave them the opportunity to do repairs and maintenance that normally was delayed. The men were still fresh. They would put them to mending some of the torn nets, caulking some of those pesky leaks, and checking the sails for worn places. They would work them for another hour and still send them home earlier than usual.

They were unaware of Joshua's presence until Andrew, turning to call to one of the crew chiefs, saw him standing about forty feet away, staring at him. Andrew squinted his eyes. He and Joshua were about the same height, but somehow Joshua appeared larger - much larger. He nudged Simon, who turned and immediately saw Joshua quietly gazing at the two of them. In that moment Simon's body slumped slightly and his hands, still at his side, involuntarily opened to Joshua.

"Andrew! Simon! Come with me and I will make you fishers of men." Joshua spoke those words in a normal conversational voice. It was an invitation. However they struck the two brothers as a command. Both of them had been hungering for some greater meaning in their lives. Every time this nephew of Zebedee's had come to the village they had been captured by the wisdom he spoke so quietly – yet so authoritatively.

They looked at one another, staring deeply into the eyes of the other. There was an almost unnoticeable nod. Then they dropped the net they were holding and walked together toward this man from Nazareth who had suddenly become their rabbi – their master.

As they approached him, Joshua turned and began walking toward his cousins whom he had seen landing their craft further down the shoreline. Zebedee had also observed the full nets and had waited for his sons to return. He was in one of the boats, reliving his active days, bantering with some of the crew. They all were absorbed in the task of securing the boat and laying the nets to dry. James looked up as the three men neared. He knew instantly what was happening. He paused in his work for a moment to reach quickly and deeply within himself, testing for one last time the decision he and John had made. When he observed this, Joshua stopped walking and waited until James resurfaced and looked again at him. He said nothing with his lips, but his eyes were asking the question: "Are you ready?" James understood it with greater clarity than if the actual words had been uttered. He reached out and took his younger brothers hand. John looked startled by this interruption. He looked at James. Then he looked toward where his brother was gazing. Without a word, he released the net in his hand, and as it fell to the sand he and James walked together toward this remarkable cousin of theirs. Zebedee watched his sons walk away from their birthrights, and bent his head so that those with him would not notice the tears he could not restrain.

Their journey had begun!

CHAPTER THIRTEEN

GETTING STARTED

Joshua led the four to the place on the hillside that he had begun to think of as his spiritual home. Although it actually lay 250 feet below sea level, the Galilean Sea was another 400 feet farther below them. The sun's rays caused the water to shimmer almost magically. The hills were lush with verdant growth. Small groves of trees bearing fruits or nuts broke the smooth symmetry of the landscape. The sky stretched out overhead like a canopy of light blue, with wisps of fluffy white drifting slowly to the west.

For a moment he paused, lifted his arms and seemed to inhale the entirety of what he surveyed. Those following him paused, almost in wonder. They had lived on the edge of this hillside for their entire lives and had never taken the time to pause and behold its beauty. If they ever had passed that way their eyes and their minds had been elsewhere.

As he turned to face the four new disciples Joshua was startled to see that there were far more than the four who had started with him. A quick count told him that there were now nine. Some of the others had seen the small procession and had tagged along out of curiosity. *Well, surprise, surprise! I suppose the thing to do is to speak to those I called, let the others listen in, then . . . well . . . then see what follows.* He seated himself on his favorite rocky perch, motioned for the others to sit around him, and began to speak.

"I could tell from your reactions that some of you have never seen the view from here, or if you had you did not take in its beauty. Am I right?"

The nodding of heads told him he was, so he continued: "What I wish to do is to give people an opportunity to view their entire lives in a fresh, new way — a way that will allow them to see the world with all its beauty, its glory . . . its wonder."

He paused to see how this thought was being received. There were a few side glances, some nodding of heads and shoulder shrugs. Then each one settled his gaze back on Joshua with looks of expectancy. "We have people in Capernaum who have never left the village. They see through narrow eyes. They look at the villages on the other side and think of them as different and dangerous. I have heard them talking. They hunch over and say things they know nothing about: 'They smell different.' 'They're lazy.' 'Watch out or they will sneak over and take our children.' Senseless ideas! In their ignorance they spread fear and falsehood." Two of the men looked angry at this. *I seem to have stepped on some toes. I imagine I will not count those two among my new followers . . . but let's see where this goes.*

"Those of us who have had interchange with the Hellenists know them to be quite like ourselves. They do speak Greek, of course, and that causes them to think a bit differently. Still, I find them to be essentially good people who do their work, care for their children, and desire to live in peace. They smell no differently, look no differently, and do not appear to be predators. Those of us who have been to Jerusalem have a different way of seeing the world than those who have not. City life is quite different from the life we live in this quiet valley. The pace here is slower. The values are different."

John raised his hand. Joshua saw him, nodded and gestured for him to speak.

"In what ways are the values different?" There was a bit of a challenge in the question; a "show me or I'll not believe" tone. Joshua smiled his approval. He would have to be able to explain and amplify what he tried to teach. This would be good.

"Possessions are more important to the city people. They spend much time in making and bargaining for things they really do not need. Their homes are more cluttered than ours. Also, there is more emphasis on clothing. Our clothes are to cover and keep warm. Theirs are to make some statement about how important or wealthy they are."

Hearing this, the group began to chuckle and to shake their heads. They simply could not imagine wasting time and effort in attempting to appear important.

A voice from the back laughingly called out: "Hey, everyone in Capernaum knows everyone else. They see how many fish we catch. They know if we own a boat or merely work on one. They know who is a good farmer and who is not. What good would it do to pretend?"

Joshua recognized the speaker. It was one of Zebedee's crew chiefs: Thaddaeus. He was average height, wiry, rough-hewn good looks . . . somewhere in his mid twenties.

"That's right, Thaddaeus! We would look like play actors, hypocrites, wearing masks to make ourselves appear better, but in actuality just playing the fool. Everyone would be laughing at us behind our backs"

He realized this was the moment to switch the focus. "However, whether we want to admit it or not we all have some values that are out of keeping with the will of God."

Suddenly the laughter abated and a look of seriousness — but an open seriousness — appeared on their faces.

This is the test. I either get my ideas across to this group or I go back and make new plans. "We have drifted away from the underlying principles set forth by Moses. They have become misplaced or corrupted by our own laziness and self-interest."

He could tell by the intent look on their faces that they were ready — eager - to hear more.

"We focus our attention on this brief life and do not consider that our heavenly father has plans for us that reach far beyond the boundaries of our imagination. We think primarily of taking care of our bodies and give little thought to eternal things. When we do we often act as though God is some judge looking down at us and keeping score of our actions. Know this: our heavenly father knows our most secret thoughts and he is not deceived by our actions."

Their surprise and confusion upon hearing this was obvious. But he continued, not wanting the flow of thought to be interrupted by questions at this time.

"In order to be able to live in this future realm that Yahweh has prepared, each of us must be quite different from what we now are. Let's be honest, even though we may not try to appear to be more than we are – because we know it would not work here in Capernaum". (He said this with a smile to lighten the message, and the men also smiled,) "do we not secretly wish we were rich or powerful and admired by others?" He received some shy, affirming nods in response. "Our heavenly father wants those who have servant hearts – not those who desire to be exalted. He wants those who are willing to give their lives for others – not those who want others to sacrifice for them. He wants those who relate and care more for the poor, rather than those who seek only for themselves. Our heavenly father desires mercy more than what we call justice." He quickly decided to amplify this. "Have you observed that Roman justice and Herod's justice are cruel, vengeful and aimed at the poor and defenseless? I would remind you that Scriptures tells us that God has decreed, 'Vengeance is mine.' By this he means it is not ours. Yahweh prefers redemption to punishment. He prefers reconciliation to exile. He wishes us to practice this in our daily lives. Our task is to create peace by refusing to practice vengeance. When we practice vengeance we perpetuate violence. You may have heard it said 'an eye for an eye.' That was an early attempt to stop the endless blood feuds that were consuming the children of Israel in their wilderness flight from Egypt. A member of one tribe would kill or injure a member of another tribe and the retaliation bounced back and forth forever, until no one remembered why it had begun. they just believed it was their task to avenge the last response from the other tribe. Moses said that the score should be made even then the violence must stop. If someone took an eye then it was proper to take an eye from the offender then call it even and cease from any further retaliation. Well I tell you that it is past time that we as a people grew up and began to act like adults. If someone slaps you on your cheek, turn the other to him."

"Hold it right there!" It was Andrew, rising to his feet and braced as though ready to pounce on a wrestling opponent. "If you actually try that you are going to get slapped silly!" The others nodded in agreement.

Joshua waited for a moment to let the emotions quiet among his listeners. He stood absolutely still, straight as an arrow, steadily gazing at him. The group settled themselves and again turned their full attention toward Joshua.

"Have you ever tried to do that, Andrew?" The question was quietly spoken without a trace of judgment. However, Andrew took it as a challenge and struggled for a response. Finally he decided to stay with his mood.

"Of course not! That would be foolish!" He stood, now glaring at Joshua for having turned this into a contest.

"Try it sometime, if anyone in the village is fool enough to slap you." He smiled at the men seated around him as he said this in an effort to close the gap he felt was developing between him and Andrew. "Try it and see what happens. Also, if, when you are on the road a soldier orders you to carry his items for the approved mile, go a mile farther and see what happens. There is a decent streak in every person, if you appeal to that instead of the violent part, you will elicit that decency and perhaps - just perhaps – you might even make a new friend. When we respond to anger with anger we only make matters worse. A threat brings out the fighter within us. Gentleness elicits a kinder part."

Andrew slowly lowered himself to the ground. Whatever struggle there had been between them was over. He was not sure how, but in some way Joshua had made his point. He did not feel defeated. *I know Joshua won, but I do not feel as though I lost. Rather, I feel as though I have been washed inside, that something within me has been made clean, and that I would, indeed, turn my cheek or go the extra mile . . . and that my life will work better if I do.* He looked at those near him, their nods and smiles told him that they also thought everyone had been a winner in hearing this new idea.

"God's realm – his kingdom is not something to be hoped for . . . something we dream about and believe may be established in the future. It is a here and now reality. In our present understanding, however it might just as well be a dream because we cannot see it or experience its wonders. What is called for is a radical repentance – a transforming of the way our minds work – our values – perceptions – our understanding of traditions. When that occurs within you, then you will discover yourselves living in God's kingdom."

"How do we go about transforming our minds to make this happen?" The speaker was a tall, rather quiet-spoken man of about thirty. His body was sinewy and graceful. Joshua had seen him among the fishermen and had admired him. When he walked he gave the impression of a mountain lion striding a narrow trail, one foot placed carefully ahead of the other. He was one of the crew chiefs who worked with Andrew and Simon.

"Good question, Thomas. Actually it is the big question – the only question that gives meaning to what I said." Thomas smiled at this public compliment. He sat, waiting for Joshua's response.

"Genuine repentance is not easily attained for a variety of reasons. Here is the main one, however: We are so immersed in our present way of thinking that we tend to believe that whatever we believe to be true actually is true. It is the other fellow's beliefs that need changing. We are so accustomed to viewing the world in a certain way that we have made that our reality. If I were to ask any of you which of your cherished beliefs or values you need to change, could you name even one at this time?"

The men responded to this in different ways. Some drew within themselves. Some began to speak with a person by them. Some just waited as though without a thought of their own, but wanting Joshua to answer the question for them.

"Another reason that full repentance is difficult is this: Even when you recognize the need to change your old way of thinking, habits of the mind and heart are difficult to make. You may know what is right, but there seems to be something deep within you that clings to the old."

At this, each man seemed to withdraw within himself. Joshua had touched a nerve: One they had never felt before. They were ready.

I suppose this the moment to wrap it up – to give an invitation and see who accepts it.

"If you wish to see the world as your father has meant it to be – if you wish to become true children of your heavenly father - if any of you wish to find your way into the kingdom, come with me."

As he walked back toward Capernaum he saw the roof of the synagogue. *Tonight begins the Sabbath,* he mused. *I suppose if I am to be a rabbi this would be a good time to begin.*

CHAPTER FOURTEEN

DISCOVERY AND CHALLENGE

Joshua was one of the first to enter the synagogue. He found a seat near the front, and when it appeared that all the men were present he rose and began to recite from the Scriptures. As he did so, he also expounded on them, explaining their meaning and relevance to their daily lives. Even those who had heard him earlier seemed astounded. They sat, quietly absorbing every word. Some in the back rows were whispering, "He speaks as one with authority, and not as the scribes we have heard who feel the need to cite ancient authorities for every thought they have."

Suddenly, one of the men leapt to his feet shouting, "What have you to do with us, Joshua of Nazareth? Have you come to destroy us?" He then paused and surveyed the room. His eyes were ablaze, with a cruel, vicious glow. He abruptly turned and stared directly at Joshua, and said in a low, threatening tone that sounded more like a growl than a voice: "I know who you are. You are the holy one of God." He stared directly at Joshua and Joshua returned his stare. Neither blinked an eye, and all present held their breath, wondering what was happening and what would happen next. Finally, Joshua raised his hand, pointing directly at the chest of the man, and spoke in a commanding voice:

"Be silent! Come out of him!"

Instantly the man convulsed as though he had been hit in the stomach with a heavy club. He emitted a loud, screeching cry that chilled the insides of every man present. Then he fell silent and lay there breathing heavily at first. No one moved; they stood almost as statues and waited. Eventually the man's breathing returned to normal and he sat up, looking bewildered but peaceful. One of the men helped him to his feet. The man rose, still obviously confused as if wondering where he was.

One of the elders asked the question that was on every man's lips: "What is this? A new teaching – with authority, and he commands even the unclean spirits and they obey him?"

Joshua was echoing these thoughts. I had known the man was possessed and I knew I could cast the demon out of him. How I had known . . . well . . . I don't know. He grinned as he thought this, but it was an uneasy grin.

A stirring of excitement surged through the crowd. No one had ever experienced a synagogue service such as this. First Joshua, this neighbor of theirs, had spoken with an authority that commanded their attention and acceptance of his words. Then this same Joshua had cast out a demon before their eyes. He had done that with a tone of totally dominating authority, as well. A unseen voice cried aloud, echoing the elder's words: "He speaks, and we must listen. He commands and even unclean spirits must obey! What has happened to him?" a voice said to no one in particular. And there were only unintelligible murmurings in response.

Joshua gestured to his new disciples, and they followed him out of the synagogue and out of Capernaum. *I need time for this to settle down or I will be turned into a show,* he thought. The group spent the night on the hillside, then they went to some of the nearby villages where Joshua told his stories and taught those who would listen.

Two days later, they returned to Capernaum. Simon had asked Joshua to dine with him that evening. He would tell his family his decision to leave Capernaum and become a disciple. There were things he must settle first, of course. He had two houses: one in Bethsaida and another in Capernaum. He had been married, but his wife had died as had the child in giving birth. His mother-in-law had become widowed and he had decided to move into her house to care for her and to be near to his work. He needed to provide for her care. Then he and Andrew had to inform their father of their decision to leave the business. There were many good men just waiting to be crew chiefs so this would not work a hardship. However, it would be a great disappointment to their father who always imagined them continuing the business he had worked so hard to build.

As the sunlight began to fade Joshua went to Simon's home, assuming he had tended to his personal affairs and that the evening meal would soon be ready. He arrived to learn that Simon's mother-in-law was ill. Some fever had come upon her and she was in bed. The meal was being prepared by a servant, and would soon be ready. Joshua saw that the meal was more of a feast and that many places had been prepared around a huge low-lying table that must have been stored behind the house. *Of course!* Joshua thought: *This is a farewell feast. Simon and Andrew must bid farewell to their many friends.* His immediate concern, however, was for Simon's mother-in-law.

"May I see her?" he asked Simon.

"Of course . . . Master." Both smiled at this new title. Simon felt proud at having said it. It was an acknowledgement that he now had someone to admire, to serve and to give him hope for the future. Joshua realized he would have to become accustomed to the title – as strange and awkward as it now felt.

Simon led Joshua to a small room in the rear of the house. He stopped at the door and gestured for Joshua to enter, assuming that he would offer words of comfort and encouragement. "Her name is Martha," Simon whispered as Joshua walked past him. As he had walked into the room where Simon's mother-in-law lay,

Joshua had thought to himself, *I know this will appear audacious to Simon. Some part of me hopes he looks away when I go into the room. But I know, I really know I can heal her. When the spirit came upon me at the Jordan, it never left. I felt it and its power from that moment. Now I am going to use it – to test it, perhaps – to see if it is real (oh, it's real. I know that). Still, I have this new power to heal. I am sure of it. It is just going to feel so . . . strange . . . yes: Strange.*

With this, he stepped up to the bed, laid one hand upon Martha's head, raised the other skyward and said, "Be healed. Be made whole. Rise and go about your business."

What followed startled both men. Joshua had expected it. Still, there was something extraordinary about the moment. Martha had simply smiled at Joshua, then she rose from her bed and walked out of the room. As he watched Martha disappear toward the kitchen, a chill spread through him. It was not a chill of fear, but of pure wonderment. *Who am I? Not the builder from Nazareth, certainly . . . and not just another rabbi . . . or even merely another prophet. "You are my son." That is what I heard. I've even admitted it to myself . . . but I had no idea of . . . this . . . when I said it. First demons! Now, fever! Where are the limits? What do I do with this . . . this . . . power?*

He turned and walked past a still-stunned Simon, and seated himself at the table. Others were beginning to arrive and were marveling at the sudden healing of Simon's mother-in-law. The village was small and everyone had heard of her illness within minutes of its occurrence. They realized it was the same man who had cast out a demon at the synagogue.

"That's the man!" Martha said and pointed directly at Joshua. "He placed his hand on my head and commanded me to be healed . . . and I *am* healed!"

After a few moments, Simon reentered, still with a stunned look on his face. A few other men rose and went to speak to him.

He mumbled what he had seen and then also walked outside, as if to clear his mind, away from the presence of his new and wondrous master.

I hope I have not become some sort of freak. Joshua attempted to appear casual, as though what had happened was just an every-day occurrence for him. He reached across the table and poured wine for the few seated around him, then he poured a cup for himself. "Your fishing was good today?" He phrased it as a question, but it was really an opening to break the awkward silence and start some conversation.

"Yes, yes it was," one of the diners answered.

"Yes! It was very good," another chimed in.

After another awkward pause a voice tentatively offered, "I don't recall it ever being better."

The silence that followed was broken by Simon's reentry. He was carrying a large leather bag over his shoulder. "Let's all have some good wine!," he shouted. "I have been saving this for a special occasion." He looked about the room, letting his gaze rest for a brief moment on each person there, and finally settling on Joshua: "And this is just such an occasion. My brother, Andrew and I have decided to pursue a new profession. We no longer will be fishing for fish . . . we will be fishing for *men!*" He said this last bit with such passion that everyone burst into cheers and clapping – although they had not the slightest inkling of what Simon meant.

"This man," Simon continued, pointing at Joshua will be our new rabbi – our master, who will guide us. By now you realize he is no ordinary person." At this he gave Joshua a nod as if to indicate that he had come to some terms with the miracle of healing he had just witnessed, and was now fully in his service and eager to follow.

Simon paused, trying to decide whether he said enough, when there was a clamoring at the door.

"Joshua of Nazareth! Come help us!" It began as a single-voiced cry, but repeated itself over and over, picking up new voices at each utterance.

Simon raced to the door to see what was causing the disturbance. He peered out into the dusk, then turned and addressed Joshua: "Master, your people await you," he said solemnly.

Joshua rose and strode to the door. There were dozens of people standing, nudging one another as though attempting to edge to the front. He looked toward the rear of the crowd and saw more coming toward the house. Some were carrying a child or helping an older person along side of them. All had looks of desperation on their faces. Those nearest, raised their hands in some form of supplication when they recognized him.

"Heal my child, please!" begged a young man as he lifted his child and offered him to Joshua. "He has not been able to see since his birth."

"No! Heal mine!" a young woman shouted as she pushed her way toward the front of the crowd. "She has been crippled for most of her life!"

"Heal me, Joshua!

"Heal my mother, please, Joshua!" Joshua turned and saw a middle-aged man holding a old woman in his arms.

There was an unbroken litany of those pleading for healing, being cried out by everyone in the crowd. Joshua stood, stunned for a moment. *I never realized there was so much pain in this one, tiny village. How could I have missed seeing the misery in the faces of these people?* He shook off the thought – *I shall have to explore that later. There is work to be done now.* He gently lifted the blind child from his father's arms, cradled him in his own, and called out:

"Line up, everyone. I will see each of you here. There is no rush. No one will be left unseen or untouched – by me."

With this, he gestured to Simon to move among the crowd to create some organization.   Simon understood, nodded assent and set about the task or creating order. Most of those within the house began to move outside. They wanted to see for themselves if this miracle worker was what was claimed.

Joshua looked at the child in his arms. *He must be six or seven years old by now, having lived his entire life in darkness.* For a moment he slowly rocked him back and forth like a loving parent lulling their child to sleep. Then, ever so gently he began to caress his eyes, as though wiping away a bit of light dust. After a moment the child opened his eyes. He instantly closed them and began to rub them as one rubs away the sand of sleep. The child opened them one more time, and stared about, wide-eyed at the crowd. His face began to light up into a grin. Then he said slowly, with a sense of awe in his voice and tears in his eyes, "I think this is what you call seeing!"

The crowd erupted into cheers. His mother, who had been standing quietly at the side of her husband, snatched him from Joshua's arms and hugged him so tightly one might think she wished to draw him totally into herself.

"Thank you! Oh thank you, Joshua. How can we ever repay you for this?" The husband reached into the bag that hung from his shoulder as though to find some coin of worth, but Joshua placed his hand on the young man's arm and said quietly: "Do not thank me. It was not I but our heavenly father who did this. Give Yahweh your thanks by passing along kindness to all you meet."

Then he turned toward the little girl who had become crippled. "How did this happen?" he inquired of the mother.

"She was playing too near to the animals and one of the goats stepped on her foot and smashed it. She was so tiny – just beginning to walk"

Joshua looked at the girl. She was about ten years of age. What a shame that this young girl has lost so much of her childhood because of a single moment. He lifted her gently into his arms and cradled her much as he had cradled the first child. Then he lifted her misshapen foot with his left hand and began to stroke it soothingly, whispering softly into her ear as he did so. Most of the crowd focused their attention upon his whispering, trying to ascertain what he was saying. Those who continued to watch him massage her foot, however suddenly were agog as the foot began to change in shape, slowly assuming a normal form. No one said a word. They were too enthralled to even move.

Joshua kissed the girl lightly; then he set her upon the earth. For a moment she stood tentatively lifting the once-crippled foot and replacing it on the ground. Slowly she put it forward and took a step. She rested on it, then she took another step. Suddenly she began to dance up and down, waving her arms, twirling and laughing as she did so.

Some cheered. Some wept. Some bowed their heads in quiet thanksgiving. Joshua had told them whom to thank, and those who heard were doing so.

Both of the girl's parents came to Joshua. For a moment they just looked at him with gratitude flowing unabashedly from their eyes. Joshua smiled, nodded and reached out to hug them. "God's love knows no limits. Remember to share that love with all you meet – wherever they are – whatever tongue they speak." They nodded, "We shall! We shall, Master." With that, they turned and rushed to embrace their daughter.

Joshua barely had time to absorb the joy of that moment when another person stepped forward, "Please help, too, Joshua."

The routine continued through the night. Some came with demons; some came with broken bones or fevers. Everyone who came was broken in some way that Joshua seemed to understand. Simon and the others who had been invited had seen their fill of miracles, so they had returned to the banquet table where they devoured the food and finished off the special wine.

Still the line continued. *Word must have gone out to some of the neighboring villages* Joshua thought. *There can't be this many people – this many ill people – in Capernaum.* As each stepped forward, Joshua focused his full attention toward that person. He listened carefully; he touched them lovingly; and each walked away whole of body and raised in spirit.

It was after midnight when the last person thanked him, embraced him and walked away.

Joshua was too weary – yet somehow too exhilarated - to even be aware that he had not eaten a single bite of the feast. If someone had asked if he was hungry he would have said, "No." Now, in this quiet moment he could not even reflect on, or bask in, the events of the evening. Instead, Joshua merely turned toward Zebedee's house some one hundred yards distant, and wearily began moving his feet in that direction. He entered the house, and without bothering to remove his sandals, he fell into a very deep and dreamless sleep.

CHAPTER FIFTEEN

CONFIRMING THE CALL

In the morning while it was still dark, Joshua arose and went out to a deserted place. It was the place he now claimed as his spiritual home. He settled himself upon his rocky perch, closed his eyes and began to settle deeply within himself.

Wherever you lead; whatever you ask; I will be faithful. Make my way clear, is all I ask.

Wherever you lead; whatever you ask; I will be faithful. Make my way clear, is all I ask.

Wherever you lead; whatever you ask; I will be faithful. Make my way clear, is all I ask.

Once settled into the quietness of his soul, he put forth his confusion:

Father, I am no longer so certain what you want of me. You have given me a message of great hope, but you also have given me the power to heal – to cast out demons – to make the wounded whole. Is there anything greater for me to do than that: To make the wounded whole?

He waited and listened for the still, small voice he had learned to heed. Surely it would utter some word to give direction to his unfolding ministry. This time, however, all was quiet – not a word.

He waited patiently for some word - some sign that would nudge him.

Silence . . . nothing but empty silence.

Minutes turned into hours. The first light of dawn began to peek above the distant hills. He watched in detached quietness of mind and body. He could see the villages on the "other side" the Hellenistic settlements as the morning light fell upon them. They had been placed there by the Romans to keep watch on the rebellious Galileans. They were called the Decapolis, The Ten Cities. There were far more now, but the original name remained. They represented the enemy, those who would dissipate the teachings of the Torah and who would betray them to the hated Romans.

Joshua observed them almost incidentally to his enjoyment of watching Yahweh turn the darkness of night into a new day. He could see tiny figures emerging from their homes. Some went toward the shore and their boats. Others came out to do their washing or cooking in the morning air. He could see children dancing about . . . and others who moved as though they were still asleep.

In this setting, the silence within him was broken:

"It is too small a thing that you should bring salvation to the house of Jacob and the remnant of Israel. I will make you a light to the nations that my salvation may be known to the ends of the earth." [1]

As this was settling into his mind, Simon and a few others appeared:

"Everyone is searching for you."

In that moment Joshua realized he, indeed, had been given a sign – a clear sign and a clear understanding of his mission. It would have been so rewarding to return to beautiful, peaceful Capernaum and become the local rabbi/healer. This, however, was no longer an option. *"A light to the nations!"*

"Let us go to the neighboring towns that I may proclaim the message there also, for that is what I came out to do."

---

[1] Isaiah 49:6

CHAPTER SIXTEEN

MOVING FORWARD

They began moving down the western side of the sea. The Hellenists on the eastern side would have to wait. He understood his own people, spoke their language and knew their history. He must first speak to them and refine his message. Then he could extend his mission outward.

Word of his healings had already reached the neighboring villages. His arrival always generated excitement and crowds quickly gathered to ask for or to observe the miracles he performed. Just outside of one village, a leper approached him, knelt before him and begged, "If you choose, you can make me clean." Joshua looked at him with compassion: *This poor fellow has stood outside, hoping I would leave by this route. He knew he would not be welcome – or even allowed – within the village. It is time that he was made to be welcome.*

"I do choose," Joshua said, extending his hand to touch this *untouchable.* His disciples gasped in horror. Some wondered if he did not realize that he, too, might be made as the leper if he so much as stood too near to him? But as they watched, the whiteness disappeared; color returned to the man's skin. The man-no-longer-a-leper stood up, gazing in wonder as the skin on his arms and legs resumed their once natural color. He looked at Joshua in sheer amazement, unable to say a word.

Joshua smiled at him and said, "Do not say a word of this to any one, but go to the priests and give the offering Moses decreed for this."

Still too overcome with emotion to speak, the man began bowing and nodding to express his thanks and his understanding of what Joshua ordered. Then he turned and stood quietly as though he was trying to decide what he should do – where he might go. Joshua understood the man's inner confusion, so he stepped forward and placed his hand lightly on the man's shoulder. He said not a word, but his touch was the first loving touch the man had experienced in more than five years. Tears of gratitude and joy began to flow from his eyes. He looked up at Joshua and for the first time since his illness had begun . . . he smiled.

For a long moment they looked deeply into one another's eyes. A bond between them had been formed. They might never see the other person again, but the memory of this moment was indelibly etched in their souls.

Joshua motioned for his disciples to follow him and he began the trek to the next village

"Why did you tell him not to tell anyone, Master?" Andrew asked.

"He must go to Jerusalem to make the offering to the priests. I do not want the authorities there to be speculating about me from hearsay. We have had too many rebellions that began in Galilee. We do not want the Romans or the spies of the Sadducees nosing about us." I have much more to accomplish here before I wish to deal with the Romans. He paused for a moment, then he added: "We have been gone long enough; I believe it is time we went home." The men nodded eagerly,

Two days later when they arrived, Capernaum looked like an encampment. Word of the miraculous healings had spread through the neighboring villages, and anyone with an illness – real or imagined – had migrated to the village in hopes of being healed. Entire families seemed to have set up temporary homes in whatever open spaces were available. When he saw the massive crowd, Joshua slipped into the house of one of the townspeople he knew, hoping to avoid being seen. He was not so fortunate, however. One of the campers saw him and sounded the alarm: "There he is! There he is! He just went into that house over there."

That was all that was needed. Individuals, couples and entire families rose up and began rushing to the house indicated. Some Scribes, who had come out of curiosity, pushed their way to the front, claiming they had special business with Joshua. The home owner was pleased at first to see Joshua enter his house. He invited Joshua to sit and offered him some fresh fruit. However, when the crowd burst through his doorway and began pouring into his house, this early welcome disappeared. The man became desperately distressed. He ran toward the rear door, but Joshua called to him: "Ezra, come here and sit down. I believe you will enjoy this."

Ezra hesitated, but Joshua smiled at him confidently and extended his hand toward him, gesturing for him to come and sit beside him. The fear melted from Ezra's face and he accepted the invitation. Later, he was glad that he did, for it turned out to be the most memorable day of his life. The people continued to pour in until there literally was no more room. Those who could not gain entrance formed a line outside that extended more than two times around the house.

Joshua decided to use the opportunity to teach the people before he began healing:

"You may have been taught to believe that your lives mean nothing, but I tell you that you are the light to the world. Your heavenly father wants you to let your light shine. Do not hide it – any of you."

At these words, the people smiled, but some looked confused.

"How are we the light of the world, and how do we let that light shine?"

"Love is the light of the world and you all have love to spare. Share that love. Share it by the look you carry on your face. Share it by the things you say – and refrain from saying. Share it in sharing of yourselves: Give to the needy, open your doors to the stranger, open your hearts to the lonely, and invite the hungry to your table."

One of the Scribes spoke up. "We are required to do this, and at least some of us already obey this demand. Does that make us light?" He said this while glancing at the others in the room with a look of mild disdain.

Joshua looked at the man as he sat there with an air of superiority oozing from his pores. *Why is there such a need for some people to believe they are better than others? It should be enough to be equal and to be accepted.* "No," he said with a tone of sadness. "That only makes those who do so dutiful. They do it because it is required. The true children of our heavenly father do not do these things as a duty – but as an expression of their love – expecting nothing in return." He let his gaze rest momentarily on each person in the room, "Let that light shine. In doing so you give glory to your heavenly father." Those in the room nodded their affirmation.

After a brief pause as if to gather his thoughts, he spoke again: "The truly joyful people are the gentle ones. Others fight for their share and more. They spend their days and their nights discontented with what they have – always wanting more. They expend their energies in plotting or fighting to get more – always more – while it is the gentle ones who ultimately inherit . . . the earth." He watched the look of confusion on the faces of some – and the looks of comprehension and pleasure on the faces of others." *That will need some work to help everyone grasp the truth of that,* he thought.

Joshua continued to teach and those within the house sat enraptured at the power and simple truth of his words. As he taught he was aware of a strange noise coming from the ceiling. It sounded as though someone – or something – was gnawing at the roof.

He made a quick assessment, while still continuing to teach: *It is quiet outside. People are not upset. I have the feeling that whatever – or whoever – it is does not present a danger . . . might as well just wait and see what happens. Then I can deal with it.*

He continued to speak, but felt he was losing his audience. The noise was increasing and small pieces of the ceiling began to fall on the floor and on some of the guests who were sitting on the floor. Some continued to try to focus their attention on Joshua, but others had obviously lost interest in his words and were totally absorbed with whatever was happening on the roof. Suddenly large pieces fell on them and those on the floor jumped into the laps of others to avoid the debris. Joshua decided to give up the struggle. He raised his hand to indicate he was through, stopped speaking, and looked upward to the ceiling. What he saw was a make-shift cot being lowered through the roof. A small figure was holding tightly to the sides in order to keep from spilling out. He peered over the edge and saw Joshua gazing up at him. His face broke into a pleading smile and he nearly fell when he lifted his hands in an appeal.

Part of Joshua wanted to laugh at the absurdity of what he was seeing. The other part flowed with compassion as he realized what was happening: *This man obviously is desperate for help. His friends have carried him here and finding the house filled, they went to the roof, dug their way through the branches, and lowered him to me. What faith they must have that I can help them! It's time, however, to demonstrate that I have come to do far more than heal tired and broken bodies.*

Joshua gazed into the man's eyes for a full minute. In that time the man began to tremble mildly – partly in anticipation – partly from fear. Finally Joshua lifted his hand as in a greeting and said, "Your sins are forgiven."

A shock wave ran through the room. The people had expected to witness a miraculous healing. Instead, they heard what seemed to be blasphemy.

Joshua sensed the simmering outrage of the Scribes sitting by him. He turned slowly and looked directly into their eyes in a silent challenge: "Why do you raise such questions in your heart?" The Scribe jerked backwards as if he had been struck. He now looked at Joshua through eyes mixed with confusion and awe.

How does he know what I was thinking? Who is this man?

"Which is easer to say to this paralytic: Your sins are forgiven, or to say, 'Stand up and take up your mat and walk?' But by that you will know that the Son of Man has authority on earth to forgive the failures of men," He turned to the man lying in the cot, and ordered: "Stand up, take up your mat and go to your home!"

Immediately the man arose, lifted the cot onto his back and walked out of the house.

Joshua then turned to those in the room who now were sitting stunned and amazed. "Who else here is in need of healing?" he inquired casually.

CHAPTER SEVENTEEN

INTRODUCING THE KINGDOM

The sun was just beginning to cast its first rays upon the quiet waters below. Joshua relished that moment when the dark surface began to shimmer, as if awakening from its nighttime slumber. Still he also felt a twinge of sadness for it signaled the beginning of the day and an end of his quiet time with his father. The others would be expecting him.

He rose from his rocky perch, stretched his arms slowly over his head, breathing in the morning air. *The sea looks so inviting; I believe I will travel along the shore today. The fishermen among us will love that.* With that resolved, Joshua began walking the narrow path that led back to Capernaum.

Salome smiled as he entered the house. She had learned to respect the quietness of the morning, allowing the conversation to awaken at its own pace – and not to rush it. As the effects of the fruits and fish set in the talking would follow. Joshua went over to where she was preparing the morning meal. He lifted a fresh fig, inspected it and popped it into his mouth. As he did so he gave Salome a slight hug. "Mmmm, nice way to start the day: Fresh fig. fresh hug." With that he found a place at the table and waited for the others to arrive.

Martha and Elizabeth continued with their preparations of the morning meal. From time to time one would look Joshua's way. They had always admired their cousin, but now they were in awe of him. They had not witnessed any of his healings, but they had heard the stories. At night they talked about what they had heard, but could not get beyond their confusion. Miracle workers were people you heard about. They were not family. Martha recounted the time she had seen Joshua accidentally cut himself while trying to help Salome with the fish. "He bled just like any man would," she had said. "Salome had to bind it with a cloth to stop the bleeding. There had been no healing miracle then." Something had changed him, but they had no idea what it might have been.

James and John wandered in. They had been at the shore helping Zebedee and the crews with the boats. Elizabeth looked questioningly at James and then at the door as though to ask where Zebedee was. John smiled and explained: "Father grabbed a piece of dried fish and a couple of figs. He said that was all he needed."

"That's right," added John. "He said he wanted to get an early start today . . . something about trying to find a new fishing area."

With that, they sat at the table and the morning meal began.

When they had finished, Joshua announced, "I believe we shall try to find a new fishing area, as well. We will walk along the beach today."

Before they could depart, Simon rushed through the doorway. His obvious agitation was contagious. It was as though an invisible rush of wind had swept through the room. Everyone stopped what they were doing and looked at Simon expectantly.

"Your cousin, John – the one they call "The Baptist," has been arrested. "

"Was it by the Romans?" asked Joshua.

"No, it was Herod's soldiers who went to Jericho and arrested him. Four days ago."

"That was just after I left his camp," said Joshua, feeling a surge of emotion as he envisioned John being led away in chains by heavily armed soldiers before his powerless followers. *John was right,* he thought. *It is the Kingdom of God versus the kingdoms of Rome and Herod. This can be dangerous business. Still, it is Yahweh's business and I must be about my father's business.* He straightened himself and stood erect, motioning to Simon and his cousin to follow him as he strode out into the morning light.

They followed him through the streets and up the adjacent hill until they came to where the disciples were waiting at Joshua's favorite rock. Prayer and teaching had become part of the morning routine. This was the time when Joshua taught in detail and the disciples never wanted to miss it.

"Today we shall talk about the kingdom of God. You will hear me speak of it often, but do not bother to look for it. It is not a place. It is far more complex, and you will have to discover for yourselves what it means. I will tell you this: One cannot rush into the kingdom. It is more like a seed that is planted. You tend it and you wait. One day it suddenly bursts forth and blooms. When it does, you will feel great joy and you will experience a new sense of freedom."

"How do we tend this seed when we do not even know where it is?" asked Thomas.

"Fair question. Think of the seed as having been planted within you."

"How can that happen? Does someone plant it there?" Thomas retorted.

"The seed of the kingdom is the Word of God, Thomas. It has already been planted within you. Now you must nourish it."

Somewhat overwhelmed, but still desiring to understand, Thomas posed one more question: "How do I do that, Master?"

Joshua smiled warmly at Thomas. He admired his inquisitiveness and persistence. "You learned to net fish, Thomas. Now you must learn to farm soul. You nurture it by feeding it through your thoughts and your actions."

"Another way to seek the kingdom is to think of it as a coin that is needed to feed the family. The wife has set it on the table, planning to take it to market to purchase the food she will need to feed the family for a week. Without thinking of what she is doing she automatically wipes the table clean with a wet cloth then she shakes the cloth. When she has finished cleaning the house she gets her basket and goes out the door. Suddenly she remembers that she has left her coin on the table. She laughs at herself for her forgetfulness, but is pleased that she has remembered before she journeyed all the way to the next village where the market was. By now she has completely forgotten about having wiped off the table, so she is rather nonchalant about looking for the coin. That is until she has looked over the entire table and has not seen it. She feels concern. 'Where could it have gone?' she thinks to herself. 'I know I set it here.' Now panic sets in. She gets down on her knees and begins to search about at the base of the table. It's not there, of course. She puts down the basket and begins a diligent search. The day is dark and so the house is dark. She finds a lamp and uses it to seek for the coin in every corner – every cranny. Hours pass and she still has not found the coin. Then just as she is about to give up and just cry until her husband comes home – she finds the coin." He paused and looked questioningly at the disciples: "Can you imagine her joy?"

The disciples nodded avidly.

"That, my friends, is how a person feels when he has found the kingdom. There also is another part to this story. Did you get it?"

John responded hesitantly: "She once held the coin, but lost it?"

"You are right, John. She once had it in her hands. There is a quality about the kingdom that you once possessed briefly, but lost. You may not remember it, but something within you remembers and still longs for it. You won't realize that, perhaps, until you find it again."

"Do you recall a time when you were younger, when everything seemed to work or fit together? It was a moment, perhaps, in which you felt yourself totally in harmony with everything and everyone around you."

He looked about at all the disciples. Some of them shook their heads in affirmation. Some looked befuddled. "Put the pieces I give you together until you can see the kingdom of which I speak. When you see it you will know how to enter it."

He stood as he said that, indicating that the morning's lesson had ended. He began to descend the mountain toward the shore. He could see Zebedee's boat near the opposite shore, still searching for a new fishing spot.

CHAPTER EIGHTEEN

No Questions Asked

Joshua always read the faces of the listeners. Whenever he taught he could discern who would listen and learn and who would not. This was a new location – a new audience. Joshua settled himself on a small mound overlooking the sea, then he quickly scanned their faces. *They are like the soil of this earth. I scatter the seeds of understanding and let them lay where they fall. Some will nurture them and they will grow. Some will listen and become excited . . . I can see it in their faces. They light up – sprout up, I suppose is a better term – too quickly. Then they will go home filled with excitement, but they will dissipate their new energy rather than nurture it and acquire depth through prayer, study and service. The first crisis will find them without good roots. They will fade away. What a shame! However, I cannot control that. I am just the sower. Others will return to activities that will simply crowd out whatever I sowed. I wish I could tend to all of them, but that is not a possibility. I can, however, select a few whom I believe to be great soil, and bring them along with me for extra care. I must keep an eye out for those. They are few and far between.*

As he was appraising this new audience he observed one he has seen previously – in another place. Last time he was sitting in the back. This time he has found a front seat. *Let's pay attention to how he responds to some of my words.*

While they were still gathering, he began to speak. His resonant voice carried across the open space and began to silence those who were still chatting with their companions:

"Your heavenly father loves you with a love that is greater than any earthly father can even imagine. He does not wish to punish you for your sins – your moral and ethical failings. He desires that you grow up and learn how to behave – how to love with a love that is genuine." *This fellow in the front row really responded to that. He must be deeply troubled by the failures in his life. Let's see how he reacts to this.*

"Just as when we were babies we had to learn to walk and to talk, so also we must learn how to love even as our heavenly father loves. Scripture tells us we are made in God's image. That is our nature: to be godly – or as God. Failure is not who you are. Sinner is not who you are. It is something you do. If you do it long enough, however, it eventually will become your nature. That is why you are to repent – to consider your lives and transform the way you now think and act. Be certain of this: God does not want your punishment. Your heavenly father desires your redemption, so that you might live in him as he lives in you throughout all time." *Oooo, look at him!* Joshua thought as he saw the man's face light up. *He's ready – perhaps more than ready.*

When he had finished speaking most listeners rose and left, but some lingered to talk with him. Joshua answered their questions carefully, thoughtfully, giving each person his full attention, realizing this was his one opportunity to tend the newly planted seeds. The man he was especially interested in, however, merely disappeared in the departing crowd. *Perhaps next time,* he thought sadly.

Later, as they left the shore and were strolling through a market, bustling with sellers and buyers haggling over prices and quality, Joshua saw his "listener." He was sitting in a booth collecting taxes from the merchants. *Oh My! He is a tax collector – a hated pawn of the Romans.* He paused for a moment to consider his options. *This certainly will cause a stir . . . even among some (or most) of those now gathered as disciples However, if I truly believe the kingdom is for everyone this will say that loud and clear!* He took a deep breath, paused again just to be clear in his mind about his decision. Then he walked over toward the tax booth. The man in the booth saw him coming and his jaw dropped open in a mixture of confusion and eagerness. Joshua stopped where he was, looked directly into the eyes of the man, and then spoke in a demanding tone: "Follow me!"

The man in the booth did not hesitate. He shoved his documents aside, rose up, and without a word to his aides he simply walked away. Thus, Levi became a new disciple.

There were looks of surprise on the faces of many disciples, but no noticeable grumbling. *Either they trust me completely, or they are too shocked to say anything at this time,* Joshua thought. Time will tell.

Levi asked Joshua and the others to join him in a farewell banquet that evening. Joshua replied: "Go back to your house and do what you must do to place things in proper order and to have the feast prepared. We will *all* be there at sundown." He placed the emphasis on the word *all*, and looked questioningly at his followers. Each nodded assent and Joshua decided the issue was settled.

Levi then departed, giving Andrew the directions to his residence.

Later that evening, as Joshua left Levi's residence he overheard some scribes complaining about his having dined with sinners.

These people do not have any idea of their own failings. They are so carefully cloaked in the self-righteous garbs they have sewn for themselves that they are incapable of grasping the underlying principles of the law. He stood facing them for a moment, then decided to confront their hypocrisy with a gentle touch. He strode slowly over to where they were standing and then with a quiet, almost confidential voice and a knowing smile he said:

"Those who are well have no need of a physician, but those who are sick do need one. I have not come to call the righteous, but the sinners." Then with a nod of his head he turned and left them wondering if they had been excluded or if he had been toying with them.

PREFACE TO CHAPTER NINETEEN

This chapter is entirely from the writer's imagination. It is non-Biblical. There is no hint of it in any of the legends or recorded speculations concerning the life of the Christ. I am sharing *my* Jesus, and *my* Jesus is fully human. Time and tradition often have attempted to neuter him – to make him a-sexual. In the Orthodox Baptistery in Ravenna, Italy, Jesus is depicted as neutered, lacking in male genitals. By contrast, in the Baptistery for the Semi-Arians (who did not emphasize Jesus' divinity to the point of denying his humanity) the genitals are visible. For those who believe such a display is unseemly, I would suggest they have been victimized by a religious view that demeans human sexuality and declares it to be dirty or naughty. The history of the Christian Church is smattered with sexual hypocrisy. Popes Sergius III, John X, John XII, Benedict IX and Alexander VI were known to have kept mistresses after their election to the papacy. Many bishops also were known to have maintained mistresses privately, while demanding celibacy of their underling priests. The Protestant Church often appears to be anti-sexual. I believe this attempt to deny human sexuality in the Western Church has contributed to the terribly distorted and unhealthy attitude toward sex we have in America. This, in turn, has contributed to the exploitation and abuse of women. The Book of Genesis declared that God created male and female in His image and told them to be fruitful and multiply. Then he pronounced all of his Creation as very good. I do not believe God meant that men and women should plant an orchard and do mathematics. Rather, it is my belief that these distortions and hypocrisies arise from man's fear of his own sexuality. Sex is a powerful drive within men. Rather than coming to terms with their sexuality and attempting to harness its energy in constructive ways, they attempt to suppress it. In doing so it results in something like an attempt to suppress the energy of a volcano: It seethes beneath the surface and eventually erupts in all the wrong places.

I hasten to add that this chapter is purely G rated. It is a gentle attempt to depict the Man of Galilee as fully human. Again: It comes entirely from the writer's mind and has no basis in fact.

CHAPTER NINETEEN

RACHEL

They had traveled for most of the morning. The sun was almost directly overhead. Some of the disciples passed the word forward to Andrew, who was walking close behind Joshua, saying they would like to take a rest, get out of the sun and have a bite to eat.

"Master," said, Andrew, "Perhaps we should stop soon to get out of the sun and eat some of the bread and cheese we have brought along."

Without looking back, Joshua replied, "No, Andrew, we are near a small town that has an excellent place for us to eat our noon fare. It is just a short way from here," he added reassuringly.

Andrew passed the word to the others and they continued to trudge along in the noon-time heat.

Nearly two hours later Joshua turned, smiled and pointed to indicate that he had seen the town and they were almost there.

"The food had better be good," muttered Levi as he wiped the dripping sweat from his forehead.

"Real good," agreed Nathaniel, as he shifted his shoulders to relieve some of the strain of the pack he was carrying on his back.

Others muttered quietly in agreement and continued to move one foot in front of the other as if they were weights to be moved by the sheer force of will.

They arrived at the town after another quarter of an hour, famished and exhausted. However, Joshua seemed to have picked up additional energy in that last stretch. He turned to his right as they entered the first street and headed directly for a small house that had a collection of mismatched tables sitting in the front and on one side.

As they entered the area of the tables, a young girl stepped out of the door of the house. Some of the disciples stopped and caught their breath. The girl was gorgeous! She had long, wavy hair, deep black with bluish highlights. Her eyes were large, almond-shaped with lashes that seemed to reach to her cheeks when she blinked. Her lips were full and when she smiled, they opened to reveal an even string of white teeth. Even with her loose-fitting tunic anyone could see she was all woman, with a tiny waist that was emphasized by the larger curves that flowed outward above and below.

"Well, Joshua the builder from Nazareth." the girl said, in a lilting voice, "I have not seen you in over a year. What brings you this way? It must be a major task if you have brought this large a crew with you."

Without bothering to explain his change in profession, he merely responded, "I told these men that you served the finest food this side of Jerusalem."

The girl, placed her left hand on her hip, gave Joshua a saucy smile and coyly inquired, "And what place in Jerusalem serves up finer fare than I offer, good sir?"

The men laughed at her reply, then turned to Joshua to see how their clever master would counter.

Joshua just shook his head and grinned, "I cannot think of a single one at the moment." With that he selected a large cushion, sat at one of the tables and indicated for the others to do the same. He struggled to appear casual and relaxed, but his heart had picked up speed at the first sight of her. *She is as lovely as I remembered,* he thought. *If she had lived closer to Nazareth life might have been different.*

"Today I have a fish broth, then lamb with vegetables. Does anyone here prefer to eat elsewhere?" she asked with a coy smile. She then turned and went into her kitchen.

"Her name is Rachel" Joshua hastened to explain. "She was the youngest of four daughters . . . arriving much later than the first three."

"What we call an afterthought?" put in Philip, not expecting an answer.

Joshua nodded. "A nice afterthought as it turned out for her mother. Rachel's father died when she was fourteen. There were no close male relatives so Rachel took over as head of the house to care for her mother who was rather aged by that time. Rachel had always been a good, creative cook, so she decided to open this place to be able to feed her mother and herself. Most of the people pay with food goods. It works out that they bring the food which Rachel cooks for them and for her own needs, as well."

"She is a lovely girl," said Nathaniel, still staring at the doorway where Rachel had disappeared.

"She is, indeed," Joshua replied. Then he quickly changed the subject. "We can purchase some additional supplies from her while we are here. Her bread is outstanding, as you soon shall see. My favorite is one that is slightly heavier and fuller than most breads. It has pieces of olives and onions mixed in, and when your taste buds encounter them they almost explode with delight. You will see that this was worth the wait."

"I have already seen that," said Nathaniel, still staring dreamy-eyed at the doorway.

Joshua had to smile at Nathaniel's obvious enthrallment. He remembered his own reaction when he first saw her. She was but a child of twelve, yet she had the appearance and poise of a young woman of sixteen. *Even then she was a beauty,* he reminisced. *I must admit that as she grew older I found her to be the most attractive of women.*

It was not just her physical beauty. Rachel's intelligence and inner beauty also is exceptional. Giving up her youth to care for her mother, when she could have insisted that one of her married sisters take the responsibility was just one example. If she had not been so committed to her mother's care – or I to my family . . . He did not allow himself the luxury of finishing the thought. The choices were made and there was no need to look back.

Meanwhile, in the kitchen as Rachel began preparing the meal, she also struggled with her private thoughts: *Why did he have to return? Every time he returns I cannot get him out of my mind for months. It is not just because he is attractive . . .* She allowed herself to dwell on this for a moment . . . *though he definitely is. It is everything about him: His fine mind, his wonderfully melodious voice that is gentle yet carries a note of authority. He has such a caring spirit coupled with a quiet inner strength that makes a person feel secure in his presence.* She looked toward the doorway, mentally picturing Joshua seated at a table, chatting with his friends. *It is more than security, though. I always feel . . . so alive – so joyously alive when I am with him. I have refused every man in this town – and many who merely were just passing through* (she smiled and shook her head at the foolish impulsiveness of some men) . . . *but if he were to ask me . . .* She refused to follow the thought. She shook her head slowly. *To him I am just a friend who cooks for him when he appears.* She busied herself by rolling the herb leaves into tiny sand-like particles.

The men had nibbled on fruit and bread, and sipped wine while waiting for the meal. When it was served they dived in as though they had not eaten for days. This was partly because of the hour, but primarily because the food was the tastiest they had ever eaten. Hours later, when they had finished the last morsel they lay back and closed their eyes. Some lay semi-awake in pleasant reveries. Others fell into various degrees of sleep. Joshua looked about at his weary disciples and made a quick decision: "Rachel, will you come back here for a moment."

Rachel wiped her hands on a cloth, straightened her hair and walked at what she hoped would be viewed as a leisurely pace to the table.

"Don't tell me your friends have not had enough – or that they are dissatisfied?" It was posed as a question, but it was obvious that this was not a concern.

Joshua smiled by way of response. He slowly swept his arm in an arc that generally pointed to his sleeping comrades: "I know the hour is still early, but it does not appear that this crew of mine will do any more walking today. May we stay here in the yard for the night, and can you prepare a morning meal for these tired men?"

Rachel smiled as she surveyed the results of her handiwork. It was not at all unusual for even some of the locals to decide to sleep in the open air after one of her feasts.

"Smoked fish, cheese, onion bread, and fruit. I will add that to your bill," she said curtly.

She looked away quickly. She did not want him staring at her, for fear her knees might become weak or she would stand there and blabber foolishly.

"Thank you, Rachel. Pleasant dreams."

The words almost froze her where she stood. She hesitated a brief moment, then turned her head toward him – but did not face him directly. "Thank you and pleasant dreams to you . . . Joshua."

She continued walking leisurely into the house. Once inside, she leaned against the wall, looked back toward the courtyard, and breathed a long sigh. Abruptly, she straightened up and walked back into the room where her mother would be waiting for her.

Had she chosen to remain outdoors her understanding of Joshua would have been radically altered that evening. Joshua looked around at the village. There were people still milling about, chatting, puttering, as they began to lay the day to rest. Still, the shadows suggested that there were a few more hours until sundown.

I suppose this place needs to hear the good news of Yahweh's accepting love, as much as any other here in Galilee. Might as well get on with it. He rose and began strolling toward the center of the town. He saw children playing to amuse themselves as their parents chatted with friends. Approaching them he said, "Would you like to hear a good story?" Happy for any new diversion, the children cheered and nodded and in as many ways as there were children, let him know they would.

"Come over here with me, then. Sit around me and let's begin." Quickly he sorted through his material to see what he might improvise that would catch the parents' attention, as well and give them the message he wished for them to hear. While he was still formulating his message he noticed a young boy who had not been playing with the others limping quickly toward where they now were seated. His eyes were eager as he had grasped what was happening. "Joshua rose and walked toward the boy. "You do not have to rush. I will meet you half way and we will walk together to your friends." Joshua continued walking until the two met. Then he reached out his hand and together they walked slowly back to the gathered circle.

My name is Joshua. I come from Nazareth.

"My name is Elijah," the boy responded proudly. I was named after one of the great prophets of Israel."

"How did you hurt yourself, Elijah? "

"I fell from the roof of my house where I was playing . . . where I should not have," he added sheepishly.

"How long ago was that, Elijah?"

"Two years ago, Joshua." He said this as a simple fact. He obviously had become resigned to the fact that he would limp for the remainder of his life. It was his penalty for disobedience.

Joshua stopped walking, knelt down and examined Elijah's leg. By this time many of the parents had turned their attention to this stranger, wondering what he was doing with their children.

"Your heavenly father does not punish you for what you did when you were younger, Elijah. Would you like for your leg to be made whole?" The question was posed simply, yet compellingly. Joshua looked deeply into little Elijah's eyes and Elijah sensed that this stranger really meant what he said and could heal him if he said yes.

With pleading eyes, Elijah nodded: "Yes . . . yes, I would . . . please, sir."

Joshua lifted Elijah and cradled him tenderly in his arms. Then he slowly began stroking the leg which had an obvious badly healed break. He was not sure how this worked, but he was confident that the leg would straighten as he rubbed it. It was as though an inner energy was being transferred into the young boy's body: a healing energy renewing the tissue. *"I make all things new,"* he quietly recited to himself as he continued stroking Elijah's damaged leg. Then, ever so gently he set the boy down. Elijah watched in awe as the leg appeared to have straightened. For a moment he stood speechless. He tentatively shook the leg, then set it down again. He lifted it again and then stomped down on it. Suddenly he let out a loud, joyful cry and ran toward his parents. "Momma! Daddy! I can walk again! I can walk again!"

No need to tell a story now. Those with infirmities will be here soon enough. For a moment he looked toward the children who were eagerly awaiting his return. He shrugged his shoulders and gestured toward the group of adults who were now rushing his way. "Sorry, my little friends. The story will have to wait." By now he was familiar with what would ensue: "Who are you? By what power do you claim to heal this boy?" Those would be the righteous ones with no infirmed relatives or friends. "Can you help . . . whomever?" He smiled as the crowd neared. The town is good sized; it will be a long night.

Hours later, Joshua returned to Rachel's house. His followers were still slumbering peacefully, blissfully unaware of the drama which had taken place.. He found an unused pillow, walked to an open space, lay down, and closed his eyes. It has been a good day. More than two hundred people had heard his message of Yahweh's redemptive love as he had placed his hands on thirty – forty?- villagers who had come to him broken and left whole. *No one even asked me who I was or what I was doing there. They only cared for those they brought for healing.* He smiled as he recalled this. *Good people,* he thought just as he slipped into a well-earned sleep.

His sleep was interrupted by the sound of earthenware being slammed on the table with no pretense of trying to be quiet. "Good morning, carpenter man," Rachel said with a smile that immediately roused him into wakefulness. "Since you and your crew are obviously moving on, I thought it best to give you an early start. Rouse your friends. I will begin bringing the fruit to awaken their mouths."

Joshua merely smiled and nodded in response. *She really is something!* he thought. *Most women are differential to men, but her beauty – and probably her cooking - has given her confidence. My guess is that most men would be pleased just to have her pay attention to them. Add her delicious dinners and she can act the way she pleases.* He rose and began shaking his drowsy disciples into wakefulness.

As they were finishing their morning meal, Joshua motioned for Judas to come to him.

"Yes, Master?" Judas inquired as he drew next to him.

"Pay her three denarii for the meals, Judas" Judas looked startled, but Joshua hastened to add, "She is the only support for her mother. The people here in town generally pay her with food goods. She can use this for the other necessities." Judas still looked unconvinced. "Think of it as a bit of charity for a deserving family added to the bill." With that, Judas stood up, nodded and went into the house, drawing his money pouch from inside his robe as he did so.

James and John nudged one another and smiled. They had heard of this Rachel many years ago from their cousin. He had described her as "a nice young girl." Now they understood why the long walk had been so necessary.

Simon, who overheard Joshua's conversation with Judas, had watched with amusement at Joshua's attempt to appear casual. Now, he stood, stretched and suggested, "Is it not time we started on our way, Master? We can make good time in the morning while it still is cool." Then he added with a sly smile, "Perhaps you would like to go in and bid farewell to our hostess?"

"I believe simple courtesy calls for that," Joshua replied. Simon detected a touch of irritation in his voice and decided never again to mention Rachel. "That is what I meant, Master," he said soberly.

Joshua entered the house and looked about at the setting. So simple, yet so neat and homey. Rachel had placed some field flowers intertwined with simple twigs in small clay vases to form a pattern of earthy beauty encircling the room. *It would be so easy to feel at home here, he thought* with a trace of sadness. *Life does not always offer us the choices we would like to have. Earlier, it was our commitments to care for family. I thought that might someday pass.* A ripple of sadness flowed somewhere in his depths. He took a deep breath, sensing this goodbye would be the last. He stepped into the kitchen area, which was more of an open area at the rear of the room. Rachel looked up, and for a brief moment their eyes met in a silent embrace. She blinked to break the moment, then turned her head away and said in what she hoped was a relaxed tone, "Thank you for your payment. You were most generous."

For a brief moment Joshua felt a strong desire to take Rachel in his arms and hold her, feeling the soft warmth of her body against his own. He quickly dismissed that thought, however, and adopted a casual tone: "Your meals . . . and the lavish accommodations (he swept his hand toward the outside tables) were more than worth price," he offered with a smile.

She grinned at his retort. *He does have a way of making me laugh,* she thought. She hesitated a moment trying to think of something to say that might cause him to linger a bit longer. "Your business must be good then?"

"It seems to be growing," Joshua replied obliquely. He wanted to say more, but decided it was best to leave it at that. Any attempt to explain further would somehow disrupt whatever relationship they had . . . and for some reason he did not care to do that at the moment.

They stood awkwardly staring at one another in an equally awkward silence. Rachel wished he would say something – do something. Finally, she broke the silence: "Be sure to drop by whenever you come this way," she said almost curtly while pretending to return to whatever task she had been doing when he entered. "Remember, I serve the finest food on either side of Jerusalem: Inside and outside" This last bit she said with a laugh, turning her head so that her hair swung out in an arc and settled on her shoulders.

"Goodbye, Rachel. Thank you again." Rachel sensed a note of finality in his voice that sent a chill rushing through her body.

"Goodbye, Carpenter man," she replied. "Take care of yourself."

Again, their eyes met for a brief moment, and a wordless message of admiration and affection passed between them. Then Joshua turned slowly and walked away.

Rachel waited in the kitchen, busying herself with nonessential tasks until she was certain they all had departed.

When she finally stepped out into the light, some of her neighbors had gathered in the area. Immediately upon seeing her, one of them approached, and with a sense of urgency, asked, "Rachel, who was that tall, good looking man with that wonderful voice that stayed here last night?"

Rachel was taken by surprise by the obvious attention that Joshua had attracted. She decided not to offer information until she learned the reason for this interest. "There were many men here last night. They ate too much food and drank too much wine, so they slept the night. "

The woman smiled, and stepped in closer, and in a gesture of conspiratorial intimacy, she whispered, "But only one fits that description. Right?"

"That does sound like Joshua. He comes from Nazareth. He is a builder. He and his crew were just passing through . . . I assumed they were on their way to some job. . . . he didn't say," she added that to indicate that their relationship was casual.

"That man is no builder!" she nearly shouted in reply. "He is a healer – a prophet!"

Rachel felt her head reeling. *What is this woman saying? I know he is a builder, a master carpenter, at that. I still have some of the tables he made for my father.*

"What do you mean . . . healer and prophet?" she eventually forced herself to say.

The woman's face softened. She could see that Rachel had no idea who that man was. She pointed to the small boy standing with his parents. "He healed Elijah of that terrible limp. They came here hoping to see him and thank him once more." Then she pointed to a young woman standing alone by one of the other houses. "You remember, Elizabeth, the blind young girl who was found abandoned years ago. Jacob and Martha took her in. She now can see." She waved at Elizabeth, who smiled and waved back.

"Everyone who came to him for healing – and there were many –were healed. He even cast out some demons. All the while he spoke to us of God as our heavenly father who cares for us and wants our love." She paused and looked directly at Rachel: "He is not a simple builder. He is a teacher, a healer. a prophet – the likes of which Israel has not seen in hundreds of years."

Rachel did not know what to say – even what to think. *How could this be? I thought I knew who he was . . . was? Yes! But who is he now? Now that I think of it, he did seem different . . . quieter – more subdued. Yet, there was a difference. He seemed to speak with more authority – more power. . . I thought it was because of the presence of the others . . .* She decided that she would have to think about it later. For the moment her mind was too confused to reason it out.

The neighbor continued to share her excitement over what she had seen: "You should have been there, Rachel. It was absolutely incredible! It was unforgettable!"

Having no response to the neighbor's proclamation, Rachel merely smiled pleasantly, turned and started gathering the remains from the morning meal. As she did so, she began humming an old, familiar melody to herself. It was one taught her by her father when she was a child. From time to time she looked toward the distant hills to see if they – he – had journeyed in that direction. After clearing the earthen ware, she began collecting the pillows which had been scattered over the area. When she came to the place where she had awakened Joshua she picked up the pillow, unconsciously pressing it her breast. For a moment she just stood quietly embracing the pillow. One more time she looked toward the distant hills. Seeing nothing, her large, almond-shaped eyes began to fill with mist. *Unforgettable . . . yes . . . unforgettable.*

CHAPTER TWENTY

MARY MAGDALA DEPARTS

Mary Magdala sat in the small room which served as her office. Her mind was not on the business, however. This was one of those days when she needed to sit in the dark. Even the light filtering its way into the room from the window seemed more than she could tolerate. *What is happening to me? I feel as though I am trapped in a pit, shrouded in darkness and some inner part of me is screaming our in desperation.* She straightened herself and looked about to see if anyone was present, as if they could discern her thoughts if they were. *Don't I make a fine picture, huddled here as though I was trying to hide . . . but then, I suppose I am trying to hide. From what I do not know. I just know that I need to be alone . . . safely in the dark.*

For some time now Mary had felt herself controlled by powerful moods. One day she might be laughing, joking with the employees - she might even be singing – yes, singing cheerful songs. The next day – or even sooner – she could be heard yelling at the same employees, accusing them of laziness or ineptness. Sometimes she cried herself to sleep. Other nights she drank herself into a stupor, crying remorsefully until sleep overtook her.

Some evenings she stayed up late, checking the company records to see precisely how much money she had earned that day, or that week . . . or that month. She seemed obsessed by each one of the many moods which simply took over and ran its course.

It is as though I have lost control of my own life, she lamented. Ruefully she returned to the company business, to see what merchandise had been ordered and what orders had yet to be filled.

I do not know how much longer I can maintain this charade. Even Silas is looking at me strangely when he believes I do not see him. He has begun being very solicitous, as well.

She turned with her back to the small window and began staring, mindlessly, at the bare wall. Her fingers were twitching and she began to stroke them as a mother might comfort a troubled child.

She had been hearing the many stories about Joshua, the builder-turned rabbi from Nazareth. They said he had performed many healings. They also said he was gathering increasingly larger crowds wherever he taught. *I knew it!* She thought exuberantly. *He really is doing it! Some men talk of doing great deeds, but great deeds are beyond their doing. Joshua now realizes who he is and the great deeds merely flow naturally from him.* She mulled this over in her mind for a few minutes. She had always sensed that he was special. She had always been attracted to that special quality within him. Mary mentally pictured him sitting on a hillside along the shore, teaching crowds, laying his hands upon them and watching them walk away whole of body and mind. She looked about her room, noting the barrenness as though for the first time. Then she rose and called for Silas.

It is time that I made myself useful to Yahweh, and to this wonderful friend I have known − but not really known, perhaps − until now. Perhaps he might even calm whatever is disturbing me so badly.

Silas appeared as if he had been waiting to be paged by Mary.

"Silas, I am giving half of the business to you now. You can manage it nicely without me. Go to the scribe and have him draw up the documents. When they are ready, bring them to me. I shall begin packing."

Silas stood stunned. Part of him was overjoyed in learning he now was a equal partner in this lucrative business. Part was overwhelmed by the thought that it now was his sole responsibility to keep it running profitably. The largest part of him was consumed with curiosity as to why Mary would abandon the comfort and security of Magdala to venture out to . . . He suddenly realized Mary had not told him where she was planning to go.

He went to the scribe's office and made the requests as Mary had told him to do. The scribe looked up at Silas with a questioning gaze. He started to ask a question, thought better of it, lowered his head, and then began writing the document in his prosaic penmanship.

When the document was finished, Silas looked at it carefully. Then he nodded his head, inquired as to the fee and paid it, carefully counting the coins as he placed them on the table. Then he rolled the scroll tightly and departed. He had only the vaguest idea what the document said, for he could not read well, but he did not want the scribe to know this. After all, he was now an equal partner in the largest, most prosperous business in Magdala. *I shall have to improve my reading skills quickly,* he thought as he walked back to where Mary was waiting.

"Silas, I want you to handle my half of the profits in this manner: You will be able to keep track of me for I shall be with Joshua. He is becoming a rather famous teacher and healer. People will know where he is. Send two thirds of the money to where I am. The other third you are to invest where you get the best rate of interest at the greatest safety. You know how to do that. I may not return for some time. It may be years. When I do return, I should like to resume some activity in the business." Mary looked at Silas to see how he was responding to this bit of information. "If all has been going well you will still be the one in charge, but I will not want to merely sit idly by." She added that to give him assurance of her confidence in him and his security in this new position of authority. *I am getting to the stage where I should like more time for reflection on life than earning money,* she thought.

As she reentered the house to complete her preparations Sada approached her:

"Mistress, you did not tell me that we were going on a trip. Let me assist you then I will go and gather what I will require."

Mary looked at Sada, much as a mother might look at her child when she has to tell her unwelcome news: "Sada, I must do what I am going to do without your help this time. It is my time to be the servant, and it would not be proper for a servant to have a servant, would it?

She nodded in agreement. Sada had not the slightest idea what Mary meant. What she did realize was that this was a moment of parting. Her mistress was leaving her and life now was going to be quite different. She had grown accustomed to the varied moods which ranged from lighthearted laughter to angry tirades. She understood that the anger was fleeting, but that Mary's care for her was lasting. Now she would have no one who really had concern for her well-being. There were friends, of course. Still there was nobody who really mattered - who had any . . . any authority . . . to watch over her.

"Now, Sada, I do not want you to worry. I will tell Silas that he is to treat you kindly and generously. Your duties will remain the same: Care for the house." She smiled at Sada and added: "It should be easier for you without me to have to watch out for." Then she did something that was quite uncharacteristic for her: She stepped forward and warmly embraced her servant girl. "Goodbye for now, Sada. I shall return, and when I do I hope I will be a better (she hesitated while groping for the right word) employer. Yes, a better employer to you."

Mary turned and began to tend to her preparations. Sada realized the conversation was over, and backed out of the room, still looking at her mistress, still trying to understand what was happening.

Mary carried her belongings out to where the donkey was tethered, and strapped them on the animal. *Am I mad, or is this really what I should be doing? Will Joshua welcome me or will he see me as an unwanted burden?* She took a long, last look at the house. Then she gave the donkey a pat to get him started. *Whatever is going to happen will just have to happen, I suppose. He may not need me, but I certainly do need him.*

Sada watched through her window until Mary had disappeared into the distance and the clopping sound of the donkey's hooves could no longer be heard.

Chapter Twenty-One

Private Lessons

Joshua stood and gazed out over the crowd that had been sitting, attentively listening to him for more than six hours. He smiled at them, fixing his gaze on a few as his eyes swept over the mixed group. Then he raised his hands in a spreading motion and said, "Go in peace, knowing you are loved by your heavenly father." This had become his way of concluding his teaching. It served a variety of purposes: It indicated that the lesson was over. It implied that it was time for the listeners to depart. It sent them out with a blessing . . . and it gave him the opportunity to stretch a bit after sitting for so long a period. He enjoyed watching the various responses to his teachings. Many rose and dutifully departed. They had been told to leave and they did. Many lingered, wanting to hold on to the moment. Some merely remained where they were, quietly gazing into the distance or laying back and watching the clouds drift by. Some gathered in tiny clusters to discuss some of the ideas they had heard. A few would work their way toward him to say something. Many of those would say simple words of appreciation. Some would add comments to his illustrations, telling him of some similar experience, e.g. "I also once spent half a day looking for a lost coin." He smiled at this remembrance. Those people did not realize they were confessing that they had no idea of the significance of what he had said. Some had been profoundly moved and wished to ask additional questions. To them, he would say simply, "If you genuinely wish to understand, follow me." Some would accept the invitation. As a consequence his entourage grew to sizeable numbers.

Joshua had decided it was time to subdivide his disciples: He had selected twelve to become part of the inner circle – the ones he would train to be the leaders of this new movement. They would be the ones especially equipped to serve as apostles – ambassadors. The others were disciples, of course. They just were not part of the inner circle with whom Joshua would share more deeply. He had selected the number twelve intentionally. They would represent the twelve tribes of the original covenant. That covenant, according to Jeremiah, had been broken and was never restored in the manner promised. Joshua had long realized that part of his mission was to restore – to proclaim, really – a new covenant in which the law would be written on the hearts of the people.

The day had been a long one. Joshua looked about and decided that they would camp where they were for the evening. Andrew gave the assignments to a few key followers. Most knew the routine, and began setting up the campsite as soon as they observed Andrew approaching them. Judas went with a group to purchase food while Thomas and Simon set about making a cooking fire. Most searched about for a comfortable place to settle for the night. Joshua motioned for John to accompany him and began a slow stroll along the shore.

Joshua enjoyed the time with John. He had watched him grow from a baby into a thoughtful, deeply caring young man. Joshua felt the need to tutor John because he believed it was John – and perhaps only John – who appeared to grasp the meanings underlying his spoken words. He intuitively went beyond the literal meaning to the symbolic. And in doing so had a far better grasp of what Joshua was trying to communicate. Spiritual truths are beyond the capacity of words to reveal. Joshua looked deeply into

John's eyes as they walked together, and thought *I wish everyone could think with this young man's clarity.*

"John, when I make reference to vines what does that convey to you?"

John considered this for a moment, then he responded: "To me you are speaking of the interconnectedness of all of God's people. We are branches of the same vine."

"When I speak about building your house on a rock as opposed to sand, what do you believe I mean?"

"We all have some foundational ideas on which we construct our lives. So many I know seem to build their lives on a belief in their superiority because they are children of Abraham, on their anger toward the Romans, on their own self-concerns, or on just trying to make it through the day. You are telling us that we need to build our lives on something more solid . . . more lasting . . . than those things."

Joshua smiled at this response, "And what would that be, John?"

John looked up at Joshua with a smile and slowly shook his head. "I do not know yet. I understand you believe it has to do with following the will of Yahweh, but I have not yet clearly seen the picture you are painting with your words."

Joshua laughed at John's statement. "Word pictures! I suppose that is what I am doing."

"Yes, it is, Master," John replied humbly.. "That is why your words will live on long beyond our lifetimes. They are masterful paintings that make indelible images in our minds. When I look at the morning landscape I see different things depending upon where my mind is. Sometimes I see the hills, sometimes the houses, sometimes I see the people. Your word pictures do that to me, as well."

Joshua was flattered by John's words. He had never thought of them in that manner. They merely were the words that flowed naturally from his mind.

"Thank you, John. Those are encouraging observations. It would be nice to believe that people would remember what I have said."

"I for one will never forget them."

"Then let us get on with our lesson, before it is time to return to the group: When I say that a person must be willing to lose his life in order to find it, and those seeking to save their lives will lose it, what thought comes into your mind?"

They walked along in silence while John gathered his thoughts. Joshua appreciated this. *He thinks before he speaks. This is good. His answers have depth and do not just fly off the top of his head. Still water runs deep, and John is still water.*

"It depends on where my mind is when you speak those words. Sometimes I sense that these new teachings of yours will upset enough powerful people that they may try to eliminate us. If that happens then those who drop out in order to remain safe will save their skins, but will lose their inner part that is eternal. Those who stay with you may lose their physical lives but will gain eternal life. Another way I understand those words is when I deal with my personal selfishness – and we all have some of that, you know." Joshua nodded. "When I focus more on myself and my own wants, and ignore the genuine needs of others I sense I am allowing something very important within me to slip away. However in my better moments, when I am willing to set my personal little wants aside and tend to the need of others, I feel more alive inside."

Joshua allowed these thoughts to settle as they walked along. Finally he stopped, faced John directly and placed his hands upon his shoulders. "You think well, my beloved little cousin.

Remember this: Events by themselves do not have meaning. Even life, simply lived without reflection, has no meaning. We give meaning or find meaning as we reflect upon life and the events of life. Our task is to help people reflect upon their lives in such a manner that they will find worthy meaning - useful meaning. We want to help them to understand that this world is good, that God loves and cares for them. We want to help them to live without needless fear, to use the gifts God has given them in worthy ways. We want to free them of old ways of thinking and acting that actually imprisons them, limiting their ability to grow into the full image of God. We can do this by giving them the tools that will allow them to see the world with fresh eyes and to hear with fresh ears. Word pictures, as you call them, can serve this purpose."

He paused, smiled and placed his hands on John's shoulders: "I believe we have traveled that path enough tonight. Let us join the others."

CHAPTER TWENTY-TWO

A GENTLE HEALING

It was three days before Mary arrived where Joshua was teaching. She saw him sitting on a low hill with a crowd of hundreds gathered around him. *Quite a crowd for so remote an area,* she thought. *Some must have walked for miles to hear him.*

As he spoke, Joshua's eyes trailed off into the distance. His peripheral vision had picked up a distant figure approaching. There was something familiar in the manner in which she carried herself: *That confident, purposeful stride – a sense of authority. I've seen that before.* The thought flashed through his mind without his missing a nuance in the parable he was weaving at the time.

"So when the day was through the owner called his manager and told him to pay each man a day's wage, beginning with those who arrived last and ending with those who came first. When the ones who had worked all day saw what the late-comers had received they expected to receive much more. However, when they were given the same wage as the others they complained to the owner saying they deserved more and it was not fair. To this the owner replied, 'Friends I am doing no wrong. Did you not agree to work for the usual daily wage? Take what you have rightfully earned and go. Am I not allowed to do as I choose with my own money? Or are you jealous because I am generous? So the last shall be first and the first will be last.' This, my friends, is true of your heavenly father. It is true of his kingdom. It is true of your relationship to him. It is good news that I tell you."

He looked again toward the distant, approaching figure: *Mary of Magdala! I wondered when you might arrive.* Some part of him wished to rise and in doing so bring the session to an end. However, these people had traveled far to hear his message. *Joshua, do not ever let personal desires interfere with this mission Yahweh has given you.* He breathed a short sigh, then turned back to address the crowd.

Mary drew near, and tethered her animal in an area just outside the ring of listeners. Then she quietly sat at the edge of those nearest her, not wanting to attract undue attention. A few turned and gave a quick glance to see who this late arrival was. Not recognizing her, they immediately returned their attention to Joshua.

I never saw this part of him before. He is spectacular! No one is stirring. Some even seem to be holding their breath. He is captivating! With these thoughts Mary soon found herself void of further personal thoughts and thoroughly enraptured by the words coming from her friend.

The sun was beginning to settle behind him, when he finally closed. "Go forth in the knowledge that you – yes, even you – are precious to your heavenly father. Do the work he has given you, and in doing so you can share the love he has shared with you."

He stood watching his listeners as they departed. Some would come to speak with him. It was this awareness that kept him from going to where Mary still sat, as if waiting for him. He looked her way as though to indicate that he saw her and would soon be available to greet her. Their eyes met for a moment and Joshua was surprised to see – not a smile – but a look of angst oozing out from her soul.

Her demons must be getting out of hand. I wondered when they would. She never really grieved when Isaac died. Instead she buried herself in the business. She distanced herself from the few close friends they had. She carries her barrenness in her heart. Success and servants have been poor companions. Look at her . . . her soul is overflowing with tears. He looked away and began to give his attention to those who were approaching him.

Mary remained quietly where she first sat. She absentmindedly watched those around her as they rose and left. Then her gaze drifted to the small groups still clustered in the area. *Who is this man I thought I knew? He holds a power over people I have never seen before. They do not want to leave this place where he spoke.* She allowed her eyes to focus again upon her friend who was now thoroughly engaged with those around him. *It was more than just his words. While he spoke, I felt . . . transported . . . yes, transported to another realm, where everything seemed to fit together in a glorious harmony. Whatever it is inside of me that causes me such pain . . . just seemed to lie dormant . . . to also be in harmony . . . with me. I felt peace . . . yes . . . peace for the first time since . . . well . . . since.* She let the thought drift off and merely sat waiting . . . content to wait. She had settled back into the mood that had possessed her while Joshua spoke. *This is far more satisfying than wine,* she thought.

When the last question had been answered and the final compliment had been graciously received, Joshua descended the hill and went to Mary, still sitting serenely in her reverie. As he neared, she saw him and started to rise, but he motioned for her to remain seated and settled himself across from her in the grass. For a moment neither spoke. Joshua gazed into her and Mary sensed that he was examining her soul. Then he placed his hands on her shoulders and said, "Your demons have tormented you long enough, Mary. Is it not time that you were rid of them?"

A flood of emotion rushed through her. She leaned forward into his arms and began to weep. For the first time since Isaac's death – she wept. She wept for the loss of her loving companion. She wept for the bitterness of her barren womb. She wept for the loneliness that dominated her nights and for the unseen distance that separated her from everyone around her. She wept for the darkness she saw in her old age when she would wither alone in her room. Tears of despair, bitterness, and even unknown guilt poured forth as from some inner spring that had been dammed up from the beginning of time.

"Yes! Oh yes! These have been my only true companions for all these years. They work with me, drink with me . . . sleep with me . . . and they give me no peace! Please, Joshua. If you can cast them out from me I will be forever grateful!" she sobbed.

"Then they are gone," he said kindly. "They shall trouble you no more. But you need to fill the space they once filled with companions who will comfort and complete you . . . or the demons will return."

Mary stopped her crying. She felt a gentle wave move through her being, washing away whatever it was that had been creating such inner pain. Her eyes widened in wonder. *Emptiness! Blessed emptiness*, she thought. With a sudden calmness inquired, "How can I do that, dear friend – no . . . dear Master?"

Joshua peered softly into her soul once more: "You have already begun. You are here, and I believe you mean to remain with us while our journey lasts. You will find many ways of filling this new void." He rose. "Come now and let us join the others."

She stood up, took his hand, and together they walked up the hill to where the disciples were assembling.

CHAPTER TWENTY-THREE

THE WOMAN'S TOUCH

When all had been fed Joshua gathered the twelve plus Mary into a small cluster. He explained that Mary would be a part of the inner circle – not to be sent forth as an apostle, but to serve as liaison with the many women who had become part of the larger group of disciples. "She has a woman's touch . . . which we lack." "Fortunately," said Bartholomew, which caused a ripple of laughter from the others.

"All right! All right," Joshua said with a note of humor. If you ever listened to the women, instead of just using them as servants, and thinking of yourselves as superior you just might find that they are as capable of learning . . . and even leading . . . as any man." The men looked startled by his remarks. "Think of it. Who really runs the house, making all the decisions that keep things working smoothly? Who often manages to get their way even though they are thought to be the ones taking orders?" The men thought this over and began to look somewhat bewildered. "Women are far more clever than most men think they are. Mary here took an ordinary trading business and turned it into an extremely prosperous business – the largest in the area. I believe that women will play a very important role in this new mission of ours, so let us show a little respect." He said this with a light tone, but his message was clear. "Now for your information – and this is not to be told outside of this circle – Mary will support our work (which means seeing that we have enough to eat without having to beg – with the earnings from her business." At this, the men sat up and took notice. Some looked at Mary with a new sense of appreciation. Others, Joshua could see, still had their doubts. *You will learn, my friends. This lady will teach you.*

"Now," said Joshua, obviously changing the tone and the subject of the gathering, "I will teach you something that will be among the most important lessons you will learn from me." At this, the men stirred and moved in closer so they would not miss a word.

"There is a significant difference between the form of a religion and the purpose of that religion. Perhaps in the beginning there is little distinction, but it grows with the passage of time." Joshua could see the confusion on the faces of most of the Twelve. *I shall have to proceed carefully with this, I see.* "Let me explain it this way: What was the purpose of the great Exodus from Egypt?" He let this question lay in the minds of the Twelve and waited while they mulled it over.

"To free the children of Israel?" offered Thomas, more as a question than an answer.

"Why free them?"

"Because Yahweh liked them and did not want them to be slaves any longer."

"What was wrong about them being slaves? They were being fed and protected, were they not?"

"But they were being abused."

"So Yahweh, in his concern for them sent them into the desert where they would suffer from the heat, from thirst and from hunger? He sent them where they eventually would have to fight and die for their land. This he did because he liked them?"

"I guess we really never thought about that," put in Andrew.

"Most people do not. They lose track of the underlying purpose and become caught up in the form. When they do that they are merely mindlessly practicing a form that no longer has meaning."

Joshua could see the looks of confusion on their faces. *I suppose I had better give them this idea in little pieces – over a longer period of time.* "I will ask this simple question. I do not want an answer now. I want you to think about it for a time. I will give you a few clues tonight, but you will have to keep thinking about this if you are to be teachers in the future."

The men nodded and sat, eagerly awaiting his words.

"The children of Israel had drifted away from Yahweh. They were worshipping the gods of Egypt. He wanted them to be back in relationship with him. The only way to accomplish that was to get them away from Egypt and their gods. Think about it. Now, I will switch subjects: "What purpose does the law about the Sabbath serve? Do not try to answer. Just listen to my words: Tradition tells us that Yahweh rested on the seventh day, so we also should rest. That is the basis for the law. No other is stated. Yahweh rested, so we also should rest." He could see the looks of assent. "It is a time for renewal and reflection. No more. It was not oppressive. Yahweh did not *have* to rest. He wanted to rest . . . so he did. His work was completed and he took a break. Nothing more –its not complicated."

Slowly the men nodded their agreement as each realized the truth and simplicity of Joshua's explanation.

"So why is breaking the Sabbath Law punishable by death? How did we ever get that far away from its purpose?" This was not a question but a statement. He continued: "We men – not the women but we men (he said this with a smile and a nod toward Mary) want power. We do anything to get power. We make laws to give us power over people – to control them." He paused to let the idea settle itself in their minds. "We even take the laws Yahweh has given us and twist them to gain power for ourselves."

"Yahweh is a loving father – not a wrathful judge. But we have twisted the rules he has given us that were designed to lead us into closer relationship with him so that they dominate our lives and keep us in fear. As a consequence we travel to the Temple and waste money giving useless sacrifices instead of using that same money to help his children who have great need. The prophet Amos told us what it is that Yahweh wants from us:

> *I hate and despise your feasts and I take no delight in your solemn assemblies. Even though you offer me your burnt offerings and cereal offerings I will not accept them, and the peace offerings of your fatted beasts I will not look upon. Take away from the noise of your songs; to the melody of your harps I will not listen. But let justice roll down like waters and righteousness like an every-flowing stream.* [1]

This is what Yahweh himself spoke through the prophet Amos. So why is the Temple a place of sacrifice and not a place where people turn for charity?"

"What we must do is to change the form as well as the content. The new understanding I am proclaiming will not fit in the old form." With that, Joshua rose from where he was sitting and strode over to where he intended to sleep, The Twelve sat quietly absorbing the radical ideas they had just heard. Mary smiled and quietly went down to where she had left her donkey. She would spend the night there.

---

[1] *Amos 5:21-24*

CHAPTER TWENTY-FOUR

SABBATH LAWS CHALLENGED

It was a Sabbath Day as they were passing through a grain field. The law allowed a traveler to pick enough food to feed himself, so Joshua began to pluck pieces of grain from the laden stalks as he walked by. The other followed his example. They collected a handful and munched on them until they were soft enough to swallow. Then they repeated the process. It made their journey pleasant, sparing them the need for making conversation and supplying nourishment to their bodies. By now, however, they had attracted the attention of the Pharisees. Joshua noticed a group of them weaving their way through the grain field, heading directly at him. He paused where he was, plucked another handful of grain and began chewing it as they neared.

Here come the self-appointed guardians of the Law. They are essentially good people, but their understanding of the Law of Moses is that must be obeyed to the letter or the children of Israel would once more lose their land and be sent into exile. They may have started off well, but somewhere along the way they have become obsessed with obedience to the letter of the law without regard for its actually consequence

When they were within a few feet of Joshua the lead Pharisee asked, "Why are you doing what is not lawful on the Sabbath?"

Joshua looked upon them with a mixture of pity and disdain. *Why is it that you people cannot think for yourselves? All you do is interpret words from long ago without any real understanding of what they meant. Let's see if this little lesson will help you:*

"Have you never read that when David and his companions were hungry and in need of food they entered the house of the Lord where Abiathar was priest and ate the bread of the Presence which is not lawful for any to do but the priests?" He smiled at them as a parent might smile at children when explaining something simple: "The Sabbath was made for people, not people for the Sabbath."

He could tell from their reactions that they did not quite understand his point. Still they realized that he had one and they could not dispute it. What he had said about David was correct, even though they did not know how that related to the Sabbath law. So they turned and left, grumbling as they went.

Later that day Joshua went to the synagogue for evening prayer. As he entered the building he noticed a man leaning against the rear wall. He had his left shoulder turned toward the wall with his right hand resting upon it, as if trying to hide it. It took only a moment for him to grasp the situation. *Somewhere earlier in your life, my friend, you hurt yourself badly and this arm of yours withered and became useless. Now you see yourself as a useless cripple, unworthy of being a part of this or any community. Well it is time to put that behind you.*

Joshua walked over to the man: "What is your name?"

Startled, the man replied, "It is Simon, sir. Have I done something wrong?" he asked with a note of fear in his voice.

"Not at all, Simon. Not at all. Stand up and let me see that arm of yours."

When two of the Pharisees saw what was happening they quickly approached with looks of apprehension on their faces.

Joshua saw them and spoke in a voice that resounded through the synagogue: "Is it lawful to do good or to do harm on the Sabbath, to save life or to kill?"

The Pharisees stopped in their tracks. They entire synagogue was waiting to hear their response. They looked at one another as though to say, "You answer him." However, the moment quickly passed when any response would be accepted. They nodded at one another, and turned and left in a huff.

Joshua turned back to Simon, "Stretch out your hand!"

Hesitantly, Simon turned and with obvious agony. He finally managed to hold his left arm before Joshua. During the time he struggled to accomplish this, a few bystanders gathered closer to watch what was happening. Joshua watched the scene and had to consciously hold back tears of compassion which welled up within him. *Look at this poor fellow! What agony he must have experienced for far too many years. Every movement was an exercise in pain. Every glance his way was another in shame and embarrassment. Well we will put an end to that, thanks be to my heavenly father.*

He reached out and gently took the withered arm in his hands. Slowly he began to stroke the arm, tenderly massaging the muscles as he did so. Then he abruptly lifted the arm straight in the air. Simon gasped – more from fright than pain. The crowd also gasped, startled by Joshua's action. Simon stood looking at his arm as though it were something apart from him. No one spoke. No one even breathed. Then – ever so slowly – Simon began to move the arm in a wide circle. He wiggled his fingers, and then lowered his arm to where it was parallel to the ground. Then he pointed it at Joshua and began to move it up and down. He tapped it with his right hand. The he smiled. "Yes! Yes! I feel it again! Oh my God. Yes! I am whole again." He fell to his knees and began to weep tears of joy. "Thank you! Thank you!"

Cheers broke out from the bystanders. Some rushed to kneel with Simon and put their arms around him. Others stood back, watching this stranger who had performed this miracle of healing, and had put those self-righteous Pharisees in their places. They would speak of him for some time in the future. This was a story to share with their children and their children's children.

When he departed the next morning half of the village followed him, wanting to see and hear more of this extraordinary man. As they arrived at the shore where he planned to teach, Andrew saw another huge crowd already gathered in anticipation. He ran ahead of the group and commandeered a small boat. When the group arrived they boarded the boat and went out a short distance into the lake so that more people would have the opportunity to see and hear Joshua. This time, rather than sitting as was the custom of teachers, Joshua stood at the bow of the boat throughout the entire session.

When he was finished, he dismissed the crowd and waited until all were out of sight.

"Let us go to a small village from here. I want to be able to sit inside somewhere and spend more time with the people."

"I know just the place," offered Philip. "It is a small village about an hour's walk from here. I have a friend there with a fairly large home. I am certain he will let us use it."

With that assurance, Joshua motioned for Philip to lead on.

CHAPTER TWENTY-FIVE

FAMILY MATTERS

Elizabeth rushed through the doorway, nearly spilling the water as she laid the huge basin on the floor. "Mother! Did you hear the news that is being spread through Nazareth?"

Mary looked up from her sewing, saw the obvious disturbance in her daughter's face, sat the sewing aside to give Elizabeth her full attention, and replied, "No, dear. What is it?"

"They are saying horrible things about Joshua!"

"Who is saying what, dear?" Mary inquired in a quiet tone, hoping to calm her.

"All the women at the well. They knew I could hear. In fact I think they wanted me to hear, even though they were whispering." Elizabeth wrung her hands and cried, "Oh, mother, now everyone in town will be talking about him. Why can't they just let him alone?"

Mary took Elizabeth's hands into her own, and slowly stroked them. *Oh Joshua, what are you doing? Ever since you left I have had this fear that you were going to get yourself in trouble.* As Elizabeth's breathing quieted, she asked, "What exactly are they saying about him dear?"

"He is breaking the Sabbath law and is encouraging others break it as well. They say he is referring to himself as 'the Son of Man,' like he is something special rather than just a man. They also claim that he has stayed in one house for days, not even bothering to eat or to sleep, and he argues with the Pharisees."

"Oh dear God," said Mary. "He *is* getting himself into trouble. When your brothers come home we will have to decide what we must do." She released Elizabeth's hands. "Now, get about your business, girl. The boys will be home soon and dinner needs to be ready for them. They will have put in a hard day's work. Joanna is out in the back, making bread. You might as well tell her now, so she will be prepared when we talk this evening." She put away her sewing, reached for a knife and began to cut the meat and vegetables into tiny cubes.

When the sons arrived home the evening meal was prepared and waiting for them. Simon entered the house first and poured himself a cup of water. "Oh it was hot today!" Judas followed, but reached for the jug of wine that sat in the dark rear corner. "You quench your thirst your way, brother. I will quench mine my way," he laughed as he poured himself a full cup, quickly swallowed it and then poured another.

"Go easy with that, my son," said Mary. "We have some family matters to discuss this evening."

Abruptly, Judas' mood changed. He walked to where she was standing, and placed his cup on the counter. "Something serious, mother?"

"Serious enough that we all will need clear heads to solve it."

James had entered the house and heard the conversation. "It's about Joshua, isn't it?" He said this more as an accusation than a question. "What has he done?"

Mary breathed a long sigh. She had wanted this to wait until later, but it now was unavoidable. "There is talk in the village that Joshua is breaking the Sabbath Law and encouraging others to break it . . ."

"What else, mother?"

"Oh, James, it seems he thinks of himself as The Son of Man, the one who is to come to repair the damage done by the first man,

Adam. They also say that he has been in a house for days, teaching without eating or sleeping, and he argues with the Pharisees. I fear for him." At this she began weeping uncontrollably. James stepped forward and took her in his arms. "There, there, Mother, do not worry. We all must go and bring him home. He must have taken leave of his senses. We will care for him until he is well again."

"This time we will not let him leave without one of us going with him" put in Simon. James, Judas and Joseph nodded their agreement.

"But what if he really is on some special mission for Yahweh?" asked Mary. "He has always been . . . well . . . different from other people. What if –?"

"Mother, be sensible." said Joseph. Yahweh does not go around picking carpenters to do his work. He has trained rabbis and priests. He does not need ordinary builders. Look at his temple. It is glorious, as is all of Jerusalem. Nothing God needs is to be found in a town like Nazareth."

"The matter is settled, Mother," said James with a tone of finality. "Tomorrow we shall all head to where he is. I am sure someone knows where he is. We will bring him back before he shames the family further and before he gets himself hurt."

"Let's eat!" said Simon. "I am famished!"

"Now that the matter is settled, let's also drink," said Judas, lifting his glass from the counter and taking a bit swig.

The family began to settle by the table, James reaching for the bread, Simon grabbing the bowl of meat, Judas bringing the jug of wine to the table and Joseph settling himself by Mary and ladling some of the vegetables onto her plate.

Elizabeth and Joanna would eat when the men were finished. Meanwhile they stood by to replenish the food, holding back their tears and giving occasional glances of comfort to one another.

CHAPTER TWENTY-SIX

THE UPS AND DOWNS OF BEING A MESSIAH

Joshua had never seen or imagined anything like this. Even as he continued teaching and healing, another part of his mind was marveling: *The people are flocking in from everywhere! It's a mob yet it is orderly – more than orderly, really. It is as though they have made some tacit agreement to spend no more time than necessary. Then they move on and let others take their places.* He laid his hand on one who had limped up to him, and felt the glow as the man straightened up, twisted his torso, grinned at his friends, then turned and humbly bowed as he backed away to the doorway. "Your heavenly father loves you and send you forth with that love," he said as the man exited the house. *I wish we had time to take a break, but interestingly enough I am neither tired nor hungry*, he thought as he turned toward a child being led to him.

"My child has not been able to see since her birth. Can you make her see?" the mother asked. Joshua could sense the quiet desperation in her voice, and he smiled to reassure her. "Her heavenly father wants her to see this wondrous world he has made, so she will be able to see with her eyes." He then soothingly began massaging the little girls closed eyes. While doing this he addressed the crowd. "There are many who have eyes that work well enough to allow them to move about, to thread a needle or repair a net, and to see all the colors and shapes of this world. Still they cannot really see. They cannot see truth and beauty because their minds will not let them. Neither can they see injustice and prejudice." He took the little girl's hand and turned to the girl's mother: "What is your daughter's name?" "It is Rachel, good master." Hearing this, Joshua smiled. "A very pretty name for such a pretty girl. Well, Rachel, open those eyes and tell us what you now see." The little girl barely knew what to do. She had been told time and time again to keep her eyes closed so she would not look . . . She almost broke into tears at the remembrances. "You will not have to worry about that ever again, Rachel" Joshua reassured her, still holding her tiny hand in his. "Try to remember now how to open those pretty little eyes of yours." Rachel stretched her neck upward as though straining to break open the eyes that had been closed for most of her lifetime.

The room was totally silent. Every person seemed to be straining with her, quietly persuading the eyes to open once more for this little person whom most had never seen before.

Slowly . . . ever so slowly the eye lids began to lift themselves and a bit of white appeared. Then two deep brown orbs emerged into view. Rachel blinked a few times, then she began to turn her head: First to the right and the slowly to the left. A look of pure amazement swept over her face. She looked down at her hand and saw it was being held by another. She slowly followed the line from the hand to the arm to the face of Joshua.

Joshua's heart melted as he saw the look of pure love the little girl's eyes so radiantly communicated to him. A tear began to trickle down Rachel's cheeks as she continued to gaze at the stranger who had given her the gift of sight. Joshua felt his own eyes begin to mist. He reached down, gathered Rachel in his arms and hugged her warmly. He looked to her mother and saw she had covered her face, but still could not hide the tears that were flowing so freely.

Still, no one in the room moved. They seemed mesmerized by the drama that was still unfolding before them.

Finally the mother lifted her head and spoke. "Thank you. Thank you, good master. What can I give you for this?"

"You can help her to learn to see with her mind and her heart what is truly good and beautiful in this world Yahweh has made for us." With this he kissed Rachel on her cheek and started to hand her to her mother. Rachel, however, quickly grabbed Joshua around his neck and planted what could only be described as a big smooch squarely on Joshua's mouth. "I love you! I love you!" she shouted in glee.

Joshua released Rachel and she quickly turned and embraced her mother around her legs, laughing and giggling as she did so.

This broke the spell for the crowd. The drama had ended – happily. They cheered and applauded – and even shouted words of approval.

Joshua laughed with them as he leaned back exhausted but refreshed by the experience.

Who needs food or sleep when they can have this? he reflected as he readied himself for the next person.

He continued interspersing his teachings with the healings, watching the orderly mob move along at its pace: Some exiting after being healed; some coming only to listen and observe, yet leaving – even reluctantly – when they sensed they had stayed their fair share of time. He had just completed the healing of a woman with crippled hands when he heard a disturbance outside the house.

Someone was shouting to the crowd still waiting to enter: "He is possessed by Beelzebub. By the prince of demons he is driving out demons."

Don't tell me they have come all the way from Jerusalem to harass me, thought Joshua. *I had best put a stop to this now.* He arose saying,

"I will be back in a moment. First I must silence these intruders who know nothing of what they are speaking."

Joshua quickly made his way to the door, stepped outside and called to the one speaking, "How can Satan drive out Satan? If a kingdom is divided against itself that kingdom cannot stand. If a house is divided against itself that house cannot stand, and if Satan opposes himself and is divided he cannot stand. His end has come. I tell you this truth, all the sins and blasphemies of men will be forgiven them, but whoever blasphemes against the Holy Spirit has no forgiveness. He is guilty of an everlasting failure."

The intruder and his companions stood listening to Joshua. Their faces were red with emotion for they were not accustomed to being challenged in their teachings, particularly by someone with no credentials. They, after all, were the noted teachers of the Law from Jerusalem. This man was but a renegade backwoods teacher – a small time self-appointed rabbi.

When Joshua ended his speech the crowd turned toward them to see what response they might have. The spokesperson hesitated. *This is an awkward moment. His reasoning is flawless. Perhaps I should have stated it in another way. We all agreed this is what I would say, however. Still we never thought it would be challenged. Most people unthinkingly accept the statements made by authorities. We got careless, I suppose, but it's too late to change that.* He turned to his companions, who looked equally perplexed. He could see the smiles appearing on the faces of those outside the house. Some folded their arms as in triumph, daring him to respond. He turned to face his adversary and saw a smile beginning to form on his face, as well.

Damn you, Joshua! You have caused me to appear the fool. I won't forget this. Eventually you must come to Jerusalem. There you will be in my territory – with my people. He turned to his companions and motioned for them to follow him. Then with as much dignity as they was able to muster, they walked toward the town entrance.

"You shall see! You shall see," one of the group shouted back to the house as they departed.

Joshua smiled at the crowd outside and lifted his arm in a waving motion. He then reentered the house to resume his work. As he seated himself he looked up to see the look of admiration spread across Simon's face.

It took minutes for the cheering to diminish enough for him to be able to be heard.

Meanwhile another small cluster was approaching the house.

"I think it would be best if I spoke with him first," said Mary.

"No, Mother, as the now-eldest son it is my responsibility. I will talk with him man to man.," said James.

"I thought we agreed that we would confront him as a united family," said Joanna. "In this way he will realize we all care."

"I think it's a waste of time," said Simon. "He is not going to listen to any of us."

"He never has. Why do we think he will now?" put in Judas.

"We settled this before we left. Let's not go through it again. I agree with Joanna," said Joseph.

Mary reluctantly nodded assent and so the group bypassed the informal line and walked directly to the door.

It seemed to Joshua that he had just become immersed in his teachings and healings when there was a new interruption: First, Joshua was aware of a small disturbance at the door, and then a group from the door pushed their way closer and shouted to him, "Your mother, brothers and sisters are outside asking for you."

Immediately he grasped the situation. He did not give an immediate response to their announcement, but paused to think it through. *They are here to bring me home. What other reason could there be? If they needed me they could have sent one or two of my brothers. If they just wanted to see me they would wait until I am finished. What is wrong with them? They know I cannot return to being a builder. My life is far beyond that! There is a stronger claim than blood. It is spirit. Yahweh is our true father and those who worship him in spirit are closer family than those who do not.* He shook his head sadly. *This will hurt them, I know. I do not wish to cause them pain. However I cannot acquiesce to them either. My heavenly father's claim is far greater than theirs.*

He reached deep inside himself to find the ability to say what he had to say with gentleness, yet with authority.

He looked toward the group that had spoken, "Who are my mother and my siblings?" Then looking at those in the room he waved his arm over them all and continued, "Here are my mother and my siblings. Whoever does the will of God is my brother, sister and mother." With that, he turned his attention on those seated near him.

Mary and the family had been standing near a window and they heard Joshua's reply. Mary's knees buckled and she quickly reached out and steadied herself by grasping hold of James. James made no outward sign of response. Only Mary felt his muscles grow tense and his entire body stiffen. Elizabeth and Joanna let out small gasps of surprise and dismay. Simon and Judas glared at each other and nodded to Joseph with a look of smug anger. Joseph bent his head and wept dry tears of pain and disappointment. With a look of total defeat the family turned from the house and began the long fruitless journey back to Nazareth. They gave more the appearance of being refugees fleeing from a tragedy than a family returning from a visit.

Joshua quieted the pain in his heart, then he turned his attention back to the crowd and, with a smile, held out his hand for the next person who needed his healing ministry.

CHAPTER TWENTY-SEVEN

PRIVATE LESSONS

When they finally left the house, Joshua and the disciples decided to go to a deserted place where they could be alone and rest for a few days. They found such a place on a shady knoll where the soil was too shallow for gardening. From this lofty spot they could watch the sun rise over the sea, and gaze into the rich valley below with no concern that any wayward traveler would wander far enough off the beaten path to bother them. They brought along ample food and enough bags of water and wine to allow them to merely linger and loaf with no other cares for a few days.

After the first evening Joshua decided it was a time for more private lessons. Late in the morning he gathered the Twelve plus Mary Magdalene and asked, "Is there something from any of my public teachings that you would like to know more about?"

"Yes, Master," said Thomas. "You said that those who blaspheme the Holy Spirit will never find forgiveness. Cannot Yahweh forgive whatever he wishes, and – if so – then why would he fail to forgive this particular sin?"

"A very good question, Thomas. I am pleased that you were disturbed by this. You were reasoning as you listened. That is a good trait. To begin with, you all have learned by now to listen for more than the literal meaning of my words. If I only wanted people to understand and respond to the literal meaning I would be lecturing – not teaching. I would be giving instructions for you to follow. If I meant to do that – which I surely do not – I would never speak in parables. I try to give tools for understanding which people can use in many different situations, in many different places. In order to understand my message, people must learn to think for themselves. A good example of that was the foolish comments made by those intruders. They teach the Law of Moses. They are accustomed to making a statement and having everyone thoughtlessly accept it as true and obey their words. Anyone with half a mind would recognize that their statement about my casting out demons by the power of Beelzebub was a logical contradiction. They, however, were so full of themselves that they had come to believe that their simply believing it – or wanting it to be true – made it true . . . or at least believable.

"You certainly made them look like fools, Master," said Simon with obvious admiration.

"I only revealed them for what they are, Simon. They are so full of themselves that they disregard or ignore anything that contradicts what they want to believe. Yahweh's children must learn to keep an open mind and examine every statement - every idea with fairness."

"We understand, Master," said one of the others.

"To blaspheme the Holy Spirit carries a few meanings: It means to rail against God - to show a disdain for God, or at least a total lack or reverence – of any respect. It also means claiming the attributes of God for oneself." He smiled at the group. "I was speaking to a band of literalists, so I chose to be literal in the meaning of blasphemy. They understood what I was saying." He shrugged his shoulders. "I can be literal when I need to be." They laughed. "People in our culture are so accustomed to think in terms of guilt and forgiveness that it is easier for them to understand me if I stay with those terms. If you listen to me long enough you will see clearly that this is not how I understand our heavenly father. By guilt and forgiveness I am trying to express separation and reconciliation. However, the model of Yahweh as a mighty king – a judge who resides in the Jerusalem Temple is so strongly embedded in our minds that people simply do not – perhaps cannot - think of themselves as being united with him in any way." Joshua paused and looked at each person in the cluster. "Let me state this clearly: God *is* spirit. When I speak of the Holy Spirit I am just expressing a different way in which I experience Yahweh's presence in my life." He stood up and strode over to one of the bags of water. No one moved. *They need to reflect on that for a moment. I hope I am not moving too rapidly for them, but they need to learn, and each major step forward in their understanding requires a rearrangement of their thinking.* He removed the cap from the bag, drank deeply, and then returned to the group which was still sitting silently lost in thought.

"Not where was I? Oh, yes. God is spirit. Now I need to clarify one other term before I truly begin to answer Thomas' question. *Sin* simply means falling short, missing the mark . . . failing in the moral/ethical sphere. It does not suggest that one is *trying* to be bad. After all, how can one fail unless one *is* trying? *Trespassing* is more intentional. *Straying* suggest mere negligence - loss of direction. Falling short is something we all do. We are like little children trying to figure out how to live in the world. When we first were trying to walk, we fell short of the acceptable standard, but we kept on trying and we learned. The same for learning to speak or learning a trade. Our heavenly father does not wish to punish us for our failures. Our heavenly father wishes for us learn from them and to grow beyond them. They are not to be punished but to be . . . well . . . healed."

"But why is it that we do not seem to be able to grow beyond them, Master?"

"That, Bartholomew, is the crucial question. At the very core of all sin is this quality of self-centeredness – of seeing the world only from our own narrow view with the primary concern being ourselves. Those intruders from Jerusalem had no concern – no awareness really – of the situation or the people they were talking to. Desperate people were being healed of their infirmities, but they did not care. Their only concern was that I was an outsider who did not play by their rules. I was not one of them. Since they were certain they were God's representatives I must be Beelzebub's servant. Therefore what I was doing must be evil." He turned to Thomas, "Now, Thomas, my observant one, here is your answer: When anyone decries the good work of the Holy Spirit they signify that they have become so centered on themselves that they are now blind to the presence of God on this earth. They are totally separated from their heavenly father, having replaced any relationship to him with a god of their own making . . . probably one representing their petty, self-centered view and values." Joshua turned again to Thomas, "Did you notice that I said blasphemies – not blasphemed?" Thomas reflected for a moment then nodded, "Yes, Master. By this did you mean that he continues to blaspheme – not that he once blasphemed?" Joshua leaned back as if in triumph. "That is precisely what I meant, Thomas. You must remember that I was speaking to people who use words literally. What I was saying about the spirit and forgiveness – or reconciliation – was as straight forward and logical as what I had said about binding Satan. As along as a person denies and decries the work of the Holy Spirit in his life that person simply continues to be alienated from God. It is that man's own rigid self-centeredness that condemns him."

He started to rise, but quickly sat back down. "One last thought since we are on the subject of sin, self-centeredness and separation: There are degrees of separation. When we are tiny children we are not focused on ourselves. We feel as though we are joined with everything and everyone. Observe little children as they play. There is a wonderful innocence in them – a trust and acceptance they lose along their way. We must become like that again . . . without losing the lessons we have learned and the wisdom we have acquired. It is when we begin to focus on ourselves as different from others that we start to sin. We try to be good, but we fall short. This is the first stage of separation. Later in life we may become preoccupied with distractions. We get so caught up in our careers that we may begin to misuse and cheat others in order to succeed."

"I understand that too well, Master."

Joshua smiled at Levi, "Yes you do. You strayed badly, and that is what was eating at your soul, causing you sleepless nights and reducing the pleasure you found in whatever you had gained. Now you are back on the path . . ." he laughed, "and are just a normal sinner again – closer to God, but not there yet."

Benjamin slapped Levi on his back and laughed, "Good to be back with the normal sinners, isn't it, my friend?" This sent a ripple of laughter through the group. Joshua joined in the laughter. *It is good to have a break from this for a moment and laughter releases the tension.*

"All right, let's be serious again, shall we?" he said quietly, not really wanting to lose the relaxed mood. "Those who do not find their way back to the path and stay there find it easier and easier to stray and stray again. The first few times they crossed the line was accidental. Eventually it becomes intentional. This is what we call *trespassing.* This goes a step beyond sinning and straying – and the separation is much greater. At this stage a person simply does not care about the consequences of his actions. It is no longer a matter of trying to do right but falling short. It now is intentional disobedience. However, the trespasser – in order to trespass – still must return on occasion to the right side. If he continues to cross over, eventually there will come the time when he no longer even desires to return. He will have crossed over to the evil side and will have become Beelzebub's man. When that occurs it is difficult to reclaim him for God."

Joshua arose, leaving his disciples somewhat stunned by this understanding. He strode over to the supplies, chose a cup and filled it with some of the rich, red wine that was there. Then he casually walked over to a little knoll, sat down and cushioned his head with his free arm. He let his mind sink into a light reverie as he watched the clouds above him drift slowly by. As he did so he felt himself nestled in the wondrous mystery he called Yahweh or heavenly father. The tensions seemed to drain from his body and he was at peace.

His disciples however, felt anything but reconciled and peaceful. *How many times have I strayed? How long did I stay on the other side? Oh, God help me, I recall the time . . . .*

Each disciple sorted through his store of memories and felt twinges of pain for the thoughtless words, the selfish acts . . . the countless times he had chosen to ignore the subtle and unsubtle pleas for understanding and help.

Forgive me, Father, for those failures – those foolish strayings – for those terrible times I trespassed.

Each vowed to make amends – to change his ways. Unaware of any terminology, all were thoughtfully determining to turn from their old ways – to see the world from a different – less self-concerned - view.

They were repenting.

CHAPTER TWENTY-EIGHT

SIMON THE ROCK

Joshua had decreed that the morning belonged to each individual. Everyone was free to do whatever he chose. After their shared morning meal and devotions. He leaned back against one of the trees and observed them in their various activities.

James would challenge whomever looked worthy to a wrestling match. Some would accept, but most declined. Joshua suspected that those who accepted did so merely to accommodate their friend. When they lost, as invariably they would, they usually just smiled and slapped James on his back, as though to say, "You are a good fellow."

John had found a scroll with Greek writing and was diligently working to make sense of it. As a fisherman he had little contact with those in the Decapolis, but he had picked up a smattering of Greek. He would read a bit then stroll over to either Levi or Judas to seek some guidance with a word or phrase. Both seemed willing to help John, as though they, also, recognized his special gift of understanding. *John tries to copy his brother's swagger, but he really is a rather gentle person.*

Thomas was one of those who would interrupt whatever he was doing to wrestle with his friend, James. Joshua felt a special affinity for Thomas even though they did not speak much in private. *He, too, seemed to grasp more fully the subtle meanings of my lessons. His questions were always worthy and showed thoughtfulness.*

Philip and Nathaniel enjoyed playing. Whatever they did seemed to have a touch of joviality to it. They laughed easily, but they also had a deeper, more serious side which Joshua could see whenever they ceased their play and entered into discussion with one another.

When Levi was not helping John he was reading a copy of the Torah which he had brought along. *Strange that this man who had served as a hated tax collector for the Romans had purchased and obviously read the books of Moses. There is much more to this man than meets the eye.*

Judas played with numbers in the earth. He might use stones, pebbles or wood sticks. He seemed to find comfort in the symmetry of mathematics. Judas liked certainty . . . a sign of someone who felt insecure somewhere within himself.

Simon the Canaanite was a quiet one who kept to himself. He had found a broken tree branch and was busily carving it. Even from a distance it was easy to see that he had some skill in doing this. *It appears that only his hands are moving, but if I know Simon, and I believe I do, his mind is just as busy shaping some understanding which he later may share with us.*

Andrew is busy as usual, moving between the groups, checking to see how they are doing, looking over the countryside to see who might be coming. He is a natural leader – quiet, but with an inner strength – a strong sense of who he is and what he believes. He has no need to be praised or even seen as a leader. He just leads by example.

Bartholomew and the other James were playing some sort of game, tossing dice and using stones to keep score. *They are both good men. Quiet men, to be sure, but dependable and smart. They should do well.*

And there is Simon. So easily aroused or persuaded. He readily moves to agree or conform. I wonder if having a strong older brother caused him to ignore his own strength. I sense that deep down within him there is a strong core, but he must find it and draw from it if he is to become the man I need him to be. Perhaps it is time we had a bit of a chat.

"Simon, my friend. Come sit with me, will you?"

Simon rose from where he had been sitting; idly watching the clouds pass by. He smiled, and walked quickly to where Joshua was seated.

"Yes, Master. What do you want?" he asked with a smile.

Joshua placed his arm around Simon's shoulder and drew him closer to himself. "I just wanted to spend some time with you, Simon. I need someone I can confide in and I believe you just might be that person."

At this Simon drew himself more upright. "I am one you can trust, Master, if that is what you mean."

"It is that, but more than that as well, Simon. I have been watching you and believe you have an inner strength that you have yet to sense within yourself. I need that strength, Simon. I need it now and I believe I will need it even more in a short time."

"Simon looked concerned, "How is that, Master?"

"I cannot say right now. It is just a feeling I have, Simon. I will need someone who can be as solid as a rock – someone everyone will be able to depend upon and look to when I am not with you. So from this moment on I no longer call you Simon- we have another Simon . . . if anyone needs a Simon." At this they both laughed and looked over to Simon the Canaanite who was busy carving and lost in thought.

"If I am no to be longer Simon, Master, then who will I be?" Simon asked with obvious confusion.

Joshua turned his body, looked directly at Simon and placed his hands on his shoulders: "You are Rock, my friend. You are Rock and that is now your name. [1] I shall tell the others when we assemble this afternoon. Now go and think about it. Search yourself and discover that solid core within you." With that, he lifted his hands from Rock's shoulders and nodded for him to leave.

---

[1] In Greek *Petros* translates as rock. *Petros* is transliterated as Peter in English.

Now, my friend, we shall see if you can bring that core to the surface and become the person I need you to be.

Joshua leaned back, no longer watching his men, no longer present to them or to the world around him. *Well, my father, we seem to be moving closer to wherever it is that you are leading me. Now I pray you that your spirit might come fully alive in that simple fisherman, so that he can continue what you have begun in me.*

CHAPTER TWENTY-NINE

CROSSING OVER

Joshua knew it was time to cross to the other side of the sea. *"I will give you as a light to the nations that my salvation may reach to the end of the earth."* That is what Isaiah proclaimed, and that is what I must do, so I might as well be about it. *(Isaiah 49:6)*.

He rose, looked at the disciples and quietly said, "It's time to cross over to the Decapolis, men. That is part of our task." With those simple words a new era had begun. The people there were Hellenists. They had been induced to settle in the area by the Romans as a means of both keeping watch over the activities of these rebellious Galileans and dissipating the power of their Mosaic Law. Their own religion was rather easy and attractive. It emphasized the sensuous side of their nature, with little demands for daily obedience. It would be a challenge, with no tradition for reference, no common understanding of Yahweh.

They abandoned their idyllic place of refuge and descended to the sea, found a boat and sailed to the other side. They landed in the country of the Gerasenes. No sooner had they landed than a strange fellow came rushing out of the tombs to meet them. He wore no sandals, but did not seem to even notice the sharp rocks beneath his feet. His hair was wild but his eyes were even wilder. Arms waving overhead, he was dashing across the landscape, screaming and crying as he approached them at what most thought was an uncomfortable speed. Some of the disciples crouched behind Joshua and Andrew as he neared them. Joshua stretched his arms out to his side as though to protect them . . . and continued walking directly toward the approaching menace.

As the man neared them they could see the bruises on his arms and legs where once shackles had been.

When he was about four feet away from Joshua he suddenly stopped and knelt at his feet. In a powerful, raspy voice he cried out, "What have you to do with me, Joshua, son of the most high God? I call upon you by God not to torment me."

The disciples were stunned at this pronouncement by a total stranger – and one who seemed possessed, at that. Joshua, however, straightened himself as though mustering his authority. He then relaxed his stance and spoke quietly inquiring of the man, "What is your name?"

"My name is Legion because we are so many." Joshua paused to consider this response.

This poor fellow needs to be freed of his demons, yet it is to these very demons that I am talking. He is so mired in the quagmire of his confused soul that he has lost touch with everything – even himself.

Joshua later was to learn that the man had been chained time and time again to control him, but every time he broke the chains with his bare hands. No one had the strength to subdue him so they had driven him out of the town into the area of the tombs, where his wailing could be heard nightly by the townspeople.

Joshua looked about to see what he might use to effect a cure. Over on the hillside he saw a herd of swine, loosely controlled by some swine herders who had strayed toward them, seeming more interested in watching this encounter with Legion than in caring for their charges.

Perhaps I can make a couple of points by using them, he thought. These Hellenists make fun of our customs. They think us weak and foolish because the Romans rule over us. Well let us see how they react to this. He smiled inwardly as the solution took shape in his mind. *Unclean spirits cannot just be cast out and left free to roam. They must go some-where. Everyone knows that.*

He looked at Legion and nodded toward the swine. His look told Legion that whatever it was that possessed him was about to be dismissed.

Legion looked toward the herd, then he opened his mouth. The raspy voice was heard once more, but this time it was shaky and pleading: "Send us into the swine. Let us enter them."

Joshua moved his arms in a sweeping motion from Legion toward the herd. With a slow, steady voice that contained a power which both silenced all who heard and yet calmed their spirits as well, Joshua said, "Come out of this man you unclean spirits." Suddenly the herd of swine burst forth from their lethargy and began to stampede down the hill toward the sea. The herdsmen jumped into action, rushing alongside them, beating at them with their staffs in a futile attempt to change the direction. They screamed at the animals, but by this time the herd was squealing and snorting far too loudly for them to be heard. Finally the herdsmen crumpled in despair and watched the swine rush headlong into the water, falling over one another as they disappeared beneath the surface.

As the last ones sank out of sight and a sudden silence blanketed the landscape, the herdsmen rose and ran to the village. It was only a matter of moments before most of the townspeople were rushing out to where Joshua was. Most looked awestruck. Some seemed afraid and began to beg Joshua to leave the area. Joshua weighed his choices: *There doesn't seem to be much purpose in staying here. These people are so upset they will not be able to hear and discern my message. If I leave them now, they will be relieved. In time they will forget the loss of the herd and only remember the wonder of this . . . which undoubtedly will become even more wonderful with every retelling.* He smiled at the thought of this curious human quality. At this moment, Legion approached Joshua and pleaded to be able to go with him.

Joshua put his hand upon the man – now no longer Legion: "No, my friend. Go back to be with your friends. Tell them what the Lord has done for you and the mercy he has shown you."

The man looked dismayed at the thought. Then he turned and saw the townspeople – no longer fearful of him, smiling and even beckoning him to join them. He squeezed Joshua's hand in a token of affection and gratitude. Joshua returned the friendly squeeze. For a moment they looked deeply into each other's eyes. Joshua saw the clarity and wholeness that had not been there when they first met. He released his grip and withdrew his hand. The man, still facing Joshua, walked backward until he felt himself being touched by his own people. Joshua motioned to his disciples and they boarded the boat and sailed back toward the Jewish side.

No one spoke on the return trip. Each disciple sat quietly, trying to understand what they had just experienced.

It was a beginning . . . only a beginning, thought Joshua. *God's love for his people must be shared. There can be no boundaries – no barriers of background or heritage.*

The wind had faded into still air. The boat was becalmed, so Joshua reached for an oar and set the rhythm of the stroke which five of the others picked up. The tiny boat began to move, slowly but steadily toward the distant shore.

Wherever you lead; whatever you ask; I will be faithful. Make my way clear - is all I ask. Wherever you lead; whatever you ask; I will be faithful. Make my way clear - is all I ask.

It makes a nice rhythm . . .

CHAPTER THIRTY

THE NEED FOR SECRECY

As they neared land, they saw a crowd gathering to greet them. The people had seen the boat coming from the other side and had heard that Joshua had sailed there earlier in the day. While the disciples were still disembarking, Jairus, a leader of the synagogue, pushed his way through the crowd and fell at Joshua's feet.

"My little daughter is at the point of death. Come, lay your hands upon her so that she may be made well and live."

Without hesitation, Joshua nodded. Jairus turned and began walking directly to his house. The crowd would not be deterred, however. They had gathered to see this wonder-worker whose feats were being proclaimed throughout all Galilee. To anyone who could watch them from a distance, it must have looked ridiculous. Everyone was pushing and shoving, trying to be at the head of whichever line they were in. Some were falling over the smaller ones in their attempt to be closer to this person of extraordinary power.

One of those struggling to be near Joshua was a woman who had been hemorrhaging for twelve years. She had traveled to every doctor and healer she could find, but even though each one had taken her money, none had been able to cure her. In desperation she came up behind him, reached out and touched his cloak. And immediately felt a surge of relief flow through her body. Instantly, Joshua stopped: *I felt power leave my body just now.* He looked about at the crowd and asked in a chilling whisper, "Who touched my clothes?"

"You see this crowd pressing you. How can you say who touched your clothes? asked Judas, almost laughing at the absurdity of the question.

Ignoring his comment, Joshua continued to search through the crowd, trying to determine if it had been a malicious act or one done in faith. The woman, now sensing herself healed, stepped forward trembling in fear, fell at his feet and told him her story.

Joshua's face immediately softened as he recognized the desperation and profound faith of this frightened woman. He placed his hand gently on her head and said, " Daughter, your faith has saved you, making you whole. Go in peace."

Even as he spoke, some men came from Jairus' house and told him his daughter had died. "Why trouble this teacher any further?" they asked. But hearing this, Joshua placed his hand on Jairus' shoulder and said, "Do not fear. Only have trust." He then raised his hand, indicating that the crowd must remain where they were. He nodded to Rock, James and John to follow him and entered the house. Once inside he saw the group of close friends and relatives weeping and wailing in their sorrow.

He sighed deeply, feeling their helplessness and hopelessness. "Why do you make a commotion and weep? The child is not dead, but is sleeping."

The group looked at him incredulously – some laughing at the absurdity of his claim. He quickly shooed them outside, but took Jairus and his wife by the hand and led them to where their daughter lay.

Rock, James and John said not a word, but watched intently as Joshua took the little girl by her hand and said in a soft but commanding voice, "Little girl, get up."

Instantly the little girl opened her eyes, stood up and began to walk about the room. Jairus and his wife stood transfixed, but with tears of joyful relief streaming down their cheeks. Rock,

James and John caught their breaths and just watched almost as detached observers as the parents scooped up their daughter and covered her with kisses.

Joshua stepped up to them and said, "Tell no one about this. Now give her something to eat." Then he turned and departed before they could gather their wits enough to even thank him.

As they walked back to the crowd John asked him, "Master, you told Legion to tell people what you did for him, but now you tell these people to be quiet about it?"

Without breaking stride, Joshua replied, "Casting out demons has been done by others, but resuscitating the dead echoes of Elijah and Elisha.[*1] This could frighten the authorities in Jerusalem. Frightened men are dangerous men. We do not need that at this time."

[*1] 1 Kings 17:17 ff, 2 Kings 4:32-38

CHAPTER THIRTY-ONE

NO PLACE LIKE HOME

It had been nearly three months since Joshua had left Nazareth. He missed Mary and the rest of his family. He had never been separated from them for so long a period in all of his lifetime. He worried about Joanna. She had been a combination little sister and daughter to him. She now was a young woman and should soon be finding a husband. Joshua had his eye on a young villager he thought would be a good catch. *I hope James has the good sense to line up Joses the carpenter's son. He is steady, kind and dependable – a good provider. Perhaps it would be good to return to Nazareth. I need to speak with James about Joanna. Also, I need to heal some relationships. The family is upset with me. Perhaps when they see what I am now doing they will understand why I said what I said back when they tried to take me home.*

Joshua called the disciples together: "We must go now to Nazareth. It is time to proclaim my message there."

Without a word, the disciples gathered their few belongings and began the trek westward to Nazareth. Two days later, they arrived at a small village near the base of a huge hill in the valley of Jezreel. "There it is: Nazareth - high and dry. Let us fill our water bags here, for there is only one well in the entire village and we may be there for a few days." In a matter of minutes the chore was completed and the group began the steep ascent to the village above. Once there, Joshua suggested the disciples keep busy by exploring the town, while he met with his family. As expected, the men were away, but Mary, Elizabeth and Joanna were at work, mending clothing and preparing the evening meal. They looked up as Joshua entered the house.

Mary saw him but did not respond. She continued to sew, struggling inwardly for a proper response. *He's back . . . but why? Has he come to apologize? Is he in trouble? Does he plan to stay? I'm still angry and hurt . . . but I have missed him so much . . . and I love him dearly. Say nothing! Don't appear to be anxious. Remain calm. He has come to me. Let him speak first.* All this raced through Mary's mind in a matter of seconds . . . before Joshua had even taken three steps into the room.

Elizabeth smiled, but took her cue from Mary and remained silent.

Joanna, however, shouted with glee and rushed to her older brother: "Joshua! Oh, Joshua! You are home again!" She flung her arms around his neck and hugged him with all her strength.

Joshua kissed her on her forehead and returned her hug. "Yes, little sister. I have come home to see all of you . . . and to attempt to explain why I ignored you when you came for me last month." He took his arms from Joanna and stepped toward Mary, who now assumed the posture of a queen awaiting a messenger. Joshua looked into her eyes, seeing the hurt and uncertainty. He immediately grasped the situation, and knelt before her. "Mother . . . my beloved mother to whom I owe my life . . . please try to understand who I have become, and what I must do. I did not intend to hurt you. What I said was to tell you and all those people who were with me in the room that the greatest claim on all our lives is Yahweh, the heavenly father of us all. It is his spirit which unites us. No matter what village we are from, what family raised us, what nation claims us . . . or what creeds we recite – it is Yahweh, our heavenly father's spirit that makes us one family. All you needed to do was enter the house and say that you also live to do his will, and I would have welcomed you with open arms." He hesitated: "as I hope you will now welcome me," he added.

This was all Mary needed. She reached out to him and slowly drew him to her, patting his head as he placed it upon her bosom. Elizabeth stepped to where they were, placed her hands on his shoulders and began tenderly massaging them . . . tears flowing down her cheeks.

Joanna just stood watching the scene with a feeling of joy. *Joshua has come home.*

His brothers would not return for hours, yet Joshua did not choose to leave the serenity that now pervaded the house. The women returned to their tasks, and he lay by the table, watching and remembering peaceful days of times gone by.

He could recall the arrival of each new sibling, and the joy each one of them brought.

He remembered the first time Joseph had taken him along to construct a home made entirely from the rocks which were so plentiful in that area. "Rocks are far more abundant and cost less than wood," he had laughed . . . "and they last much longer." "Joseph had carefully taught Joshua to select and chip the rocks to fit snugly together.

He relived the first evening that Joseph had taken him to the synagogue – to sit as one of the men. How proud they both had been. Later, at supper Joseph had asked him to give the blessing.

How long he continued in this peaceful reverie, he did not know. Suddenly there was the sound of men's voices and the four brothers came into the house, still laughing over some joke Judas had told them. When they saw Joshua, however, the laughter stopped. The men froze where they were and one could feel the tension sweeping through the room.

"What do you want?" demanded James. "You don't live here any more." He added with a hint of scorn in his voice. His other brothers, Judas, Simon and Joseph, moved closer toward James as if to present a strong, united front.

Mary quickly intervened before Joshua had the opportunity to respond: "Your *brother*" (she emphasized the word, brother) "has come to visit and to explain the misunderstanding we *all* had about his words." She looked squarely at each of her four sons as she spoke. Then she rose and placed her arms on Joshua's shoulders. "He has taken time from his important work to spend some time with us. Now, no more about this matter. Get yourselves ready for supper." With that, Mary turned and began stirring the fish stew she had prepared.

Joshua gazed at each of his brothers with an open, neutral expression, and each returned his gaze with equal neutrality. Joshua took a place at the end of the table and his brothers opted for the other end even though it meant being crowded.

There were a few failed attempts at making small talk during the supper. Primarily it was eaten in silence, however. When it had ended, Joshua stood and walked to the door saying, "I need to tend to my disciples. I will sleep with them tonight." Mary quickly said, "Please join us for the morning meal, and give my love to James and John." Joshua nodded ascent and disappeared into the darkness.

The disciples had gathered a short distance from the house and signaled to Joshua as he appeared through the doorway. "Well, Master and cousin," said James, "How did the reunion go?" Joshua shook his head by way of response, "Not well. The women welcomed me, but you may have felt the chill from the men even where you were."

"It will take time, but they will get over it, Joshua," James offered, slipping back into the role of relative for a moment. Joshua was relieved by this change of tone. He had become somewhat weary of being called Master by these cousins he had known for most of his life as companions. "I hope so, James. I truly hope so." He looked at the disciples, then turned to Rock, "You have eaten?"

"Yes, we assumed that when you remained in the house you would dine with them so we prepared a meal for ourselves and ate it over by the edge of the town," he added, pointing toward the open area a few hundred yards distant.

"That might also be a decent place for us to spend the night. James, gather the men over there. We will have an evening prayer and then retire for the night."

"I will do that, Master," responded James, now slipping back into his role as disciple. He turned and walked over to where the others were gathered, as Joshua, John and Rock strolled over to the open area. Joshua looked about for a suitable spot and laid his few belongings there. He then found a small knoll where he could conduct the evening prayer. Then he sat and waited for the disciples to gather. The lengthening shadows told him the daylight was about to fade. He looked back toward what had once been his home and felt a twinge of sadness.

Wherever you lead; whatever you ask; I will be faithful. Make my way clear, is all I ask.

With a sigh, he turned his attention to the disciples who had begun to gather at his feet.

"Tonight's prayer will be focused upon resting ourselves in Yahweh's presence and drawing from his grace."

CHAPTER THIRTY-TWO

WELCOME AND NOT WELCOMED

Joshua arose before the sunlight had lightened the sky. He had purposefully slept near the edge of the clearing in order to avoid disturbing the slumber of the others. He donned his sandals and headed toward the village. Once there he began to retrace the path of his morning walks, wending his way through the streets toward the northern edge where he could sit and survey the Valley of Jezreel. There was something utterly peaceful about the scene. The wreckage of so many once-powerful fortress cities sitting on the northwest edge created a sharp contrast with the lush serenity of the valley. *It is the gentle ones who prevail. It never is might that makes right. Rather it is right that makes might – the enduring mightiness of Yahweh.*

His thoughts were interrupted by the light sounds of footsteps approaching him from a distance. Joshua turned his head to see who his visitor might be. *Brother James! Well this is either going to be very good or very uncomfortable,* he thought. The two had always been close, but as brothers there also had been a bit of a rivalry between them – more from the younger than the older, as one might expect. Joshua, as the eldest son, was a favored one, but he also was one who challenged authority and did the unexpected. James found his niche by accepting authority and doing what was expected and desired. He had even become somewhat obsessive about obedience to the Law of Moses. He had even been given the unofficial title of "James the Just" by many of the townspeople. At Passover he was the one who would conduct or lead the search for leaven within the house. On a few occasions Mary had intentionally left some where he could find it. James then would admonish Mary for her carelessness, feeling particularly righteous because he had saved the family from sinning. Joshua always watched those proceedings with interest and a bit of humor. He knew it was Mary's way of affirming James as a loving and caring son. He also wondered why James had not figured that out. When Joseph had died and Joshua had become the de facto head of the family, there was an occasional tension between them. James had thought that by virtue of his example he at least should have been consulted on the more important family matters. When Joshua had abandoned the family to pursue his own interests James immediately filled the void and assumed the role of head of the house.

James approached Joshua, and without a word sat down by his side.

He's walked all this way to be with me. I'll wait and let him say what is on his mind.

The two sat in awkward silence for a few minutes. Finally James spoke:

"Mary told us what you had said about those doing the will of Yahweh being your true family."

Joshua said nothing. *Let's see what he wants to make of that. Did he understand or was he still so caught up in himself that he missed the point?*

"Joshua, it was my fault that the family walked away from you then. I was so certain that you were going to resist us – even deny us – that I misunderstood what you were trying to tell us. We *are* part of a greater family than mere blood ties give us. I realize that now. I knew it then, but I could not accept it when it came from your mouth." He leaned forward and turned his head to face Joshua. "I have always admired you, big brother. But I also have resented you at times. You took charge so easily, as though you were born to do so. You made decisions, gave advice – gave orders . . . as though . . . well as though you were some sort of royalty - - - as I said: 'born to do so.'"

James had said what he came to say; now he waited for Joshua's response.

Joshua lifted his arm and placed it on James' shoulder. "James, I also have always admired you . . . and I shall always love you. Brothers have differences, of course. We have ours. We also have fierce loyalties to one another." He hesitated, as if deciding whether to continue the thought. "James, my brother, I shall need your loyalty, your wisdom . . . and your leadership qualities – oh, yes. You do have them. That is why we butted heads like a couple of goats on occasion." They laughed, and whatever tension still remained was swept away by that laughter.

James shook his head. "You don't need me, Joshua. You have a group of strong followers who will do whatever you ask of them."

Joshua responded by nodding his head affirmatively: "Oh, but I will need you, James – sometime in the future. You will know when. These men I have are good men and loyal men, but they do not have some of the qualities that you possess. Andrew is loyal and a good assistant, but not a leader. His brother, Simon, still has a way to go before he can be a leader. Cousin James is a leader. Yes, but a bit rough around the edges. Cousin John is more of a thinker than a leader. The time will come when I must call on you."

James was both taken back and flattered by his brother's appraisal. "If you ever really need me, you know I will make myself available to you, big brother."

"The time will come. You will know. You will respond. I am certain of that." He leaned back, resting on his elbows, gazing at the valley below him. James, too, leaned back and relaxed. For a time it was enough just to be together again, just to be at peace with one another – and with one's self.

Memories of bygone days floated through their minds – childhood days, when Joseph was alive and vigorous. There seemed to be more laughter then. Life itself seemed much simpler.

Finally, with a note of reluctance, Joshua stood up. "Come, James. It is time to rejoin our family for the morning meal. This talking has made me hungry."

James rose, and together they made their way back into town. Rock saw them as they passed by, laughing and chatting. He immediately turned to find James and John, to tell them the family crisis had passed.

When they entered the house it was apparent to all that Joshua and James had reconciled and were as close as ever. The women smiled and breathed a sigh of relief. So did Joseph. However, both Simon and Judas looked a bit skeptical. James saw this and noted, *I shall have to talk with them a bit, I see. They always were somewhat envious of the close relationship Joshua and I enjoyed.*

Joshua noted their coolness, as well. *I will let James handle that. For the moment I shall just enjoy the family.* He found a place at the table, lowered himself, tore a piece of bread from the large loaf that still was hot to the touch, poured some honey over it, and exclaimed, " It is good to be home – so good to be home again."

He had barely taken his first bite before he heard his name called from outside: "Joshua? Joshua, are you there?" the voice inquired.

"It's Rebecca." said Mary. "I recognize her voice." She raised her voice and called back, "Yes, Joshua is here, Rebecca. Come in." Mary quickly poured some herbal tea and met Rebecca as she entered. She handed it to Rebecca and offered her a place to sit, but Rebecca refused. She approached Joshua and knelt at his feet.

"We heard you were here, Joshua. Please, please would you come to the house?? My Abigail is sick with a fever and I do not know what to do for her. We have heard of the wonderful things you have been doing. Please come. Come and heal her . . . please." The last please was uttered so plaintively that even Simon and Judas looked to Joshua with faces agonized – pleading on her behalf.

Joshua laid his hand on Rebecca's head, as though he were blessing her. "Do not fret, good neighbor. Of course I will go with you. We cannot have little Abigail sick or suffering, can we?" He walked past her and led the way to the house of Isaac the Tailor.

He could see Abigail as he entered. She was wrapped in a blanket and being held by Naomi, the baker's wife who lived down the street. Little Benjamin and Mary were playing unconcernedly on the floor – apparently oblivious to the concern of their mother. *Ah, the innocence of children*, thought Joshua. *Where does it go? When does it go?* He wasted no time but walked directly to Naomi, lifted Abigail from her arms, cradled her in his own, and opened the blanket to reveal skin that was pink and spotted. He laid his hand on her little head, and began to hum softly into her ear, rocking her gently as he did so. She had been sobbing quietly, but gradually hushed and started murmuring almost as though she was trying to sing along with Joshua. Rebecca and Naomi watched in silence, barely daring to breathe as they sensed they were witnessing some sort of wonder. After a few minutes Joshua opened Abigail's blanket again, stared down at her now clear skin, smiled and handed her to Rebecca. "There is nothing wrong with her. She is fine," he said. "Your love . . . and your faith," he said, looking at both women, "has healed her." Then he added, "Sometime faith and love is all we need." With this he turned and left the house.

"Do you think we just witnessed what I think we just witnessed?" asked Rebecca in awe. Naomi could only nod affirmation in her stunned silence. After a few moments, in which Rebecca constantly unwrapped and rewrapped Abigail's blanket, continually reassuring herself that the fever and the spots were gone, Naomi spoke: "We have all heard the stories of the wonders Joshua has performed, but I thought they were exaggerations. He never did anything like that while he lived here." She walked across the room to where Rebecca and Abigail were and laid her hands on Rebecca's shoulders. "Now I know that they were true. Something has happened to our Joshua. He always seemed special, but now . . . well . . . he is more than special."

Joshua returned home, knowing the inevitable crowd would soon gather. He had grown accustomed to this, but this time he felt a pang of disappointment. *I had hoped to spend time with Mary, Elizabeth and Joanna. I have dearly missed them and did look forward to . . . well just being with them again. We never required many words. The feeling of closeness – the odors from their cooking – the familiarity of surroundings – sufficed to know that one was safe, accepted . . . and loved. I could use that right now. Some part of me keeps whispering warnings that I am not as safe – as accepted or loved as I would care to be.*

The sounds of voices at the door interrupted his thoughts and – somewhat reluctantly – he rose and went to see how his service was needed.

There were the elderly with their blurred eye sight, painful joints and inevitable fears. He placed his hands on their eyes and joints and spoke words of assurance to their fears. The lame were made whole. The fearful were given courage born of trust. Simple little cures of the body and the soul. Their needs were met and sooner than expected Joshua was free to return to Mary and his sisters. This time he hugged each as though he had been long-absent. *We do gain fresh appreciation when we fear we have lost something, do we not?* he asked himself rhetorically.

Their time together passed quickly and soon the men returned from their day's labor. The evening meal was served. It was eaten just before sundown which would start the Sabbath.

After the meal they walked to the synagogue. Upon seeing Joshua, the leaders of the synagogue immediately invited him to give the lesson. He spoke with such clarity and gentle power that his listeners began to whisper among themselves: "Where did this man get this wisdom?" "What deeds of power are being done by his hands?" Then the detractors began responding, "Is this not the builder, the son of Mary?" "His brothers are here among us." In various ways they were saying that Joshua was no one special – that his words carried no authority. People being what they are, many adapted to the mood of the more insistent critics. As quickly as he had been admired for his wisdom he now found himself disdained for being who he was in their sight: The questionable son of Mary and Joseph . . . a mere product of lowly Nazareth. The people's negative image of themselves and their village had poured itself upon him. Recognizing this dramatic shift, Joshua stopped his teaching, looked at the audience with sympathy – yet his personal hurt also was obvious.

He paused to gather his composure. Then he slowly let his gaze sweep over the crowd. As he did do he recognized each one and nodded to affirm that recognition. "Prophets are not without honor, except in their own hometown, and among their own kin, and in their own house." He looked at Simon and Judas as he uttered those final words.

Both brothers avoided his gaze and dropped their heads in tacit acknowledgement of the truth of his words. Shoulders slumped in embarrassment, they did not move again until later, when the room was empty.

Then ever so slowly Joshua stepped from behind the speakers' stand and made his way to the rear of the synagogue. Few eyes followed him. Most stood facing the front, nervously waiting for him to depart. Something had radically altered the mood of the room – from light-hearted celebration to profound sorrow. Some of the very young men felt it and began to weep. As he walked past one, Joshua paused and patted his head, instantly calming him. When he reached the door he turned and surveyed the scene. For a moment his eyes misted over with sadness. Then he turned and disappeared into the gathering darkness.

CHAPTER THIRTY-THREE

TRIAL RUN

Early the next morning Joshua aroused his disciples before sunrise. "It is time for us to move on. I will join my family for the morning meal then we shall depart. Make ready!"

"But, Master, we only arrived yesterday." Andrew responded. "It's time, I said." replied Joshua with a touch of testiness in his tone. "It probably was a mistake coming here."

"I am sorry, Master. We all hoped it would go better." Joshua nodded; then he shook his head. "People insist on living with past impressions. This makes them blind to see what actually is. The people of Nazareth are essentially good, decent people. They just live in too small a world, Andrew; a world seen only through narrow windows.

Within the house, Mary and the two girls were preparing the morning meal. Joshua could smell the tantalizing aroma of fresh bread while he was still some distance from the house. Elizabeth was laying out the smoked fish and fresh fruit as he entered. As soon as she saw him she put the items down and rushed to give him a gentle, loving hug. "Oh Joshua, I am so sorry about last night. I do not know what got into them. There were so many people there who know and respect you, but they seemed to be swallowed up by those who are jealous of you and those who do not know you well." As she spoke she caressed his hair, as though straightening it.

Elizabeth! Elizabeth, my darling sister. You probably know me better than anyone. I know why you never married. There have been many men who wanted you as their wife. However, in many ways we shared the role of caregiver for this family. Just as I could not abandon my role, neither could you. He hugged her gently, and for a moment they gazed into one another's eyes, each open to the other; each seeing deeper than others were allowed to go.

Finally, Joshua broke the silent intimacy of the moment: "It is best that I go." Elizabeth had prepared herself for this. She had slept fitfully, knowing that he would leave, perhaps forever this time. Still, she gasped when he said the words.

"Oh, Joshua, my Joshua." For a brief moment she just stood, staring into his eyes while her own began to fill with tears. "My mind understands but my heart does not. I do so want you to stay. Yet, I do believe you when you say that it is Yahweh who has made this claim upon you. So go, if you must, but know you carry my heart with you . . . big brother" (she added this with a poor attempt at a smile). Then she turned, re-gathered the fish and fruit and began again to distribute them around the table.

The men entered in silence, as though they had anticipated the mood of the morning. Simon and Judas approached Joshua and placed their hand on his shoulders in a passive attempt to compensate for their earlier actions. Joshua turned and hugged each, patting them on their backs as a return token of his affection for them. Without a word the men took a seat and the women began to serve them: Fruits in abundance, smoked fish, cheese and fresh bread laden with honey. Mary had prepared a huge pitcher of an herbal drink which she sat in front of Joshua. "It is best with a bit of honey,' she offered in an attempt to break the silence.

"Thank you, mother," Joshua said, grateful that someone had broken the silence which had dominated the room. Then he reached for the pitcher. "I suppose everyone knows this but I need to say it: I shall be leaving after the meal. There is much work I must do."

"Joshua, do not be hard on the townspeople," said James. "We expect out prophets and heroes to be people from the past – or at least distant places. We hear about them or we read about them, but we never expect to meet one – particularly if it is someone we watched growing into manhood." He leaned toward Joshua and looked directly at him. "To so many of these people you will always be Mary's son – someone they remember tagging along with Joseph or running errands . . . or playing some mischief" he added with a knowing nod at Joshua.

"I understand that, James. I suppose I accept it even though it is so foolish and wasteful. People form opinions and then cannot see clearly enough to change them when the situation - - - or the people change. That accounts for so much of the hatred and prejudice we live with." He let this thought sit for a moment then added: "People need to grow up and act like adults. They need to use their minds for more than remembering and reciting old sayings . . . and passing along outdated truths that probably never were truths." He suddenly arose. "I'm sorry, my dear family. I love you dearly but I sense there is little time and much to do. I must go." He stepped over to each of the women and kissed them on their forehead; then he waved broadly to the men." Farewell. I shall remember you all in my prayers."

"But you haven't finished your meal yet," insisted Mary. "I am fed mother. The love here has done that for me." He turned and disappeared through the door.

Once outside, he motioned to the disciples to make their way toward the street where they would assemble. They quickly gathered their belongings and gathered before him. They descended the road from Nazareth into the valley below. They entered the first village, and Joshua stopped and announced: "It is time now to test what you have learned." He said. "I am sending you out in pairs to separate villages. Leave everything here except a staff."

"But we shall need some supplies, Master – at least some mon-" Levi was stopped midway in his protest. "I said '*nothing!*' Joshua interrupted curtly. If you have learned anything from me you will need nothing. All you will require will be provided you. Now listen carefully: When you enter a village and are invited to enter a house, you will remain there for the duration of your stay." "What's the point of that?" asked Judas. "If you do the things I believe you can do," replied Joshua, "you will receive many invitations from people who want the prestige of hosting you. Forget them. Remain with those who brought you in as a stranger – no matter how humble their dwelling . . . or how meager their meals."

"What if no one offers hospitality, Master? What are we to do then?" Good question, Andrew. "If no one receives you, shake the dust of that village off your feet and go elsewhere." He smiled and continued in a conspiratorial tone: "They will hear later what they missed, and perhaps learn a lesson in basic hospitality." The men all laughed at this, though it was obvious that some were skeptical of the experiment.

"Come, now," Joshua commanded. "Each of you take turns standing before me." As they did so, he laid his hands on each, saying, "Take the authority to heal and to cast out the unclean spirits." As each man received that commission he straightened and assumed a more commanding attitude which revealed itself in his speech and posture.

When the last disciple had been commissioned Joshua said casually, "Find your partner, then go and find your village. Return here when the moon is full." He watched them mentally sorting through the group to select a partner. Some choices were obvious. Others were hesitant to ask, for fear of rejection. Eventually, however, each teamed with another and they departed. With a smile of satisfaction, Joshua turned to Mary Magdala, "The children are on their way, Mother Mary. Let us make ourselves comfortable here and wait their return. If you wish to secure some quarters for yourself, I suggest you go over to the well and begin chatting with the women."

Mary smiled, "I know how to care for myself, sweet master. I know you do, as well, so I shall see you when the moon is full." She began to walk away, and called over her shoulder, "Enjoy this quiet time. It will end soon enough."

CHAPTER THIRTY-FOUR

REFLECTIONS WHILE WAITING

Joshua watched as Mary strolled down the street and turned a corner. Then he turned to survey the area. He could spend some time in the village. That would eventually lead to his teaching and healing, however, and he wanted to use the time for something other than that. He found his way to the market, purchased some smoked fish, olives, bread and dried figs. Then he left the village and began to scale the nearest hill to where he found a flat space, adequate for a brief camping stay.

After setting up his temporary camp, Joshua found a comfortable place to lay back, gaze at the sky and contemplate how he would pass the next few days. *This seems a good time to reflect upon what has taken place, and to set some plans for the future.* He let that thought linger as he lay quietly, watching the clouds overhead as they passed slowly by. As he did so he felt himself slipping into a peaceful reverie in which he felt himself resting in the hands of the One he called Father.

Father, I believe I have come to understand you more clearly, now that I sense you as a constant presence in my life. The psalmist, who asked where he could go to flee from your presence, did not envision you as some relentless pursuer, trailing behind him, but as an all-pervasive Presence. To speak of your spirit is but another way of speaking of you – of understanding how we experience your presence in our lives. When I sensed your spirit descending upon me, engulfing me, I now believe it was more of an awakening on my part than a reaching down on yours. There is some portion of you that resides in me – in every one of us, I believe. I reside in you and you reside in me – in everyone. We just are unaware of that, and so we fumble around in life, looking for something outside of ourselves to fill what we feel as a void within ourselves . . . simply because – well because we are too self-absorbed - too full of ourselves to recognize your presence.

It is we who cut ourselves off from you, casting ourselves adrift – fearful of tomorrow – fearful of your judgment – fearful - - - of death, itself. Yet because you live in us there is some part of us that never can die. Joshua raised his head to gaze about the landscape. On a distant low-lying hill some workers were picking fruit from a tree. On the nearby hillside that ascended to Nazareth there was a woman tending a small herd of goats. His mind stretched into the village and he imagined Mary chatting with some of the women in the market area. A bird crossed his path of vision and he absentmindedly watched it settle on the ground and begin its search for some form of nurture.

We all are beloved creatures of Yahweh, he thought: *People, goats . . . even birds. Yahweh is aware of each of us and cares for each of us. We live out our days – our lives – and then our bodies fade and we pass from this earth, but we do not pass from His love.*

Joshua was surprised to hear these thoughts. *We know far more at a spiritual level than we understand. I suppose this is what gives rise to that we call intuition. It is not until we articulate these vague thoughts – give them words – that we learn the wisdom that lies buried somewhere deep within us.* Again, he was startled – but pleased – to hear himself express these ideas. *What is happening to me – within me, Father? I seem to have tapped into some deep reservoir of wisdom that gives me an entirely new understanding of . . . well of life.* He lay with his eyes closed for a long moment, allowing the excitement within him to subside and to rest himself again in the continuing presence of a loving Yahweh.

I am immersed in God! God is immersed in me!

We all are awash in Yahweh's blessed love! We just do not know it. To know it is to live within His Kingdom: outside of Rome's; outside of Herod's. It is to be free of the restraints put upon us by mere mortals: to fulfill the image of the One in whose image we have been created.

All of us are God's children.

He paused and then looked upward again; this time not at the clouds, but beyond.

This is the message you wish for me to share with the world, Father? Your spirit resides in each of us. We have only to awaken to it? We are all beloved children. Death does not have the final claim to us. We are to treat one another with kindness and respect. The world claim upon us is not equal to your claim upon us. Love – not fear – is the key to our actions. Is this true?

Joshua stopped abruptly. He felt he was becoming carried away by his own speculations.

We shall see, soon enough, if I am right on this. When the Twelve return they will have performed wonders on their own . . . if I am correct.

He lay back, absent-mindedly gazing at the clouds as he let the impact of this new revelation sift through his mind.

The time until the fullness of the moon would pass slowly now that he was eager for their return.

I must find Mary, he thought. *She is a good and wise listener. Life has taught her many lessons. She is someone I can confide these thoughts with – someone I trust and respect.* With that, he rose and headed into the village.

CHAPTER THIRTY-FIVE

WAITING WITH MARY

He spied Mary where he thought she would be, by the village well, chatting with the women while they waited their turn. The wells in most villages served as a central meeting place for the women. Fresh water was a necessity for every household, and it was the women's chore to provide it. Over the years this thankless task had evolved into the daily gathering place where family matters and gossip could be exchanged, and the boring routine of the day could be interrupted for a moment of friendship and sharing.

Mary recognized him as he approached from a distance. Before she could discern his features she recognized his gait. Even when weary there was always a hint of a swagger, as that of a prince strolling among his people or surveying his land. There was nothing arrogant in this. It was more a matter of confidence and comfort within himself that gave this impression.

When she saw him she excused herself from the group and began a casual stroll to meet him on his path. "You must excuse me. My rabbi wishes to speak with me." This caused many heads to turn in the direction Mary was looking.

"Her rabbi?" someone whispered as Mary departed. "What is a woman doing with a rabbi?" "How can she be a disciple? That is not done by women."

"She did not seem to be an ordinary woman, did she? This woman was very knowledgeable."

"She had a very good mind – and was quite confident as she spoke among us strangers."

Now the eyes turned from the departing Mary to the approaching stranger. They gathered closer together. One of them giggled and whispered into the ear of her companion. They would find much to speculate about for the next few days.

Joshua could see the activity behind Mary as she approached him. He laughed at the realization that their gossip was about Mary and him. *People are funny creatures*, he thought. *What they don't know or understand they guess at, and quickly they have a way of turning those guesses into fact. Well, we won't be here much longer, so their gossip should not have any effect upon Mary's standing.*

As Mary drew near, he said, "They are talking about you – probably about us, Mary. Turn back and wave good bye to your friends."

Mary, turned, smiled and waved a final goodbye, and the women stopped their chattering and acted as though they had been caught doing something wrong. Quickly, however they regained their composure and waved back.

They both had a good laugh over that as they walked toward Joshua's camp site.

Mary proved to be the good listener Joshua wanted. Her questions helped to clarify some of his thoughts. Her obvious acceptance and enthusiasm for his ideas helped to reinforce his confidence in them. Over the days their bond became stronger. Both felt a deep and lasting friendship being formed. They cared for each other, not in a romantic manner, but in a familial way. They had known one another for many years, and had watched the other grow and go through good time and bad times, difficult and painful struggles, and little victories. All these shared experienced seemed to coalesce into this new, comfortable relationship. Mary still admired him greatly, but her affection and concern for him was equally great.

Probably without realizing it Joshua had found a replacement for Joanna. She had been his confidant, his sounding board, his trusted companion in Nazareth. Unlike his brother, James, she was non-judgmental as she listened. She would ask good questions – sometime for clarification and sometimes to force Joshua to think deeper on a subject. All the while she would be emotionally in tune with him, encouraging him in his endless pursuit of truth.

Joshua and Mary quickly fell into a comfortable routine. The morning hours were spent discussing the Scriptures and their deeper meanings as Joshua saw them. Mary relished these moments. Not only did she gain new insights on the will of Yahweh and his working in human events, but she was treated as a person of worth by a man she admired. In the afternoon hours she walked to the village for water and food supplies while Joshua busied himself with cleaning the camp site and exploring adjacent areas. Later, he would return and lie on the hillside, staring at the passing clouds while his mind sorted through the goals he set for the return of the Twelve. Mary used this time to sew and mend her clothing. Sometimes she remained in the village to speak with the women. At first, the women who had seen her depart with Joshua treated her with a slight touch of disdain. Mary quickly dispelled this by sharing some of the insights Joshua had given her.

"He treats me as a person of worth," she said. "He teaches me as he teaches the men who also are his disciples."

"I do not believe you," replied one of the women. "No man ever treats a woman as equal to men."

"My master does," Mary responded. "He knows men will not listen to me, so he did not send me out with them, but he includes me in all of his teaching times." She hesitated to see how this was received, and then plunged forward, "He speaks of Yahweh – not as a judge – but as a loving father who cares for everyone: His sons, his daughters and even the little children." She decided not to speak of his healings, lest Joshua be disturbed. *He needs this time of rest*, she thought.

"But Scripture tells us that Yahweh will judge us," one of the women protested.

"My master says that Ezekiel corrected that thinking and told us that Yahweh is not concerned with who we once were, but with who we are now, at this moment. * (Ezekiel 18) My master says that the past in not important to Yahweh: only the present really exists."

"That is true," said one of the women. "I never thought of it that way, but it does sound reasonable. I remember how some of us were as young girls. We did some naughty things, but we grew up and learned better." She looked about at some of her companions. "I like some of you a lot better today than when you were little."

A few of the women covered their mouths and giggled at the remembrance.

"Maybe Yahweh likes us better today, as well," one of them offered.

"That is what my master claims," said Mary. Yahweh is loving and forgiving. He does not want our punishment. He wants us to grow up and act like responsible children, living – not in fear of him, but in loving obedience."

One of the women stepped from the crowd, put her hand on Mary's shoulder and said, "You are a fortunate person to have such a wise master."

"Thank you. I agree, but by now my master must be thirsty." With that, she nodded goodbye and departed.

Once back at the camp site she felt compelled to interrupt Joshua's reverie with a question. "Good master, can you tell me why it is that Yahweh chose to make women inferior to men."

Joshua had sensed that this question would come from her some time, so he was prepared. "Mary, it was not Yahweh who did that. Do you not recall the Scriptures telling us that Yahweh said, 'Let us make humanity in our image: male and female he created them.' Later he looked at all he had made and saw that it was very good?' It seems obvious that women are also made in Yahweh's image. That is basic. It was men, not Yahweh - who decided your sex is inferior."

"Why would they do so?" Mary asked almost plaintively.

"We men are threatened by you women. Did you not know that?"

"Why should you be threatened by us? We are much weaker," Mary replied.

"Only in body strength, Mary. I have learned that their minds are as good as ours. My sister, Elizabeth, has a better mind than any of my brothers, and Joanna certainly is as smart as Simon and Judas. I believe the issue is tied up with sexual attractiveness. We men are terribly attracted to women." At this, Mary lifted her right eyebrow and smiled reflectively, remembering the many suitors who wondrously appeared immediately after her husband's death. "I thought they were interested in my money," she laughed. "No, Mary," Joshua laughed. "Money may have been a part of the attraction, but it was you they desired – probably had secretly desired for years." Mary blushed at the thought, then shook her head and turned her attention back to Joshua.

"Many men often have difficulty controlling their sexual urges, Mary. We blame this on you women, calling you temptresses and the like when it really is ourselves that are the problem. We have all sorts of demeaning terms for women with loose sexual control, but for the men we are far more lenient." He continued: "Because we are the stronger sex and strength is important to survival, we do what is necessary to earn a living and have given you women a subservient status, making you do the menial work we do not wish to do. You bear the babies. I believe that was Yahweh's choice because you make better parents than we men. You truly understand your children and do what is necessary to help them grow as Yahweh wants them to grow. We men would just teach them fishing, hunting, wrestling . . . and drinking," he added with a laugh.

"Joshua, I had no idea you thought like that!" Mary gushed, resisting the urge to hug him in her enthusiasm.

Joshua looked directly into her eyes: "Mary, have you ever seen me mistreat or talk down to a woman?" he asked.

Mary paused to relive the many encounters she had observed, then she shook her head. "Never!"

"And you never will, Mary. You know why I kept you here while I sent the others out. I know the world is not ready for women apostles and prophets, so I include you in my classes, knowing you are the quiet, unnoticed apostle to the women you encounter."

Mary felt a surge of feeling rush through her when he said this. *Does he know what I say to the women in the village? How could he know?* she mused. *He's guessing – or assuming – or perhaps he just has a clear understanding of how life works – how people work.* She patted her hair and smiled at him, "You've been peeking, "she said.

"No, Mary. I only am aware of who you are and the gifts you bring with you." He suddenly adopted a more serious tone: "Mary, you will need to be careful to whom you speak and of being seen as one who is too close to me. It could prove dangerous to you."

Mary was startled by this sudden warning. "Why should that be, Master? You are much admired wherever you go." She blushed slightly: "I am proud to be seen with you," she said somewhat self-consciously, lowering her eyes to hide her embarrassment for making such an admission.

"It is not those to whom I speak that will pose the danger," Joshua replied. "It is those who will hear about me and will feel threatened by my message. "

"Who could possibly be threatened by what you say or do, good master?" Mary asked innocently. "Your words speak of Yahweh's love and care for us, and your actions bring healing to many, many people."

Joshua had to smile at her naiveté. "There are those who will think I am leading people astray from the faith given us by Moses. There will be those who profit from the people's fear of Yahweh who will hear my message as a threat to their livelihood and positions of prestige. Then there are those who simply will see me as a danger to the existing system – which has become so badly corrupted over the years." Joshua softened his tone: "Just be careful, Mary. I do not want you to get hurt by my actions."

"I will be careful, Master," she said, still looking away from him. "But I also will be true to my belief in what you say and who you are."

Then she raised her head, gazed at him and smiled.

Joshua merely returned her smile and lay back on the hillside to watch the clouds roll by.

The conversation had ended.

CHAPTER THIRTY-SIX

CELEBRATION AND BEYOND

Herod received word of the teaching and powerful signs Joshua was doing in Galilee, and he was disturbed. He began pacing through the palace walls, wailing: "The man has to be John the Baptizer. No one else could do or say the things he does." His advisors tried to calm him. "No, sire, the crowds seem to believe he is Elijah or one of the profits. You have nothing to fear from him." Herod would have none of their explanations, no matter how appealing they might be. It was he who had ordered the arrest of John. Although he never meant to harm him, primarily because he feared him, he was tricked into ordering his death by Salome, the daughter of his wife, Herodias. She hated John because John had warned Herod against marrying her since she was the widow of his brother. In spite of the warning, however, he had married her, partly to stabilize the government and partly from lust. Even years later, when she should have felt secure in her position, her anger toward John was not lessened and she longed for his death. Her opportunity came one night when her daughter danced for Herod. The king, in his incessant lust, bombastic pride and sated with wine declared before his guests that whatever the girl wished he would grant. After conferring with her mother she announced to Herod that she desired John the Baptizer's head on a platter. In his alcoholic confusion he saw no alternative but to grant her wish. The memory of that had haunted him daily since that fateful night. He therefore determined to have this Joshua watched to see what danger he might pose.

It was at this time that the full moon appeared and the Twelve returned from their assignments. Each one was eager to share his experience. They were a combination of exhilaration and weariness. Joshua calmed them down and suggested that they retire to some deserted place where they might have the opportunity to rest, while sharing and reflecting on their adventures. Thaddeus suggested a place, and having no reasonable alternative, everyone accepted the suggestion. They quickly packed their belongings and headed for the place Thaddeus recommended.

Unfortunately things had changed since Thaddeus last visited the area. There were new villages and many small farms. When the people saw or heard of Joshua's arrival in their area they passed the word and rushed to see this miracle teacher and healer.

As he came ashore he saw the gathering throngs and immediately felt compassion for them. *They are like sheep without a shepherd,* he thought. *Good people but with no guidance. Hard workers, probably, but so caught up in their work that they have no time to contemplate the real meaning of their existence here on earth.* He strode partly up the first hill, turned, sat down and began to teach them. As he did so he observed their faces. At first there was some confusion as his words appeared to contradict the popular understandings of what was good, what was beneficial and what was worthy of attainment. Rather than riches and power he seemed to be calling them to be humble servants. Rather than seeking vengeance for wrongs committed, he called for forgiveness. All the while he spoke softly yet firmly as one with authority, using his words to paint new pictures of Yahweh upon their consciousness. With the passage of time he could see the looks of understanding beginning to spread across their faces. Some began nodding in tacit agreement. A few nudged their companion and smiled as they pointed toward him. *They are beginning to understand. The word stories do work with those who are willing to look beyond the surface meaning of my words,* he thought with silent satisfaction. "If some Roman soldier orders you to carry his burden for a mile, carry it for two miles. His authority only allows him to order one. You become the one in charge when you go two. You give him a gift that is unwarranted. See what happens – within yourself and within him." Some laughed aloud at the thought. "Treat all people as neighbors . . . and treat all neighbors as family. Yahweh is the father of us all, so we all are family . . . unless, of course, you choose not to be Yahweh's child." As he had come to expect, the crowd began to move closer together, no longer needing distance between themselves. *This closeness will remain. Some barriers have definitely been torn down,* Joshua thought. He had seen this in village after village. *They seem to grasp an underlying tie that is stronger than they had ever imagined.*

The time seemed to pass quickly. Joshua was being energized by the enthusiastic response of the crowd. He wove his tales with the skill of an experienced weaver, adding little nuisances which would catch the attention of those with reflective minds, while adding interest for the others. He told of workers being hired at various times during the day, each anticipating how they might use their wages as they toiled in the vineyard. Some were security oriented, some were pleasure oriented. Others were considering sharing their earnings with their neighbors who had no work that day. Still others were praising themselves for being hired early and therefore earning a greater wage than their lesser fellows. When he came to the part in which each received identical wages, Joshua could see the look of disbelief, consternation, and outright indignation on the faces of some. He paused for a long time, as though that had been the end of the tale. Then, looking directly into the eyes of those who seemed most disturbed, he added the punch line:

"If it pleases the owner of the vineyard to reward the men equally, where is the unfairness? Did he not promise each a fair wage? Was a full day's wages unfair in any way to those who worked a full day? Was it not better to have been hired early and know you were worthily employed, rather than to be idle, wasting the day, and hoping for gainful employment? Those who began their work early had the benefit of knowing their day would be well-spent. The others lived with uncertainty."

He stood and stretched himself, waving his hand to indicate that it was a momentary interruption. Actually he did so to allow his listeners to discuss this among themselves. He had learned that this was an essential part of the teaching. It was in expressing their views and reactions that they actually assimilated the ideas he had poured forth. He had come to recognize, also, that these little clusters had a way of becoming continuing groups when he gave them the opportunity to meet one another at a deeper level than they normally encountered each other. He smiled to himself as he observed their agitated interaction. *If you wish to cause consternation just mention a form of justice that is beyond people's petty rules and customs,* he thought. As he watched them, he noticed that the sun had taken on a softer hue and had long-since passed the middle of the day. He looked again at the crowd, now totally involved in their discussions. *Mmmm, it is past the time for these people to become hungry. We have all been so engrossed with the ideas I have been serving them that we have forgotten about mere food. Still, they must be fed or they will soon become restless, even irritable, and that does not help them to learn what I still must teach them.*

He looked about for someone to call, and saw Andrew. *He is not a powerful thinker, but he is dependable and resourceful. He can be entrusted with this task of finding food for the multitude that has gathered.* He motioned for Andrew to come to him.

Andrew came running as soon as he saw Joshua's gesture. He was half way down the hill, so it took him a moment to work his way free from the crowd and then to sprint up the remainder of the hill. He arrived gasping for air, but with an eager smile on his face. "Yes, Master?"

Joshua smiled inwardly at his earnestness. It was a smile of satisfaction, knowing he had men like this who willing obeyed his every command. "Andrew, we need to provide food for these people, and we need to do it quickly. It already is past their noontime meal. "

Andrew looked about quickly and then turned back to Joshua looking completely perplexed: "Master, there is no place to purchase food for these people. Even if there were, we do not begin to have the money needed to buy all that is necessary".

"Well, then, Andrew, inquire among the people and see if they brought some food along with them." Andrew nodded, but shrugged his shoulders as he did so, thinking, *Good luck on that, master. If any did, I doubt they will want to share with a pack of strangers.* He started down the hill, making a cursory inquiry of those he passed. Most avoided his eyes and muttered something about not having anything. Andrew began to be disgusted at their selfishness. *This started off to be a good day, but it's going to end poorly. We need to plan more carefully for these huge crowds.* He paused at this thought, and surveyed the crowd carefully. *The word is getting out. Anyone can see that. These crowds are larger every time he speaks.* Finally he gave up the quest and returned to Joshua empty handed.

Strangely, Joshua was not disturbed, but accepted the news with a smile of satisfaction. "Andrew, the people are about to learn a lesson in the abundance of God's graciousness. What do we have remaining from our supplies? "

Andrew had already ascertained that and quickly replied, "Five loaves and two fishes, Master."

"That should do. Now watch what happens, Andrew." He took the loaves and fishes and lifted them high so that all might see. Then in a loud and clear voice he called to the crowd: "My friends, let us give thanks to our heavenly father for his abundant love and care for us. The people bowed their heads as he continued: "Gracious and loving father of us all, who calls us to live as brothers and sisters in his eternal family, bless these elements of food that they may provide nourishment to us all. Lift us to higher levels of loving that we may live in harmony with all your children and share in the abundance of your gracious care."

There was a rustle of stirring among the people as he prayed. Then Joshua lifted his eyes toward the sky and broke the bread into small pieces, and handed them to Andrew who began to distribute the pieces among the people nearest him. When the bread was gone, Joshua did the same with the fishes. Those who received the food broke off small pieces and passed the remainder along. All the while, Joshua kept his eyes directed heavenward. Many among the crowd broke their food into multiple pieces and distributed the pieces to four, five or even six different people. Still the remaining pieces always were large enough to divide and distribute.

The crowd grew silent. It appeared to be a combination of embarrassment and wonder that had covered them like an invisible blanket. Only the soft sounds of arms moving inside of clothing and the gentle munching of bread and fish could be heard.

Joshua lowered his eyes and surveyed the large crowd of people quietly devouring their simple meal. He smiled at Andrew, who was standing transfixed in amazement.

"Faith, Andrew. Faith," he whispered. "It just takes faith."

Andrew nodded as though in agreement, but his eyes betrayed the fact that he had no idea what had just occurred.

CHAPTER THIRTY-SEVEN

CONFRONTATION

A group of the Pharisees and scribes from Jerusalem discussed investigating the renegade rabbi from Nazareth whose teachings were leading the Galileans astray. It was difficult enough for the Galileans to maintain even a semblance of obedience to the Mosaic Law. The many Hellenistic settlements planted in the region by the Romans offered so many attractive alternatives. They had managed to integrate the zodiac symbols with the twelve tribes, confusing their history with superstitious rot. With this popular rabbi discounting the need for ritual observances the very fiber of Jewish discipline was disappearing.

The Pharisees were good people as a group. They paid their taxes. They observed all of the laws and rituals of their religion. They were well-versed in the Holy Scriptures, and were the ones who served as teachers and leaders in the synagogues. A few of them, as with any large group, were taken with their own self-importance and self-righteousness. For the most part, however, they were decent, well-meaning people. They understood their role to be the guardians of the Law. It was the failure of their fore-fathers to maintain the dictates of the covenant made on Mt. Sinai that had caused them to be sent into exile in the days of Jeremiah and Ezekiel.

Their glaring weakness, of which they were blissfully unaware, was that they had allowed their vigilance to deteriorate into a set system of actions. The zeal and understanding which had given rise to their movement was gradually displaced by rigid adherence to the outward symbols. Obedience, they understood, but they had lost the sense of the underlying dynamics which had shaped their rules and rituals.

Isaac, their self-appointed leader, had called the group together, because he also feared that Joshua might be attempting to muster a band of rebels in still one more futile attempt to drive out the hated Romans and restore the Davidic kingdom of old.

Galilee was a hot bed of insurrection. The people there were far removed from the authorities in Jerusalem. They were more independent in nature and more prone to ignore the demands of both the Romans and Herod. Through the years more than 30 would-be messiahs had incited a group to join them in a rebellion. Inevitably all of those who participated were slain.

"This Joshua of Nazareth could cause the death of many of our people," Isaac warned. That was all that was needed to push the group into action.

"We must gather some supplies and go there immediately," said Amos, one of the younger members of the group.

"Then let us do so," Isaac said with a note of finality that ended the discussion. "We shall meet at the Temple tomorrow at dawn" He nodded and each member nodded back in agreement.

The matter was settled and the group departed the next morning. The trek would take four days, for they took the long route by way of Jericho. The thought of going directly through Samaria never occurred to them. A good Jew would never set foot on that hated soil, even though it would save more than a day's journey by doing so.

When they eventually arrived in Galilee and were able to locate Joshua, they moved their way forward through the crowd in order to observe him closely. After listening to him for more than an hour they gathered at the back of the crowd and shared their observations. There was no unanimity among them. Some were impressed by Joshua's demeanor and the power of his words. Others had focused on his actions and the lack of adherence to Jewish customs. Young Joses overflowed with enthusiasm. "This man is not just an ordinary person," he exclaimed. "He has no formal training as we have had, yet he seems to have grasped deeper meanings from the Scriptures than any of the elders I have heard."

Isaac and a few of the older members of the group were affronted by this unintended criticism of their scholarly skills, but Isaac managed to mask his feelings. He had not become a leader among the Pharisees by giving way to his emotions.

"Do not be so easily deceived, my lad," he said to Joses. "His words sound good on the surface, but underneath serpents lay waiting to strike out and poison those who listen too intently." He looked about to be certain he had the attention of all present, then stepped toward Joses and announced quite dramatically: "This uneducated carpenter from Nazareth - This Joshua – for all his fine words - is unwittingly undermining the law given to Moses by almighty God at Sinai. He is a fool, leading fools away from Almighty God. He disregards the Sabbath. He ignores the rituals of hand washing. He eats food that is prohibited. He is unraveling the very fabric of our faith!" With this, Isaac turned and solemnly nodded at the entire group, who solemnly nodded in return.

The next day, Isaac and his companions decided to confront Joshua in the village he would visit. "We will question him publicly before he has the opportunity to win the people over with his smooth sounding voice and powerful personality. They will hear for themselves how empty his reasoning is."

Joses smiled and rubbed his hands together in anticipation of revealing this backwoods imposter for who he was. Amos looked apprehensive, remembering how powerful and incisive Joshua had been in dealing with the questions for the people over the last three days. He sensed himself outnumbered, so he remained quiet as the others nodded or voiced their agreement. He did decide, however, to stay at the back of the group rather than presenting himself as a target for the response he was certain would come from Joshua when Isaac attempted to corner him.

The next village was along the coast and held about a hundred families. Joshua and his followers had entered the village early to purchase supplies and to announce their presence and the teachings that would begin at the third hour. Isaac and his companions found them at the market. *A perfect place to show this misguided, uneducated would-be-rabbi for who he is,* thought Isaac.. Without any hesitation he approached Joshua and addressed him in a voice intentionally loud enough to attract the attention of all the shoppers: "Why do you and your disciples not live according to the traditions of the elders, but eat with defiled hands?"

The sneak attack I have been expecting, Joshua thought. *I have been watching them the past three days as they circle the crowd like wolves waiting to pounce. Well, you have me precisely where I want to be, my unknown adversary. Let us see now how well you hold up under what I shall pour on you.*

Joshua looked over his shoulder when he heard Isaac's voice. He had instantly determined not to turn to face him, but to treat him as an interruption, so he began by responding to Isaac, but as he spoke he became inclusive, voicing his response to the other Pharisees, and finally to the crowd in general.

"Isaiah prophesied correctly about you hypocrites," he said with a tone of disgust. "As it is written, 'The people honor me with their lips, but their hearts are far from me. In vain do they worship me, teaching human precepts as divine doctrines.'"

Now he turned his body toward Isaac and looked directly into his eyes. "You abandon the commandments of God and hold fast to human traditions." Before Isaac could gather his thoughts, Joshua continued, now walking slowly toward him as he spoke.

"You have a way of rejecting the commandments of God in order to hold fast to your traditions. Moses said, 'Honor your father and your mother.' But many of you tell your parents that what you might have given them to support them in their old age has been designated as Corban – an offering to God. This makes you appear pious and good in the eyes of others, but you deprive your parents of their deserved care in doing so. That is God's greater priority."

Isaac was stunned by his words. He, himself, had dedicated much of his estate as Corban. As a result, his parents had been forced to move to a lesser part of Jerusalem where he rarely saw them. His mind was a confused array of questions: *Does he know? Who would have told him? How could he have known? Did one of us tell him? Amos? If anyone did I would wager it was Amos.* He stood speechless, shoulders slumped in defeat.

Joshua observed his reaction, *I see I scored a damaging blow without even knowing I was doing so.* He quickly turned from Isaac, with the air of a victor addressing his adoring audience.

"There is nothing that can go *into* your mouths that will defile you. It is the things that *come out* of you that can defile."

With that, he turned his back on Isaac and the other Pharisees and strode toward the landward edge of the village where he would prepare for the morning's session. He was well aware that the crowd would be enormous after this show.

His disciples beamed at him as they left, knowing that he had bested this self-important hypocrite. Judas, however, cringed inside. *When we meet this group again,* he thought, *it will be in Jerusalem. That will be their home town. We will be the strangers . . . and they will want revenge for this public humiliation.*

Amos stood watching Isaac, still standing quietly with slumped shoulders . . . staring into the dirt, not wanting to face the crowd or his comrades who knew of his dedicated Corban offering. His humiliation slowly evolved into smoldering anger, and his thoughts began to echo the fears of Judas: *The next time we meet, Joshua, the shame will be yours – not mine.*

CHAPTER THIRTY-EIGHT

TEACHINGS AND WARNINGS

"It is time to take a respite from teaching the crowds, to spend some time together where I can speak to you about spiritual matters you must learn." Joshua nodded toward a distant hillside clustered with uncultivated trees.

That was all that was needed. No further instructions were required. The group had begun to think as one body. Joshua, of course, was the head. His strong will and dominant personality seemed to flow out to the others and few words were needed. Simon the Rock gathered his meager belongings and began the slow climb. The others followed without a word. They, too, were weary of the constant routine. They were tired of being crowded and bumped by the many people who clustered tightly together, each pushing and shoving to get closer to Joshua, so they could touch him or hear him better. Afterward they served as makeshift counselors for those who remained, weeping or praying. It was worthy work, they knew. Still it wore them out, somewhere inside, as they attempted to soothe, comfort and give guidance to these earnest people. Joshua looked over his disciples reading their thoughts. He sighed silently: *There are only so many messages I can give and they have heard most of them by this time. A few, such as John and Peter, realize they were being "schooled" in the message I proclaim, so that they can one day be the teachers. I can see, though, that some of the others are, frankly, somewhat bored by the sameness. They will prove to be less effective in future days; their messages will become lost.* He paused and looked upward: *Father, is this really the group you have given me to proclaim this revolutionary good news?* He had asked it before and no longer waited for a response. *What is — is. I must work with what I have.*

After they had arrived at the indicated area and settled their camp they gathered to where Joshua was seated on a small mound.

"It is time to speak more clearly about forgiveness. The misunderstanding of this causes so much heartache and fear. You will need to be good interpreters of this message, so listen carefully: I have given you the name *Father* by which you are to understand the nature of Yahweh. People still think of him as a judge who keeps score of your wrong doings and will some day punish you for them." The disciples nodded silent agreement. "This, however, is not how a loving parent treats his children. Your fathers were more concerned that you grow past your petty misdeeds and learn to behave as responsible men . . . and women," he added, as he spotted Mary at the edge of the group. "Now James and John, I've known you long enough to have seen the occasions when one of you mistreated the other. Don't be embarrassed. It's something brothers do to each other while growing up. James, Judas, Simon and I have had our moments. But that kind of abuse is behind you now. Am I right?" They nodded assent, looking somewhat embarrassed at being singled out. "Of course it is. When we are children we act like children, but when we become men we put away our old childish behavior. Zebedee no longer is concerned over how you acted then. He holds no grudge for your childish behavior, does he?" He looked directly at his cousins in a way that required a verbal response. "Of course not," they replied in unison.

Joshua let their response settle over the group as he looked intently at each, then he whispered, "Neither does your heavenly father remember and begrudge your once childish misbehavior."

"This does not mean that your misdeeds were unimportant — that you did no harm. Many times your thoughtlessness and selfishness has hurt others. When it did – or does – your heavenly father is hurt just as Zebedee – or Jonas," he added, looking at Andrew and Simon the Rock, "were saddened to see their children hurt one another. What you need to do to set things right, however, is not to ask Yahweh's forgiveness by making sacrifices at the Temple. Rather go directly to the one you offended, apologize and ask his forgiveness. If you damaged something that can be repaired, make the repairs or pay for them. If going to that person is impossible, then find another way to set things right, even if it means giving aid to someone entirely different. Your heavenly father will know you have changed your ways and are trying to return to him."

"What we call sins are moral and ethical failures. We may want to do better, but we find ourselves doing things of which we will be ashamed. That is because we have a long way to go before we actually mature into the likeness of the One who made us in his image. Remember, even in those bad moments, that you are made in His image. That is your real nature. It is the essence of who you are. Try your best to live up to that image, but be assured that when you fall short, Yahweh still loves you and is eagerly waiting for the time when you will walk faithfully in his ways."

Thomas spoke up first: "Master, do you mean that we are not basically sinful people? We have been told by the teachers of the Law that we are."

"They are wrong, Thomas. They do not know how to interpret the Scriptures. The first book of Moses, the one we call Genesis, clearly says that God made us – both the men and the women – in his image." He glanced at Mary as he said these words, and noted her pleased response. "Image of God is who we *are*. Sin, or failure, is what we *do* while trying to become the fulfillment of the promise placed in us by Yahweh."

He paused to look at each of the disciples. He could see that they were attempting to reconcile this concept with the teachings of the Scribes and Pharisees. *It is time to conclude this lesson and let them think about it.* "God never meant for us to fear him as some bearer of judgment. Obedience should arise naturally from our love for him." He said this with an air of finality, then he lay back on the grass to show that the time of teaching was over.

The men sat there for a few moments and then began to drift away. Some wanted to be alone; others wished to talk and so they gathered into little clusters.

Only Judas remained.

Joshua sensed his presence. He had become fond of Judas Iscariot. Judas had been raised in Jerusalem and so was better educated than most of the others. This was one reason Joshua had made him the treasurer. Another was to make a statement that he was trusted and accepted. Judas was a bit of a loner. He was more of an observer than a doer. As a young man he had grown weary of city life and the cold winters in Jerusalem. An uncle of his owned a small farm in Galilee, so Judas had requested permission to work for him. He had met the daughter of a neighboring farmer. She was his only child and she was a reasonably attractive young woman, so he had spoken with her father, promising to work for seven years to pay for her hand in marriage. The time had passed, the father had died and Judas was the sole owner of the farm. When he felt the desire to join Joshua he had arranged to have one of the village men farm the land, keeping a third for himself and giving the rest to his wife. *He has a sense for business and a sense of responsibility,* thought Joshua, admiringly. Without raising his head he whispered, "You wish to say something, Judas?"

"Yes, Master, I do," responded Judas, and he edged his way over to where he could speak privately. Joshua waited patiently for him to speak. Finally, as the silence was becoming awkward, Judas realized that he was the one who must begin the conversation. *Of course! I am the one who said I wanted to speak. He is waiting, probably wondering why I am not saying something.* He almost slapped his head in his embarrassment and anger at himself. "Master, I worry about the time when you will take us to Jerusalem." *There, I said it. Now let him speak,* he thought with a sigh of relief.

He had not long to wait. "Why would that be, Judas?" Joshua asked this, already knowing what the answer might be. *Still it is good to get his fears out in the open. He also might bring some fresh insight into the issue, since he is more familiar with Jerusalem than I.*

Judas rummaged through his mind for a moment, seeking the right words. He did not want to appear cowardly, but he also did not want to let Joshua and the group stroll into Jerusalem innocently anticipating that their presence would not disrupt many of those in power. "The city is entirely different from any of the towns and villages in Galilee."

"How is it different, my friend?" Joshua asked with genuine curiosity. He had visited Jerusalem many times and had always enjoyed the excitement and energy of the city, but had never examined why it felt different to him.

"There are many differences, Master." He paused to gather his thoughts. Judas had felt thrilled when Joshua called him "friend." He had adored Joshua from the moment he first heard him: His keen mind, his warm spirit, his vision. Perhaps it was this adoration that kept him emotionally detached. The thought that Joshua could ever genuinely care about him had been too much to hope for, so he had maintained a proper distance. Now he mustered his courage and edged even closer to Joshua as though to share some secret: "City people are more competitive, less cooperative – less neighborly - than the people in the villages of Galilee. Strangely, they also are more conforming, less independent, more easily swayed and led. It is the crowded conditions, I suppose. One fiery spokesman can turn a crowd into a mob in a matter of minutes. In the villages the people cherish their neighbors. In the city, some also do, but far more cherish their privacy first." He paused to consider this. Then he nodded, more to himself than to Joshua. "It is the crowded conditions shaping their inner lives as well as their outer."

Joshua sensed where Judas was heading, but he wanted to hasten the journey and deal with the issue. "Why should this concern either you or me, Judas?" he asked with an obvious openness to whatever Judas might say.

Judas sensed this and took heart from it. *He really respects what I might think – me: Judas Iscariot – an outsider and loner at best. I wish I might know you better, Joshua, but there is some barrier, probably within myself, that does not allow this. You have selected Simon, you call Rock, and your cousins.* He sat quietly pondering how to say what he believed he needed to say.

Joshua observed him in his silence. *Poor Judas. He yearns to be accepted but does not know how to fit in. He probably has explained it without realizing it. He was shaped by the city and simply does not know how to relax and be comfortable – and natural – with the others.* He continued to wait quietly until Judas had gathered his thoughts.

Finally, Judas broke the silence: "Master your presence and your message will be seen as a terrible threat to the established order that rules Jerusalem." Joshua understood this, but he waited, looking directly into Judas' eyes with an intensity that seemed to Judas to be penetrating into his soul. *He's reaching deeper into me than even I have ever reached*, Judas thought, and felt a shiver race through his being with the thought, *I wonder if he knows who I really am . . . I wonder if I know who I really am.* He took a deep breath and continued: "The Romans may see you coming as another would-be messiah. Galilee has produced far too many renegades who thought they were the second king David, anointed to drive out the present-day Philistines and re-establish the great empire of old. I know you have used the term Son-of-Man in a wonderful way to confuse them while making some claim to the Jews who understand the term. Still, any collaborator can explain that to them and you will be arrested merely on suspicion." Joshua nodded, indicating that he should continue. The Pharisees see you as a threat to the covenant made at Sinai. The Hellenistic influence in Galilee has made it difficult enough for them to maintain the observance of Moses' Law. You have broken Sabbath laws and dietary laws and encouraged others to do the same. They do not have much influence in Galilee, but they are a power in Jerusalem. Be careful of them, Master. They want to be rid of you and your influence. They are good people but they are rigid in their beliefs. This makes them even more dangerous because they genuinely believe they are acting for the good of the society and according to the will of Yahweh." Again Joshua nodded. He had considered this. Judas' warning served to confirm his concern.

"Herod also will be threatened by you. Your talk of God's kingdom sounds like a call to a religious rebellion. Be careful how you speak about this subject while in Jerusalem."

"What about the Sadducees?" Joshua asked, still gazing intently into Judas' eyes. "I have always trusted and respected the priests," replied Judas. "Their positions are secure. However, they are in Herod's camp and might need assurance that you do not intend to incite the people to revolt."

Joshua sat, staring into Judas' eyes. By now Judas was beyond his self-consciousness and felt a deep understanding and acceptance from this mysterious man to whom he had tied his life.

Joshua, reached out, touched Judas' shoulder gently. Then he smiled. "Thank you for your wise counsel, my faithful friend." Now Judas returned the gaze, and for a long moment they sat in silent acceptance and appreciation of a bond of friendship and trust that had been formed.

Chapter Thirty-Nine

Moving On

Joshua rose early and went to a private place for his morning prayers. He sensed he had settled into a routine which, while meaningful and satisfying, was not what he needed to be doing. *Father, I must sharpen my sense of direction. I realize these things I have been doing are but a prelude to what you would have me do. I am becoming a mere teacher and healer and I know – I am certain – you have more in mind for me than that.* He closed his eyes and began to repeat his mantra, allowing his mind to drift to wherever the spirit led:

Wherever you lead; whatever you ask; I will be faithful. Make my way clear, is all I ask.

Wherever you lead; whatever you ask; I will be faithful. Make my way clear, is all I ask.

In the intimate quietness that followed, Joshua felt his mind clearing and images began to appear, fuzzy – blurry – at first. Then they emerged: Certain and unambiguous.

He rose and walked back to where the disciples were preparing the morning meal.

"Andrew, take Bartholomew and Philip and go to the town of Sarepta in Phoenicia. It is a quiet village that lies between Tyre and Sidon. The rest of us will remain here to teach the people in the area. Then we leave tomorrow. I want you to find a quiet place where I may spend a few days undisturbed. When you have found it, have Philip camp outside the town to guide us to you when we arrive there."

Andrew responded, "As you wish, Master." Then he nodded to Bartholomew and Philip. They picked up their belongings, grabbed a handful of nuts and fruit and started down the hill.

The rest seated themselves for the morning meal. A ripple of excitement moved among the disciples. They sensed that this signaled a change in their routine, one that moved them nearer the fulfillment of whatever calling Joshua had. There was talk of coming into glory through the wondrous power Joshua displayed. Joshua watched as the men silently jostled one another, each disciple seeming to be wearing smiles and expressions of eagerness. *They have no idea where this is heading. Actually, neither do I, but I am beginning to suspect that there is not going to be much glory associated with it.* He searched in the basket and found some fresh figs. Absentmindedly he tossed one in the air, opened his moth and caught it cleanly without it so much as touching his lips.

CHAPTER FORTY

DEFEAT AND DISCOVERY

Philip sat by the city gate as he watched Joshua and the disciples approaching the village of Sarepta. For a brief moment, Philip felt the urge to rush to them, but hesitated as he appraised the situation. *Wait a minute, Philip. They're coming this way. They have to come this way. Let them come. There's no need to rush off; they'll be here soon enough.* He chuckled to himself at the thought. *Let him come to me for a change.* He smiled and waved at them, and was pleased to see Joshua smile and wave back. Philip had been following Joshua for months now. He sometimes wondered why he had abandoned his home and his livelihood to follow this man he really did not know. *There is just something about him that is different from anyone I have ever encountered,* he thought. *He speaks quietly, but with a power – and authority - I have never experienced. I feel so whole – so complete – so very much at peace in his presence . . .* He smiled as he recalled how he had rushed to find his friend, Nathaniel, and bring him to Joshua. *Like someone who had found a treasure and wanted to share it,* he thought. *And that is what he is: Joshua of Nazareth – a treasure to be shared.* He nursed this thought for a moment, and then concluded: *Being with him is home for me. Serving him is my livelihood.* Philip lifted his gaze to watch Joshua striding toward him. Then, forgetting his resolution to have Joshua come to him, he arose and rushed to greet him.

Andrew had negotiated a brief rental of a house at the edge of the village. The owner had a widowed sister nearby and he would reside with her while Joshua used his house. It was a small building, adequate for one or two occupants. The disciples would camp outside. There already was a small oven and a table-of-sorts made of a few stones and a piece of driftwood. Joshua had noticed this as Andrew led him into the house. *The owner is a man who does not like to feel cooped up, I see,* he thought. He paused to look about and reflected briefly on what the owner experienced as he prepared and ate his evening meal. *The sunsets must be magnificent,* he thought as he looked out over the huge sea that stretched further than the eye could see – or the mind imagine. This will be restful . . . restful and quiet. He smiled with satisfaction at the thought. He enjoyed teaching and healing the people, but it had worn on him. He relished the thought of a time of respite when he could reflect and recover his energy.

What Joshua had not planned on was the owner, or really, the owner's sister, Nina. Her daughter was believed to be possessed by a demon. She cried and screamed throughout the day and wailed late into the night. Nina had gone to every priest, holy man or known healer in the area, but none had been able to help her. When her brother told her of the man who had rented his house she knew he must be the Jewish miracle worker she had heard of who roamed Galilee. "Oh, dear brother," she almost screamed, "please watch over my little one while I go to beg this miracle worker to cast out her demon."

"No, no, Please do not bother him," her brother pleaded. "I promised his friend, Andrew, that I would not tell anyone of his being at my house. I only told you because I had to explain why I need to stay here for a few days."

Nina ignored the panic in her brother's voice as she rushed off. "He will not mind," she assured him. "He is a healer – some say a prophet of his God. Surely he will want to help." She rushed off, moving at a pace somewhere between a walk and a trot, hoping against hope that this man might be able to accomplish what everyone else had failed to do.

Most of the disciples had drifted off, searching for firewood or going into the market area to purchase food or merely to browse through and pass the time. Only Simon Peter and Andrew remained to witness the scene that unfolded.

Oblivious to the drama that was developing, Joshua had taken off his sandals, washed his feet, found a few old cushions that had been scattered about and had fashioned them into a make-shift reclining couch. He had just settled back, placed his arms behind his neck and was beginning to drift off into a quiet reverie, when a woman burst through the door, crying and pleading with him to save her daughter from the demon.

What in the name of heaven is this?!! thought Joshua, as he was startled from his reverie into a moment of chaos.

Nina was so totally focused on her daughter's need that she failed to notice the surprised, angry look on Joshua's face. "Please, sir," she repeated, falling to her knees and bringing her hands together in prayer. "Please cast out the demon that has taken possession of my daughter."

From somewhere deep within him, old feelings were aroused. Words he had heard in his childhood – words laden with long-forgotten emotions – came pouring out of his mouth:

"Let the children be fed first," he practically shouted, "for it is not fair to take the children's food and throw it to the dogs!"

Nina was shocked and momentarily frozen by the vehemence of his response. However, she quickly gained control of herself. *This man may be my last chance to save my daughter. I need to win him over – to soften his anger – and let him see me as a person.* She thought for a moment. Then she put on a smile and lifted her head so Joshua could see her face. "Sir," she said with a noticeable tremor in her voice, "even the dogs under the table eat the children's crumbs."

Joshua looked at her, then into her, and he saw the fearful pleading that lay just behind the smile. He heard the soft tremor in her voice as she spoke.

What in the world have I done to this poor soul? She is not some foreigner breaking into my house (if anyone is the foreigner here, it must be I, he mused). She is a person – a mother – like my own mother, desperately trying to help her child . . . that she undoubtedly loves as dearly as Mary loves any one in her brood. He focused his energies inward and directed them toward the unknown daughter of the woman before him. Then he knelt down, looked into Nina's eyes and nodded: "For saying that, you may go. The demon has left your daughter."

Nina remained where she was. *What does he mean by this? He has not even seen my daughter. He has not confronted the demon as the others tried to do. Is he just trying to get rid of me?* Then she looked again into his eyes and saw such tenderness and truth as she had never seen. *He is not trying to deceive me. I can see that,* she thought with an air of certainty. *My daughter is healed. He knows that. I believe that. Yet . . .* Her face suddenly shone. Laughter of pure joy sang from her lips. Nina arose abruptly and rushed out the door. She did not think to say thank you. She simply ran to see the miracle she knew had occurred – to see her daughter, calm, happy as she had not been in years.

Joshua watched this process of disbelief transformed into certainty and joy, and when the woman had rushed away a flood of calmness engulfed him. He followed her path to the doorway in time to see her disappear over a small knoll. The moment she disappeared from his sight Joshua's entire mood changed. Instead of satisfaction, as he often felt when he had healed someone or ousted some demon, he felt defeated . . . beaten and weary. He shuffled his way back into the room which now seemed darker, less comfortable, than he had previously experienced it to be. *This won't do*, he thought. *I need some sunlight to take away the shadows from my soul.* He turned and stepped out into the yard. Simon was standing quietly, awkwardly . . . attempting to give the impression of being absorbed in some distant scene.

He heard my interchange with the woman, Joshua thought. *He's embarrassed . . . as I am.* He paused for a moment, deciding whether to return quietly to the house or to share this mutual embarrassment.

"Rock," he called. "Come into the house with me."

Simon followed sheepishly, wondering what his master had in mind. His mind began to race: *Should I deny hearing the conversation? No, Joshua is no fool. He knows I heard. Perhaps I should agree that these foreigners are as dogs.* He hastily dismissed that idea. *I just will promise to say nothing. That's it. I will promise to say nothing.* He almost smiled in relief at having come up with what he believed to be a suitable response.

Meanwhile Joshua had walked over to where he had stacked the cushions against the wall. He selected two that seemed suitable, placed one down in front of him at the table, and tossed the other to Simon.

"Rock, you heard me. I know that you did. What happened to me when that woman burst in?" He shook his head in dismay. He rose and began pacing the room like a caged animal. " I sounded as bad as any of those ignorant fishermen I have heard in Galilee who rant and rave against those Hellenists in the Decapolis." I don't feel that way . . . or at least I didn't think I felt that way." A look of consternation spread across his face.

Simon started to respond, but realized his pre-planned response was inappropriate, so he just looked up and gazed attentively. Joshua stopped pacing, looked intently into Simon's eyes, as though trying to read his thoughts. Then he lowered his head, and shook it again in dismay. Slowly he lifted his head heaven-

ward, and stretched his arms as though seeking to embrace whomever it was he was addressing: "Father, help me. Like all of the
others who walk this earth I, too, have drunk from the poisoned
well of prejudice that is invisibly placed in every town – in every
city – in every nation throughout your world."

He bent over, lifted his pillow, walked directly to Simon and
sat down, taking Simon's hands as he did so. "Oh, Rock," Joshua
said, "most parents and other adults unthinkingly pass along the
bitterness and fear of those different from themselves. We rarely
examine what we pass along in order to test whether it is justi-
fied and worthy. We merely unthinkingly accept and pass along
the distorted beliefs as eternal truths." He released Simon's hands
and leaned back on his cushion, hands cupped behind his head.
"Although I do not recall Joseph or Mary spreading poison they
probably did so in ordinary conversation. I certainly heard enough
while in Nazareth." He paused and decided he might as well
teach while trying to sort through his own feelings.

"This anger toward other people, Rock, always arises from
fear." He watched Simon's face as he said this, and determined
that this idea needed elaboration. "Anger is a natural reaction to
any threat, Rock. Recall when you have felt anger. It always was a
response to some sort of threat." Simon began to react, but Joshua
waved his hand to silence him.

"It might have been a threat to your idea of who you are. It
might have been a threat to what you perceived as your social
standing. You may have felt insulted, or perhaps your manhood
was belittled." Simon's eyes began to show understanding. He
nodded. "Oh I see what you mean, Master," he said. "Yes, I have
had that happen."

"Anger equips you to respond and defend yourself. It doesn't
care what kind of threat it is. It just appears when you feel threatened." He paused and smiled. "Either anger or fear is what we feel

when there is any danger. I did not bother to mention fear, Rock, because you don't experience that." He paused again, and then continued with a twinkle in his eye: "Except when a sudden bad storm erupts on the lake." They both laughed at that.

For a moment Joshua was tempted to let the subject rest on that light note. *No, I've opened the door,* he thought. *I might as well carry this idea through to as far as Rock can go with it.*

"When we have anger to an entire group of people, Rock it usually is because we have a lot of anger within us that we cannot properly express because it would cause us difficulty. We may be angry at our employer but we know we will be dismissed if we express it. We may be angry at our lives, the way they are turning out . . . but we can do nothing about it. We may be angry at our wives or parents but we know better than to start that fight." Simon smiled and nodded agreement at that. "Ah, I see you understand where I am going with this, so let's just say that people tend to redirect this anger to something or some people where it is safe. For instance, in Capernaum there is always some cause for someone to be upset with someone, right?" Simon nodded. "Instead of starting family feuds we hate the people in the Decapolis. We redirect our anger to where it is safe. The people in Jerusalem know it is not safe to be publicly angry with the Romans, so they hate the Samaritans. There is no reason to do so, except for the need to have someone to whom we can direct our anger."

He sat watching Simon's reactions as he processed the idea. Finally Simon raised his head and responded, "Is it really that simple, Master?"

Joshua knew the cause was more complex, but he answered, "No, Rock, it is more complicated than that, but this is a good, brief explanation and should serve to help you – help us both - to understand what happened with that woman a moment ago."

He paused to consider what he had said, and then he continued, "This blanket judgment of all people comes from ignorance, Rock. By that I do not mean that these people do not have good minds. They may have very good minds, but they have no real understanding or experience with the people they dislike."

For a long time Joshua just sat, holding Simon's hands, gazing into his eyes.

"In spite of what I thought – what I believed – my thinking has been too narrow. I think of myself as a Jew – a child of Abraham. I look on everything – everyone – from that perspective. If I pushed the thought further I probably think of myself first as a Galilean." He paused for a long moment. "If you are honest, Rock, you probably think the same way: Galilean, Jew . . . then a member of the human race." Simon nodded in sad agreement, as Joshua continued: "We draw circles, starting with the smallest: ourselves, then enlarging to family, the tribe or village. We may increase beyond that, looking for the similarity and common interest. Yet the smaller circle always is the favored one."

He smiled ruefully "Simon, do you recall how I spoke to the men on the mountain just outside of Capernaum? I spoke so blithely of the prejudice of some of the village, sounding pretty self-satisfied at my own broad acceptance of all people." Simon nodded, and smiled knowing for he could see where Joshua was heading with this. "Well, I proved myself to be really no better than the rest, did I not?"

At this, Simon interrupted. "Master, you are too hard on yourself. Yes, you reacted badly at first. I must admit I was surprised to hear your harsh reaction to her plea. But by the time she spoke again you had changed. You saw her as a mother, a person in need, and you responded caringly." He paused to let this sink in. Then he added: "You healed her daughter. That is what she will remember. That is all you should remember."

Oh, Rock, Joshua thought, *you are a faithful friend, and you have a kind, generous heart, but you need to think more deeply.* "Thank you, my friend. I appreciate your support, but we both need to learn something from this encounter." He paused, reflecting on his decision. *Yes! That is what I will do. I must learn their language better. I know enough to do business with them, but not enough to teach them — and to share my vision of God's kingdom with them.*

Then he continued: "Rock, you and I — and all the others with us are ignorant. We need to experience these people we call 'Others.' So we will return from this excursion by way of the other side: The Decapolis. We will spend time in every village on the way. We will share what we have and accept whatever hospitality they offer."

Simon nodded his understanding then he added, almost in a conspiratorial tone: "I shall say nothing of this to the others, Master."

"Do as you wish, Rock, but I do not mind if you share this. It may help them to understand and learn from our return journey."

Chapter Forty-One

Reaching Out

They spent a month on their return to Capernaum. Joshua insisted on remaining a few days in every town and village of the Decapolis that they encountered on their journey. He left the disciples to shift for themselves, which also gave him the opportunity to observe and appraise how they spent their time. At first some of them merely gathered together in groups of two or more. Eventually, however, he saw that they entered into the life of the community, chatting as best they could with the villagers and playing with the children.

For his part, Joshua sought out the most learned men and discussed their philosophy.

He also spoke with groups of women as they gathered at the village well. He was a quick student and his command of the Greek language improved daily. At one village the people brought to him a man who was deaf and had a speech impediment. Joshua took the man away from the crowd. He put his fingers in the man's ears, spat on his finger, and touched the man's tongue. Then he looked at the man, smiled and gestured for him to speak. The people watched in amazement as the man began to speak plainly, with no trace of an impediment. One said to the small crowd gathered there, "He does everything well. He makes the deaf hear and the dumb to speak." The word of this deed traveled faster than he did, and when they entered a new town the people were eagerly anticipating his arrival. There were always a few sick or lame among the people, and he laid his hands on them and healed them.

By the time they arrived at Capernaum Joshua had seen an obvious transformation among the disciples. There was a new respect for the Gentiles, as any none-Jew was called. Joshua also was pleased to note the change that had occurred within himself. *I no longer feel like an alien when I speak with them. I truly believe I no longer see them as different. They have different ways of thinking about life, but they love their wives and husbands – and their children as we do. They worry about the same things we worry about. They have dreams and aspirations that are similar to ours. My message of God's love and acceptance lifts their spirits, even though they are not sure of there being only one God. Now that I understand their language better I believe I can teach them what they need to learn.* He smiled in satisfaction as he reflected upon their brief sojourn in the Decapolis. *Yes, it was time well spent. I am more certain than ever of what my task is.*

CHAPTER FORTY-TWO

REFOCUSING

Immediately upon his return a group of Pharisees met him and asked him to produce some sign that might prove the claim that he was from God. Joshua looked at them in disbelief. *What are they after? I have healed sick, cast out demons, fed multitudes with only a few scraps of food.* As he paused to consider this he looked deep within the eyes of their spokesman. *They are laying a trap. I have never claimed to be more than a man. Still, I have heard that some of the leaders of these Pharisees have made false charges and wish to have me arrested.*

"No," he said with a calm voice. "No sign will be given to you – or to this generation," he added as an afterthought. With that he turned and went to the shore and boarded a boat. He signaled for his disciples to follow him. When all were aboard they returned to the Decapolis.

As they disembarked he said, "I need some time to consider what we are to do. It should not take long. Find something to do for a few hours and then return." He saw their looks of concern and added, "Do not be afraid. You will not be in any danger." With those words of assurance they turned inland and began to search for some activity by which to pass the time.

Joshua watched them as they wandered away. *You will not be any danger, my friends, but I fear that my own time is shorter than I might have wished.*

He sat where he stood, leaned back on his elbows and stared into the sea. Then he lifted his eyes to the sky and quietly – inwardly – spoke: *Father, I sense things closing in, drawing to an end. So soon? I am really just starting to understand what it is you want of me. You do not want me to start a movement or organize the people for action of any kind. You simply want me to change the way they think . . . and the way they act toward one another.* Joshua lowered his eyes and drew inward for a long time, pondering the words he had just formulated. Then he shook his head slowly and lifted his eyes to the heavens. *Father, it really would be easier to incite them to action or to organize them into a new faith. We are so caught up in or own little circles of concern for ourselves that I am not sure my words have lasting impact . . . even with some of the Twelve who are with me daily.* He shook his head again. *I just don't know how to do that, Father,* he admitted. Again he paused and went within himself, searching for some course of action that would use his time well.

Father, lately I have been hearing the words of Isaiah resounding deep within my being:

He was afflicted, he submitted to be struck down, and did not open his mouth.

He was led like a sheep to the slaughter. Like a ewe that is dumb before the shearers. Without protection. Without justice he was taken away, and who gave a thought to his fate; how he was cut from the world of the living, stricken to death for my people's transgressions? [1]

Father, I sense that in fulfilling my mission I shall find myself upon a Roman cross. Pleadingly, he added: *This is not what I want. It is not what I planned on. But, Father, I have learned to trust myself to your will.*

Spontaneously Joshua began to mentally repeat his mantra from the early days:

Wherever you lead; whatever you ask; I will be faithful. Make my way clear, is all I ask.

---

[1] Isaiah 53:7-8

Wherever you lead; whatever you ask; I will be faithful. Make my way clear, is all I ask.

Wherever you lead; whatever you ask; I will be faithful. Make my way clear, is all I ask.

When the disciples gathered again Joshua said simply, "We must go to Caesarea Philippi where we can spend some time together without being disturbed." By this time the disciples had stopped even attempting to discern Joshua's motives, so they merely nodded and followed him back into the boat.

CHAPTER FORTY-THREE

RECOGNITION AND REVELATION

When they arrived at Bethsaida the people of the village brought a blind man to Joshua and asked him to touch the man. Joshua looked about at the gathering crowd and decided he had best work with the man without a crowd. He took the man's hand and led him away from the village, and when they had arrived at what Joshua believed to be a reasonably private area he spat on the man's closed eyes and laid his hands upon him.

"Do you see anything?" He asked. The man rubbed his eyes, gazed back at the crowd outside the village gate and responded, "I see men, but they look like trees walking." Joshua smiled at this. *You are no different from many who have good sight, my friend. They also see people, but not as people . . . more like trees walking about — objects to be used or ignored.* Joshua laid his hands on the man once more, and then inquired, "What do you see now?" Again the man rubbed his eyes like someone who had just awakened and needed to rub the night's sand from his eyes. He looked again toward the village. Then he turned and grinned at Joshua: "I see everything — Everything — clearly now.

They left Bethsaida before more people could pounce upon him for healings. He needed to be away to spend time with those whom he might be able to teach.

As they neared Caesarea Philippi the landscape became more verdant. They were nearing the source of the Jordan. The snow-capped mountain of Mt. Hermon provided a steady stream of water. Additionally, there were springs which flowed into the small streams which merged to create the Jordan. With this abundant supply of water the earth took on the appearance of a near-jungle, overflowing with vegetation. Faded and worn images of Pan, the god of nature could be seen along the way – left there by long-forgotten earlier settlers. Amidst all of this, Joshua stopped his disciples and asked them, "Who do people say that I am?" This startled them and there was a brief pause. Then one answered, "Some say you are John the Baptist." Another spoke up, "Some believe you are Elijah." A voice behind Joshua offered, "Many say you are one of the prophets."

Joshua raised his hand to indicate that he had heard enough. Then he looked squarely into their eyes – one by one – challenging each to think for himself. "But . . . who . . . do . . . you . . . say . . . that . . . I . . . am?" he asked slowly and deliberately.

Then was a long, awkward moment of silence. Finally Simon spoke up with a barely contained excitement: "You are the Christ – the Anointed One of God!" He almost shouted this. The others looked first at Joshua and then at Simon who was still gazing at Joshua in amazement. Slowly, almost comically, each one of the men gave a look of startled recognition, realizing for the first time the nature of the man they had been following.

Mary Magdalene, who had been at the outer edge of the group, merely smiled and nodded her approval.

Joshua observed the signs of recognition as they appeared in each of the men. I believe they are beginning to understand. Yet I have done none of the things most people expect of the Messiah. These disciples of mine have grown more than they – or I – realized. He looked over and saw Mary giving her nod of approval, and he smiled. *She had it figured some time before this,* he thought. *I love her mind and her spirit.*

Joshua allowed the emotions of the moment to calm down. Then he motioned for the men to draw nearer, and to sit down.

This is the difficult part, he thought, looking at their expectant faces. *I can see that some of them still have no grasp of what being the Messiah means.* Still standing, he began to explain to them what to expect.

"The Son of Man, he began, "must undergo great suffering, and be rejected by the elders, the chief priests and the scribes. He will be killed, but after three days he will rise."

As he was speaking, each of the men – and even Mary – sat stunned.

Mary gave a quick gasp of dismay.

Judas narrowed his eyes, imagining the scene: Golgotha – Joshua on a cross.

Thomas thought, *Never! I will defend him.*

Andrew waited passively for Joshua to continue.

John felt a bolt of fear sweep through him.

Judas Iscariot thought: *This will start the revolution and we will be rid of the Romans.*

Each quietly processed this news in his own way.

Simon, however, jumped to his feet, grabbed Joshua's arm, drew him to one side and scolded him, saying: "You can't go! Stay here with us where you belong."

I wish it were all that easy, Rock, Joshua thought. Then he snatched Simon's hand off of his own and ordered: "Get behind me, Satan! You are not thinking as God would think, but of the way ordinary men think!"

Simon appeared to visibly shrink in size. He stepped back – shocked by Joshua's reaction. Then he turned toward the other disciples, and shrugged his shoulders as though to say, "I was only trying to help."

There had been a group of people following Joshua at a distance, hoping he would speak to them before he had gone too far beyond their village. They had witnessed the scene, but had no idea of what had transpired. Joshua saw them and thought, *I suppose it is time to share some of this with those other than The Twelve,* so he motioned for them to gather near. As they approached, Joshua placed his hand on Simon's shoulders and smiled at him sympathetically. *I don't want to hurt you Rock,* he thought. *I am counting on you to be a rock in the days ahead.*

When the crowd had gathered, Joshua addressed them along with The Twelve: "If anyone wants to become my follower he first must deny himself and take up his cross – and then follow me. Those who want to save their lives will lose it, but those who are willing to lose their lives for my sake and for the sake of God's Good News will find it. What does it actually profit a person to gain the whole world and to lose his life? Really now, what can a person exchange to get his life back?"

With that, he nodded at the crowd and waved his hand to indicate that they should depart. As they departed, he thought: *You have no idea what I meant, but soon – too soon – you will understand.* Then he turned and motioned with his hand for the rest to follow him.

CHAPTER FORTY-FOUR

A PLACE OF REFUGE

As they walked along the road some of the men asked one another why they were going to Caesarea. Judas listened to their discussion, grinning inwardly as they did so. *None of them has the slightest idea,* he thought. They are Galileans and have never had need of a Caesarea in their lives. Well, here's my chance to show them I am more than a poor, misplaced city boy.

"Caesarea is a Refuge City," he said rather casually, as though this should be common knowledge.

"What is a refuge city?" inquired Thomas.

"It is a place where you can go and no one will arrest you . . . as long as you remain there."

"I never heard of such a thing," said Andrew.

"You never had to, Andrew," Judas answered with a laugh. "There are so many places to hide out in Galilee, and few, if any, of the people would be willing to inform on you to either the Romans or Herod's people."

"But why does Joshua take us to a refuge city?" asked Philip. "Surely none of us is in danger of being arrested."

This time Judas stopped, shook his head and said, almost in disgust: "Haven't you been paying attention to what is going on? The Pharisees are all over him. They see him as a threat to all of Israel."

"What are you talking about?" asked James. "Some of the Pharisees have asked him questions, but none have made threats or indicated that he is a danger of any kind."

"You really do not get it, do you?" Judas responded. While waiting for a reaction, he explained: "They fear that Joshua is trying to destroy people's respect for the Law. It is difficult enough for you Galileans to obey the letter of the Law, what with Decapolis so near at hand. Their people have no Sabbath; they ignore our ways and practice their own, which is far less demanding than ours. They have introduced astrology as a means of guiding their lives." He laughed. "That's certainly a lot less demanding than prayer and Torah. When the Pharisees question Joshua they are trying to find ways of charging him with blasphemy and treason. Don't you see that? My guess is that they have already complained to the priests, Herod and even the Romans about him. We've had many false messiahs sound some call to arms and lead a mass of ignorant followers into a disastrous battle against the Romans. No one wants that to happen. Add to that the fact that Jeremiah had told the people back at the time of the Babylonian Exile that the reason for losing the land was that they had broken the covenant." Judas paused to let them absorb what he had said. Then he summed it up. "If they fear him enough, and I believe they do, then they will even falsify charges against him to be rid of the danger he presents. So," he took a long breath, "we go on to Caesarea Philippi." With this, he resumed walking . . . and the others followed . . . with a dramatic change in mood.

Simon mused to himself: *So that is what Joshua meant. He knows they intend to kill him when he goes to Jerusalem. Why then will he choose to go? I really do not understand him or what he is doing. What is this about dying and rising?* Unconsciously, Simon began to stroke his chin. *I hope he will tell us more before we go — and I know we must go — to Jerusalem.*

CHAPTER FORTY-FIVE

PREPARING APOSTLES

When they arrived at Caesarea Philippi they immediately began to set up camp. "We will be staying here longer than usual, so look for a good spot and make it more permanent," Joshua ordered. Judas gave Philip a knowing nod which was acknowledged as they both set about their tasks. John and James mumbled between themselves as they searched about for a suitable location. "James, I don't like the thought that Judas seems to know so much about what is going to happen," said John in a voice that was only slightly above a whisper. James nodded his agreement. "I've never felt comfortable with him," James replied with a touch of bitterness. "He thinks we haven't noticed how he keeps trying to worm his way into the inner group." He paused for a moment to mull this over. "I just don't trust him. He may have lived in Galilee for many years, but he is still an outsider – a Jerusalemite – to me."

"Me, too," agreed John, and they let the matter rest as they split up to search further.

Joshua found an open area and lay down in it and gazed at Mr. Hermon in the distance. *It seems strange to see snow so close*, he thought as he observed the upper portion of the mountain buried beneath huge piles of snow. *I've never felt snow, or walked in it, he mused. Before we leave this place I shall have to see what it feels like.* His mind drifted back to the first time he had seen Mt. Hermon. He was about seven years of age, and Mary had taken him when she went to Capernaum to visit her sister. He had met James at the time. He smiled as he recalled how very young James had been at the time. *He was barely able to talk . . . and John had not been born. Where do the years go?* He asked himself idly as he looked over to where John could be seen setting up a site at the edge of a clearing.

Behind them was the lush greenery that distinguished this area from any other in Israel. *What magnificent intertwining of trees, vines and flowers of all kinds, he* thought. *Our heavenly father has given us such a variety of beauty and wonder . . . I just cannot fathom why people cannot be content with what is so readily available to them. Why they must scrape and fight to gain more . . . for the brief time they shall spend on this earth.* This last thought seemed to jerk him back to reality. *I must use these days well, for I now believe they shall be about the last that I shall spend upon this earth.* He thought this with a twinge of sadness – not fear.

Joshua rose and called over to James and John: "Find Simon and Mary and tell them to join me here. Leave setting up to the others. I need to speak to the four of you." He then lay back and waited for them to join him. He did not have to wait long. Mary was behind him gathering wood for the fire. Upon hearing him she stopped searching about and brought what was already collected to where Joshua lay. James knew where Simon was and only had to walk a few paces to find him gathering armfuls of long, soft grass to use for bedding. He brought what he had to the clearing where John was standing, dropped them in what looked like a suitable place. Then walked directly to where Joshua was lying.

"Sit with me, my friends. I want to share some thoughts with you." Joshua waited a moment until each was settled comfortably. Then he spoke in a voice barely above a whisper, as though what he was about to say was for their ears only. "You are the ones I have selected to teach as a small group, answering your individual questions until I am certain you genuinely understand what I tell you. I will teach all of the Twelve – plus you, Mary," he said with a nod toward her, but later you all will have the opportunity to share more deeply with them." He paused and looked deeply into each one's eyes. "It will be later – and you will know when that time is" he added hastily to avoid questions, "when they will be able to understand more fully."

Each of them: Mary, James, John and Peter, reflected briefly on what he had just said. None of them grasped the meaning, but each assumed he or she would as he spoke with them. Each simply nodded quietly as Joshua continued speaking.

"Rock," Joshua said, pointing his finger at him, "You said I was the Messiah – The Anointed One of God." Simon lowered his head, embarrassed to be singled out for having made such a grandiose statement. "You were right, my friend." Joshua spoke slowly and deliberately so that the impact of his words would be felt by each one there. Then he proceeded to tell them of his baptism by his cousin John, the experience of the Spirit driving him into the wilderness, his visions while there and, finally, his absolute certainty that Yahweh had claimed him as His son and anointed him to be the bearer of the new covenant and the good news of Yahweh's unconditional love of all his children.

When he finished, he leaned back to observe their reactions.

Each sat stunned - - - lost in thought - - - deep within some portion of their minds that had been hitherto unexplored.

Maybe I told them too much too quickly, Joshua thought. *They all seemed to accept my earlier statement, but perhaps the actual telling of how it came about was too much for them to accept.* This worry quickly faded however, as each one smiled and nodded understanding and acceptance.

Mary reached out and touched Joshua's hand lightly. "Thank you for sharing that moment with us, Master. You have given each of us a precious gift in doing so." He glanced at the others and saw each one smiling as he met their eyes. A warm, comforting feeling swept though Joshua's entire being as Mary had spoken her words. *They understand. They truly understand,* he thought. Now I know I can move forward with them quickly.

He picked up his teaching, "It took me some time to understand just what my mission was to be and how I might go about accomplishing it." He stopped for a moment and inserted. "I am so glad that each of you accepted my invitation to become a part of this mission. You bring energy, intelligence and special talents into the group – as do each of the others", he added quickly so as not to give them the impression that they should be over the others. "James, John and Mary, perhaps it is because I have known you so well for so long a time, and . . ." at this he stared and smiled at Simon for a long time. "Rock, I saw something very special in you when first we met." Simon again lowered his head in embarrassment. "Don't be embarrassed, my friend", Joshua said as he laid his hand on his shoulder. "Special gifts are needed in life. Yours was buried deep within you, but I see it emerging daily. When it does, you will discover, perhaps, why I call you Rock." Realizing that what he had said might cause the others to feel less important, less loved, Joshua quickly turned to the other three. "Each of you has some special gift which is why you are here with me, right at this moment." He turned again to look at Mary. "You, Mary, you may find obstacles that will hinder you in using your gifts fully in this mission. The men in this society have great difficulty in their relationships with women." Mary nodded knowingly, as he continued. "Many are afraid of the attraction they have for women. Some are afraid that, if given the opportunity, the women would prove themselves equal – and perhaps even superior in some areas – to men. At any length, Mary, be certain the men will do their best to quiet your voice . . . now and even later," he added as an afterthought.

Next, he turned his attention on John. "John, my young cousin, you seem to see the world differently than most people do. You speak only after careful thought. What you say always seems to come from a different place than where the others are. It is as though you are looking from above, while others are stuck on the ground. You will be a teacher, teaching another view of the same event. Give yourself time." John appeared somewhat confused by Joshua's assessment of him, but silently understood and agreed that he did, indeed seem to see life from a perspective quite different from his companions. This had always caused him to feel a bit apart from whatever group he had been in. It is one reason he had been eager to follow his cousin. Joshua had always understood him and spoken to him in terms he readily grasped.

Now Joshua turned toward James. The two stared silently at one another for a long moment, each recalling scenes from earlier days. Their smiles blossomed into full fledged grins and seemed about to erupt into laughter when Joshua spoke: "You, my cousin, have always been one to speak his mind and act on his thoughts. You make things happen. It never is dull when you are in the area." James just continued grinning, as Joshua spoke. "You will need to be careful," he cautioned. "You will do – and you *must* do – what is most natural for you. But, again, be careful. You bring many valuable gifts to the party. Do not leave it too early." When he finished, *he thought: Where did all of that come from? James is a strong, capable leader. He is impulsive, yes, but he is dependable and he is trustworthy. Where did this need to caution him come from?*

James was having something of the same reaction: *What was he trying to say to me? He knows me well enough to know that I never back down from a fight or from anything just because some think it might be dangerous. Why didn't he just tell me what he wants me to do? He knows I would do it for him – no matter the cost!*

Joshua observed the four, *Let them mull over what I have said. They need to come to terms with that before they will focus enough to pay full attention to what I want to say.* He lay back for a moment and closed his eyes, signaling to them that they were getting a short break from the teacher.

CHAPTER FORTY-SIX

TEACHING ON THE KINGDOM

When he believed he had given them enough time to at least begin to digest what he had told them, he sat up and began to speak: "When I speak of the Kingdom of God I hope you realize I am not talking about an actual place. Oh, yes, I realize the political implications – choosing Yahweh over Caesar or Herod – opting for the values of a heavenly ruler rather than the values of our present society. What I really am trying to communicate, however, is more profound than those ideas." The four leaned in simultaneously, almost causing Joshua to laugh as a quick vision of conspirators flashed across his mind. "It's not a secret, but it will mean a lot more to people if they figure it out rather than if I – or any of you – tell them. To become a part of God's Kingdom rather than an earthly kingdom requires a fundamental change in perspective and understanding. You constantly hear me call the people to repent." He waited for them to acknowledge this. "People often think of it as meaning change direction. However, the term quite literally means to transform your mind. This is the only way a person can actually change the course of his life for an extended period of time. Everyone one of us has made resolutions to do better at something or another, only to revert back to our old ways, right?" Again, he waited for acknowledgement to be sure they were following his thinking. "Mary, it was when you realized that your life was not working as you wanted it to that you came to me and began to change." It was not spoken as a question, but Mary responded, "Yes, I knew I had to change in order to find peace within myself." As she spoke these words her mind raced back to the time when she had decided to leave Magdala and her business and seek Joshua. She added. "I had given it a lot of thought and finally admitted I needed help. Since then I have begun to see the world through very different eyes. I no longer worry about myself, but feel part of something much larger – much greater."

Joshua smiled and nodded his appreciation of her words. "Was it not the same with each of you, as well? You felt empty - that your life was without meaning or purpose? Each silently nodded affirmation. "Since you have been traveling with me have you not sensed that your understanding of life and what is important has changed dramatically?" Again, each silently nodded agreement. *Now to make my point,* Joshua thought. "Did I have to tell you to change your minds or did it just begin to happen?" They sat in silence while each recalled the significant events he had experienced as a disciple of Joshua's.

James recalled the early gathering of the disciples: *When I first heard him begin to speak of heavenly treasures I had no idea what he was talking about, but as I watched how he interacted with complete strangers – as a friend, and how he maintained an uncanny calmness in the confrontations with some of the Pharisees, I began to see his world – and not just the little one I had been living in.*

Simon also was remembering: *I was just a poor, ignorant fisherman, stumbling my way through life – trying to find some joy – trying to explain to myself at times why I was even alive. Other people could catch fish; I wouldn't even be missed. But now I see the world more through his eyes and realize how precious I and everyone else are to God. I know – or at least I sense that I will live . . . in some way . . . far after this body of mine is worn out.*

John had tried to recall when he first sensed there was something different about his cousin – something he admired and coveted: *I think it was the way he entered into the games . . . and the work. He always worked when he visited. Cheerful – never competitive, but always successful and productive. I always had the feeling he saw things and heard things that we did not. Until he said this –right this minute – I never stopped to realize that I now see what he seems to always have seen. This world is not just a place of toil, each person struggling to see that he gets his share. Yahweh has created more than any of us need. It is only a matter of understanding that and changing our lives to care and share more. Yes. Yes!! I think I understand what he is doing! What a wonderful gift he wishes to give to all of us!!!*

Joshua watched patiently as one by one, each of the men came back from deep within himself and indicated understanding and agreement.

I think I made some good choices with these four, thought Joshua with satisfaction. Then he indicated that he was about to speak again.

"When anyone begins to grasp the idea of loving and caring for others – even strangers – as they would care for themselves and their own family, then they are at least nearing the Kingdom of God. You see, it is not a place but a state of mind – deeper than the mind, though. It runs to the very core of who we are. So I call the people to repent, and to the degree that they really wish to change their lives – and to the degree that they are capable of comprehending what that radical change entails . . . they will respond."

"Master, do you really believe everyone can and will do that?" asked John quickly.

"You ask two different questions, my young cousin."

"The first is do I believe everyone can transform their minds? The answer is yes, I do. The second is trickier: Do I believe everyone will? Unfortunately my response to that must be, no I do not. You heard me give the parable of the seeds many times. That has been my warning to the listeners who jump eagerly at my words. For one thing, we do not change our deep inner selves merely by an act of the will. It is by acting on our beliefs that we are transformed. For each of you it has been in serving me and serving the many people we have encountered. You have found yourselves more worried about some utter strangers than about yourselves. You have lost all your concerns about your possessions. I have seen you dip into your personal coins and select some for children and others who have touched your hearts. It has been your actions — not your listening that has changed you. Many who hear me — or, someday will hear you - will listen and then go away and go on the way they always have. Still others will begin with good intentions but become sidetracked by life's other demands. And there will always be those who expect too much too quickly. Their faith may appear strong, but they will fade when tested by life."

"Then what will happen to them, Master?" inquired Mary after a moment's hesitation while she weighed whether to explore that possibility.

Joshua looked at Mary with sad, momentarily tired eyes. He breathed a long sigh and then said, "Mary, that is a long and complicated story. You have heard me speak of heaven and hell. I use that model because most people only think in terms of reward and punishment. Our heavenly father, however, is too compassionate and loving to set hell as the final resting place of our souls. Some people live but a few days or weeks or months . . . or years. Yahweh will not give eternal judgment based on so short a time. Even for those who live long and full lives, we must remember that David wrote, "But a thousand years are in thy sight as but a watch in the night." [1] Simply put, God's time is not our time. In the same way, *our* judgments are not God's. We think in finite terms, but God does not. We have a need to punish wrong doers;

---

[1] Psalm 90:4

God does not. Our heavenly father is more concerned with forgiveness and redemption than punishment. Our Scriptures speak of Sheol as the realm of the dead. They do not distinguish between the good and the bad. They do not divide the realm into a heaven and a hell. That is man's doing – not God's."

"Those people who live lives centered on themselves may appear successful but I would call them unsuccessful. A person is not successful until he is content –at peace - within himself. Herod is not a contented person. His killing of John betrayed his fear. Caesar is not content and at peace or he would not need to surround himself with armies and constantly require more and more things for himself. When the life of a narrow, self-centered person comes to an end – well, you have heard me speak of a final judgment when everyone will be judged simply by whether they could care enough for others to provide for their needs. No creeds. No temple sacrifices. No observance of religious rules. Actually it is a simple matter: Did you feed the hungry, clothe the naked, welcome the stranger, visit the sick and those in prison? Those who did are with God in spirit and those who did not have wandered away and are out somewhere in the darkness. I speak of God sending them there, but they really just wandered out there by themselves – by their selfish selves. A simple understanding is this: Those who grow in their capacity to care more for others will live more contented lives than those who do not" he hesitated, then decided to add, "and they will find more joy in their lives beyond this earthly journey. However, those lives, whether well-lived or wasted, will continue to develop in our future existence. Yahweh will continue to try to redeem them and make all of us truly whole."

"There are many people – far too many – who seem to be unaware of the spiritual realm wherein God dwells. It is as much a part of our world as the physical realm that we can see, smell, touch, taste and hear. These people simply have eyes but really do not see. They have ears but cannot hear. Living without the spiritual dimension distorts their understanding of life. They seek short term, rather worthless goals and rarely, if ever, feel genuine contentment. I have come to make them aware of that spiritual realm and to show them how to enter into it. I also have come to let them understand that God is not so much a judge as a loving parent. They should heed his word out of love – not fear."

Joshua looked at their faces. *I may have given them too much to think about. They will need time to sort through what I have said. I probably ought to stop for the time being.*

Without another word, he rose and walked over to the clearing where the others were setting up their camp ground.

Mary, James, John and Simon sat as though glued to the ground by their thoughts.

CHAPTER FORTY-SEVEN

MORE PREPARATIONS

When all of the disciples had settled into their personal sites and they had gathered for the evening meal, Joshua decided to use the moment for another teaching session. He looked over and saw Philip, staring contentedly at the landscape as the shadows lengthened and the setting sun changed the hue of the greenery with a soft, pinkish light.

"Philip," he called. "What message would you give to the people if I sent you off on your own?"

Philip almost choked on the piece of bread he was chewing. Upon hearing the question he cringed inside. *Oh goodness, why me? What should I answer? Keep chewing as though you are attempting to clear your mouth before speaking, Philip. Now think.*

Every eye had turned his way. Each disciple stopped eating while watching for Philip and waiting for his response. One could tell by looking at their faces that each was happy his name had not been called. Yet each began to ponder the question for fear that Joshua might say their name next.

Having taken all the time to swallow he thought was allowable, Philip turned to Joshua and replied, "Yahweh, your heavenly father, invites you to live with him in his kingdom. You can do this by loving all his people, caring for them as he cares for them."

Joshua nodded his approval. Then he turned to Bartholomew: "Can you add anything to that?"

Fortunately Bartholomew had used his time well. "I would add that Yahweh is far more interested in you turning from your old ways of selfishness than in punishing you." He said with a sense of confidence.

Again, Joshua nodded approval. Then he looked about for his next selection. He spotted Levi slouched near a tree like some schoolboy attempting to hide from the teacher. "Levi, what do you have to add to the discussion?"

Levi straightened up and spoke in a clear voice, "Master, I would remind them that the final goal is to be able to care for everyone else as well as you care for yourself." Then he resumed his slouch with a satisfied smile.

"You have spoken well, Levi. Few people may ever really be able to do that, but it is the purpose of this earthly life to begin growing and living in that way."

"Would anyone else care to put another idea forward?" He asked this in a gentle, inviting manner, so the others would not feel pressured.

There was a pause, almost an awkward silence. Then Thomas spoke up: "Yes, I believe it is important to stress the idea that any person – at any time – can choose to abandon his old life and become like a new person in the eyes of God."

Joshua's eyes lighted up as Thomas expressed his idea. "Very well spoken, Thomas. Yes, we must always hold out hope of God's acceptance and forgiveness for anyone - - - anyone at all. Your heavenly father is a God of love and mercy."

Judas blurted out his reaction: "But surely Master there are sins that even our loving father will not forgive?"

Joshua paused for a long time, formulating his response. Finally he looked directly into Judas' eyes. Then he looked directly at each person seated there. "Listen carefully to what I am going to say. Our heavenly father is saddened by our misdeeds. He mourns for those whom we hurt or even slay by our wanton actions. Our misbehavior is very important to him. Make no mistake about that. Now, having said that: Yet, God does not think as we think. There is some perverse quality within us that demands retribution. We need to balance the scales. That is not the way our heavenly father thinks. Oh yes, some of the prophets of old thought that God acted as we act and so they thought God demanded retribution. They thought God wanted to punish the unjust, and most of us thought that was fine. Hosea saw beyond that, as did Ezekiel, but most did not. [*1] Trust me when I say that God wants your redemption. God wants you to dwell with him in harmony. God did not create you just to punish you forever for some misdeeds in your brief time upon this earth. If anyone – anyone at all – truly regrets his old ways and turns from them, then Yahweh – your loving heavenly father – will forgive that person and bring him into his kingdom."

Everyone sat quietly for a prolonged period of silence. Finally, in a voice barely above a whisper, Judas asked, "Then why should anyone want to spend his entire life sacrificing for others, if they can turn at the last moment and be saved?"

Others nodded their heads in agreement. Mary watched their reactions. *They are still like little children,* she thought wistfully. *They really do not grasp the essence of what Joshua is trying to teach them.*

Joshua looked about at the entire group and quietly inquired, "Do you recall the parable I told about the two sons: The younger claimed his inheritance and left home and the elder remained?"

"Yes, Master, we've heard you tell that one many times," replied Philip.

"Do you remember the conversation the father had with the elder son after the younger had returned?"

"Yes, I do," he replied, waiting for Joshua's next question.

"Do you still not understand?" Joshua asked, looking about at the entire group.

[*1] Ezekiel, Chapter 18

Again, there was silence.

"I believe I do," offered John. "The elder son thought he should have been given extra things for his loyalty, and never understood that his reward was simply that he had been with the father all of the time."

Joshua said nothing. He merely smiled and nodded slowly at John. *I knew he would understand if anyone did, he thought. He will be one who can carry on my work after . . .* He let the thought fade.

CHAPTER FORTY-EIGHT

A FRIGHTENING FORECAST

The days passed quickly, following the same routine. Joshua rose early, found some quiet place and spent most of the morning in quiet conversation with his father. At times he felt uncertainty and anguish. At other times he felt calm and confident. Whenever he reflected upon his morning prayers he realized he was preparing himself – being prepared, actually – for what lay ahead.

In the afternoon he called together his four confidants. He always took them to a different locale. Sometimes it was in a clearing. Sometimes they went into the woods where they had to brush back branches to clear a way for themselves. Once settled, Joshua spent time tutoring them and interacting with their questions. Intuitively he understood that the success of his mission rested more on them than upon the others, so they needed to have a more thorough understanding of his thoughts and his sense of mission. One reason he selected different places for their gatherings was to keep them from developing a sense of remaining static. *They will need to be ready to move at any moment,* he thought.

The evening meal was the start of the group discussions in which Joshua served as moderator, posing questions and then inviting the others to generate the discussion. He always allowed the discussions to continue until he believed a proper understanding was expressed. He then would switch to another topic.

Over the days he was gratified to note that everyone had become more attuned to his thinking, and apparently more aware that they were being prepared to act on their own and become leaders of others.

One evening, while sitting at the evening meal, Joshua changed the format: Joshua looked about the group to silence them and gain their attention as he did each evening to begin the discussions. *It is time*, he thought, *to say it again. I believe they dismissed or forgot what I told them earlier. No one has mentioned it. Nobody has questioned me about what I meant. They need to know what is going to happen. They must begin to prepare themselves.* When he was certain that he had their attention, instead of posing a question, he quietly and calmly said, "The Son of Man will be turned over to the authorities. He will be executed, but will rise again in three days. Do not worry. This must happen before God's Kingdom can come in all its glory." Then he crossed his arms, leaned back and silently observed their reactions.

Nothing! Nothing at all. It was as though he had never spoken . . . except that no one was moving. Each one there sat quietly – not even looking at one another. It was as though they were afraid to even make eye contact with anyone for fear of being seen in their confusion and fear.

Their thoughts were many and diverse, but they all shared the same confusion and uncertainty.

Is he referring to himself . . . or is someone else going to appear?

Is a kingdom going to wondrously appear? What kind of a kingdom will it be?

Since we are here in a place of refuge, is this Son of Man some-one we know?

Who would turn Joshua over to the authorities? None of us . . . I hope.

Joshua watched the scene: *Perhaps I spoke too abruptly, but it is important that they are prepared to accept what will happen – and I now* know *it is going to happen. They will be in for bigger shocks than this soon enough.*

For a moment he hesitated, deciding whether to say something that might ease their confusion and fear, or merely to rise and leave them as they were, wrestling with the vague awareness that their easy lives were about to change - - - dramatically.

He watched for a while as each agonized over his words. *There will be much they must decide and learn for themselves,* he thought. Then he stood up and left quietly.

CHAPTER FORTY-NINE

JERUSALEM CALLS

Camp life had taken on a simple order. While Joshua was at morning prayer some of the disciples prepared the morning meal. Many of them began following their leader's example and also spent some of the time in prayer. In the afternoon when he spent time with James, John, Peter and Mary, they gathered into small groups to discuss Joshua's teachings and to speculate on where he was leading them.

There still was no consensus on the meaning of The Kingdom of God or Joshua's declaration about the Son of Man being killed and rising again. In this regard, some signs of petty jealousy and ambition often appeared. They were kept under control primarily because of each person's great devotion to Joshua.

For his part, Joshua was pleased to observe a greater cohesiveness within the group. Even Judas was considered less of an outsider.

The Passover is approaching, he thought. *It is time that we journey back to Jerusalem. Before we do, however, I have to walk in snow.* He chuckled to himself at the thought. *I've longed to do that since I first saw Mt. Hermon and was told why it was so white.* Then – more solemnly – he mused, *I want to go up to the mountain of the Lord . . . to ascend to Him at the highest place . . . and spend a moment . . . before I . . . leave.*

He called for the disciples to gather, watching each with tender regard as they put aside what they were doing and came toward him. *You all have been so loyal . . . so trusting and trustworthy.*

Then searching each approaching face, he questioned: *Will you continue to be so?*

Once the last disciple had gathered, Joshua gave these instructions. "James, John and Rock: I want you to accompany me to Mt. Hermon. The rest of you are to break camp and go to the small village at the foot of the mountain. We will meet you there shortly.

The men nodded or voiced their assent and scattered to do his bidding. James, John and Simon looked at each other questioningly, but, without a word, immediately followed Joshua.

Although Mt. Hermon appeared close it was more than a day's journey. The four walked in relative silence. For those who have bonded in profound ways words are unnecessary to maintain the sense of contact and closeness. Each was caught up in his own thoughts for most of the journey.

They were ascending now. Actually, they had been ascending gradually for some time, but now they became aware of a chill in the air. When they looked back toward where they had been the landscape lay below them, complete with miniature villages strewn along the low lying hills and shorelines. *I wonder if this is how Yahweh views his people?* Joshua questioned, but he quickly dismissed that idea. *No, he is never distant, but always present.* He shook his head at the thought and chuckled as he asked, *So why am I climbing the mountain to be closer to him?* He let this lay quietly until the answer rose into his consciousness. *Because I still think of Him as far, far above me.* "*I was glad when they said to me let us go up to the mountain of the Lord*". *[1] That's what David, God's anointed said. Then I believe I must go up as he did.*

Eventually they arrived at a place where the ground was covered with snow. Joshua looked at his open sandals and the open sandals of his companions. "There is no need for all of us to freeze

---

[1] Psalm 122:1

our feet," he said. "You remain here, and I will go ahead alone." He saw the beginning of a protest form on their lips and raised his hand to stop them. "No, please," he said firmly. "I really would like to do this alone." He noticed a slight sign of relief on their faces as they nodded their agreement and began to search about for a place to rest during his absence.

As Joshua continued his climb, the walk became steeper, and the air cooled rapidly until he could feel the chill beneath his tunic. The sky above had clouded over, shielding whatever heat the sun might have offered to diminish the chill. Still, he continued his ascent, doggedly as one determined to finish what he had undertaken, regardless of personal discomfort. *"I was glad when they said, let us go up to the mountain of the Lord,"* became something of a personal mantra as he rose higher and higher and the landscape below became a blur of greenery dotted by specks of brown and grey.

Finally he arrived at a point where his inner voice said, *Far enough.* He looked down toward his companions and could not discern one from the other as they sat huddled together in the distance. Then he turned and faced the mountain top and raised his arms as though to embrace the unseen presence he felt so strongly.

For Joshua it was enough just to be standing where he was: High on the mountain, feeling the presence of his father. Mentally, he began to repeat his mantra: *Wherever you lead; whatever you ask; I will be faithful. Make my* – Abruptly, he stopped mid sentence. He turned to face Galilee in the distance. For a brief moment his mind's eye saw a kaleidoscopic variety of scenes: He pictured the village of Nazareth and the lush valley below, then he saw the inside of his home and each family member as he had bid them farewell. He saw also Zebedee's home at the moment around the table when he had made the announcement of his mission. Finally – more distant, yet startlingly clear - he briefly glimpsed

Rachel as she stood in her kitchen when he departed. He silently whispered a final farewell. *I am called to a cross. It will only be when I publicly die and rise again that anyone will actually believe – will begin to understand – that this earthly life is but a step in a never-ending journey. Only then will they be able to grasp the meaning of my words. Our heavenly father loves us all and never will abandon us – to death - - - or anything else.*

His eyes were misty as he turned back and faced the mountain top. Slowly but with a firm certainty he picked up his mantra. This time it was abbreviated: *Wherever you lead; whatever you ask; I will be faithful. Wherever you lead; whatever you ask; I will be faithful.*

His three traveling companions had been quietly watching his ascent, wondering how high he would go . . . and when he would return. Just as they saw him turn away from them, and before they saw him lift his arms, the sun broke from the clouds with radiant brilliance. The entire snow-covered area of the mountain reflected the sunlight in such a manner that the men were nearly blinded. They quickly shielded their eyes and squinted in order to observe what their master was doing.

Joshua's white tunic also reflected the light, multiplied many times over. The sparkling snow surrounded him. His arms raised but moving slightly also reflected their presence to those below.

"What is going on up there," John whispered as though entranced by the sight.

"I don't know," exclaimed Simon. "Everything – even our master – seems to have been transformed into brilliant whiteness."

"Aren't there two figures by him?" asked James, seeing only the dim outlines of Joshua through his squinted, shielded eyes."

"Who would they be," asked John, more in disbelief than actual curiosity.

"I will have to think on that," responded his elder brother.

"Why don't we just ask him when he returns?" put in Simon, trying to bring some rational order to the speculations.

"Perhaps this is the reason he wanted to go alone. He wanted to meet them without us present," responded James, holding fast to his theory more out of stubborn pride than belief. "I don't think we should act as though we saw anything."

Agreed," said John, and the subject was dropped . . . but not forgotten.

CHAPTER FIFTY

BACK TO REALITY

For Joshua the time spent alone on the mountain was a rich, memorable moment. It had fulfilled a childhood ambition. Far more importantly it was the time of intimate encounter on the Mountain of the Lord. In many ways, of course it was no more intimate than the time of morning prayer, in which he sat in his father's presence and silently discussed his task. Yet, there on the mountain which he had struggled to climb he had felt more in tune with his relationship to Yahweh, his father. Perhaps because it had been he who had worked to approach The father and he was not merely sitting and waiting for Yahweh's Presence to be felt — with no effort on his part.

In any event, when he returned to his traveling companions his face was aglow – with far more than the effects of the chilly air. This only served to reinforce their belief that Joshua's encounter on the mountain was far beyond the normal. So it was with renewed and energized spirits that all four descended to the village to join the rest of the disciples.

On arriving at the village they heard sounds of commotion. Fearing the worst, Joshua immediately headed toward the noise and saw his disciples apparently arguing with one of the villagers. He immediately stepped between them and inquired in as calming voice as he could muster, "What seems to be the problem here?"

The villager stopped his harangue and turned toward Joshua. For a long moment he stood, silently appraising him. After what was more than an awkward pause, he spoke:

"Teacher, I had heard of you and your mighty healing powers, so I brought my son to you for you to heal him. He has a dumb spirit within him who seizes him and causes him to foam at his moth and become rigid. You were not with them but they said they were your disciples. I asked them to cast out the demon, but they could not do so. We were arguing over whether they – or even you – actually had any healing powers."

Joshua turned toward the disciples, who shame-facedly lowered their eyes as though to examine whatever might be on the ground. *Oh, my poor, poor students,* he thought,. *Have you learned so little? Have you been with me this long and not yet discerned what sets me so apart from those whose thoughts are only on their stomachs, their possessions and their work?* He decided to voice his dismay and concern for them. " Oh you faithless generation!" he said. "How long am I to be with you?" He saw their shame, and gentled his tone, adding, "How much longer am I to be with you?" Then he turned toward the father of the young boy and said, "Bring him to me."

The man walked over to where his son was lying, inert with foam seeping from his mouth. He carefully lifted him and brought his son forward. Joshua felt a deep sense of compassion for the man as he watched him carefully cradling the boy in his arms. When they arrived before him he inquired, "How long has he been like this?"

"Since childhood," replied the father. "If you can do anything, please have pity on us and help us."

Joshua looked steadily onto the father's eyes and replied with a slow, soft voice, "All things are possible for those who genuinely believe."

The father practically blurted out, "Oh I believe." Then he added in a tearful, pleading voice: "Help my disbelief!"

You have more honesty and faith than most men, my friend, thought Joshua. Then he looked away and saw a large mob coming his way. Quickly he called out to the spirit within the boy and rebuked him, demanding that he leave and never return. Then he took the boy who was unconscious and appeared to be dead. He lifted him by his hand. The boy's eyes opened. He looked about and grinned at the crowd, unaware of the miracle they had witnessed.

Joshua turned to the father and looked deeply into him as though probing his soul. The father stared back in silent wonder and thanksgiving. Without a spoken word there was an interchange of understanding. *"You have done far more than help my disbelief; you have caused it to melt away into nothingness. I thank you. I trust you. I would follow you anywhere if you call me."* Joshua nodded his understanding. Then he gave a swift glance about at the man's son and the village, tacitly indicating, *"This is where you belong now."* Then he turned and walked off with his disciples gathering closer to their master.

"Why couldn't we do that, Master?" one of them asked.

Joshua stopped and let his eyes rest on each of the men. Then he replied in a matter-of-fact way, "That kind cannot be driven out by anything but prayer."

The men walked along in silence.

"I didn't see him pray. He just commanded the spirit to leave and it left." Bartholomew whispered to Philip as they moved along.

"He didn't pray. I don't understand," Philip whispered back.

Mary was walking close enough to overhear the exchange. *He did not pray then and there because he did not have to,* she thought. *He fills himself in prayer every morning.* Then she added to the thought: *When will you understand who he is . . . and why he is who he is?*

In the early evening, once the group had found a place to settle and the evening meal had been prepared, Joshua decided he needed to be clearer - more specific – with his disciples.

"Just as there is a physical world filled with abundance and beauty, so there also is a spiritual world that underlies and maintains all physical life." He paused to let his words filter into the consciousness of the others. He had given no preparation that he was going to speak. He just had spoken the words quietly, as though to himself, and let those who were not lost in their own thoughts or wrapped up in their own conversations hear them. Some heard him immediately and stopped whatever they were doing to listen. Others noticed their reactions and also turned to focus their attention upon his words. It seemed as though Joshua was thinking aloud and allowing those who would to eavesdrop. He continued his soliloquy: "Most people are oblivious to this spiritual realm. They ignore it and live only in their physical nature. They can only believe what they can understand, and they can only understand what their narrow perspectives allow. They are prisoners to tradition and to popular thinking." He stopped speaking aloud, but all who were present were aware that Joshua's mind was still at work. Finally, he spoke aloud again: "We are made in our heavenly father's image – His spiritual image, for God is Spirit – pure spirit." Again he grew quiet, but still lost in thought. After what seemed an interminable time of silence, he again spoke aloud: "The more time we spend in the spiritual realm – the more we immerse ourselves in it – the more we draw from its knowledge and its power."

Again he fell silent, but continued to ponder as the darkness of night began to gather and engulf them.

Each person there sat entranced as he drew them closer and closer into a realm they have never imagined.

The silence was broken again with these words: "It is in the realm of the Spirit where we encounter our heavenly father most fully. It is in this realm where we encounter our heavenly father most intimately." He slowly shook his head and continued, "God does not want us to obey his commandments out of fear. First and foremost . . . He wants our love – our companionship. Everything will follow correctly when He has that."

Again – silence.

Again – the silence is broken by the sound of Joshua's voice.

"Do the right things, of course. Avoid doing that which hurts others: Yes! Do them for the right reasons, however. Not out of fear of punishment or hope of a reward. Not just because someone – long-ago – said this should be done. Do these things as a gift to the One who gives us life and loves us without restraint."

He rose and without a glance at the others strode off into the darkness. "I must go now to spend private time with Him . . . Him whom I call Father."

CHAPTER FIFTY-ONE

STILL NOT UNDERSTANDING

The morning light spread across the land, setting it aglow with fresh vitality. By this time, Joshua had completed his morning prayers and was waiting by their dining site for the disciples to gather. "Today we return to Capernaum," he announced with a sense of excitement. It had been a long time since they had seen their families. He knew that many of them were in need of seeing their loved ones. He would not stop by Nazareth. There was nothing there for the others and he felt no need to see the family and stir up old memories. His mind was set for Jerusalem; he did not wish to be distracted.

As they walked, Joshua could hear some of them arguing. Whenever he looked back at them, they immediately stopped, and tried to give the impression that they were one happy group. *Boys will be boys, I suppose,* he quipped to himself. *They seemed to be invested in whatever it was they were arguing about. I'll have to find out . . . though I imagine it was nothing more than who is doing his share of the chores.* With this, he refocused his mind toward what lay ahead.

They arrived later that day in Capernaum and gathered for a moment in Zebedee's house. When the last of the Twelve had entered the house, Joshua grinned at them as one might at a group of boys who appeared to be up to some sort of mischief: "All right, men," he said, looking about at each of them. "What were you arguing about on the way here?"

Joshua was surprised to see their expressions suddenly turn from curious to guilt. *I seem to have touched a nerve*, he thought. Then he waited for someone to respond.

There was an awkward pause, as each of the disciples looked about to see if someone else would volunteer an answer. Finally, Philip spoke in a hesitating voice – barely above a whisper, "We were arguing who among us was – or would be - the greatest."

Joshua was startled by his answer. *Have I been with them this long, and they still do not understand?*, *h*e thought. "Whoever wishes to be first must be last – and servant to all," he said with a note of disgust in his voice. Then he looked away, and noticed a small child playing outside of the doorway. Without a word, he strode out the door, walked over to the child, gathered him in his arms and walked back to the center of the room. He raised the child and slowly turned so that all could view him. "Do you see this child? Whoever welcomes one such child in my name, welcomes me, and whoever welcomes me, welcomes not me but the One who sent me." He then walked back into the yard and set the child down where he had seen him.

During all this, the disciples seemed as stone figures. Not a one of them spoke or moved. Some even appeared not to breathe. They sensed they had been discovered as they were, not as they wished to be or to appeared to be. They were still sitting shamed-faced when Joshua reappeared.

John attempted to rescue the moment and he offered "Master, one evening, while we were traveling here, we had seen someone casting out demons in your name. We tried to stop him because he was not a follower."

Joshua looked at him and felt compassion, realizing what John was attempting to do, but knowing he had to correct – to broaden – all of their understandings of what he was doing. "Do not try to stop such people – any of you. For whoever does a worthy deed of power in my name will not be able to speak ill of me. Remember this: Anyone who is not against us is for us."

He had not intended for this homecoming in Capernaum to begin on a sour note. Still, it had happened. *It might have been easier just to have said nothing,* he thought. *Saying nothing when the situation calls for speaking the truth, however, is how all evil begins. It is time now to end this and send them to their families and friends.*

He smiled and waved his hands. "Five days. Five days and I will meet you here at Zebedee's house. Enjoy your time here."

Grateful that this emotional ordeal was over, they rose up, and left without a word.

Chapter Fifty-Two

Encounters Along the Way

As they journeyed into Judea, some Pharisees approached him and tested him with this question: "Is it lawful for a man to divorce his wife?" They knew the Law, but they wished to see how Joshua would respond, half hoping he would advocate violating the Law so they could accuse him of advocating against the Law, but also half hoping that he might have some greater insight that might help their personal understanding.

Joshua seemed to sense this blending so he responded directly: "What did Moses command you?" They dutifully responded, "He allowed a man to divorce his wife if he gave her a certificate of dismissal."

And what good is that certificate? he thought. *How will she live after she is divorced? She will be unwanted by respectable men. She can only return to her home, if there is one . . . and if they will accept her..* He looked at the Pharisee who had posed the question and replied, "He allowed that because of your hardness of heart. He knew that too many men would wish to be rid of their wives, not because of what they had done or not done, but only because they selfishly desired another, younger, more attractive woman. God made them male and female, 'For this reason a man shall leave his mother and father and be joined to his wife and the two shall become one flesh so they no longer are two, but one flesh. Therefore what God has joined together let no one separate.'"

He looked deeply into his questioner's eyes, observing his inner wrestling with Joshua's answer. *I hope you have the wits to understand what I am telling you, he thought. A woman is completely dependent upon a man for support in this society. No man has the right to take a woman from her home and then discard her like an worn out robe.. He also has no right to use his position to abuse her in any way. What is needed is for people to act toward each other as they would wish for others to act toward them. They should work together to create a safe, loving family in which to raise their children.* He turned his thoughts upward to address Yahweh: *When, my father, will we humans ever learn to care – to really care for others as we care for ourselves?* He turned from the Pharisees and walked away, sad of heart at the thought.

One Pharisee remained where he stood, still wrestling with Joshua's response, knowing it contained a truth he was not quite able to grasp – or ready to accept. *I wish I had the courage to let go of my position and possessions and follow you,* he thought. *I believe you understand life far better than I.* He hesitated for a brief moment, feeling an urge to follow after him. Then, thinking better of the idea, he straightened himself, looked at his companions and said with a trace of a sneer: "The man is no prophet. He just talks nonsense."

As Joshua walked farther into the village, women began to bring their babies and small children to him, asking that he touch them and bless them. There were so many that they began to hinder Joshua's progress so a few of the disciples stepped into the crowd of women and began to shoo them away, saying, "The master has no time for these children. He is on his way to more important things."

Hearing this, Joshua called out: "Wait! Let the little children come to me and do not hinder them. To such as these belongs the Kingdom of God. I tell you truly that those who will receive the Kingdom must do so as a tiny child . . . or they will not enter at all." He said this in a tone that obviously was admonishing those disciples who had just spoken.

As they were about to leave the village and continue on to Jerusalem, a man rushed up to Joshua, knelt before him and, almost pleadingly, asked him, "Good teacher, what must I do to inherit eternal life?" Joshua looked at him and thought, *this fellow's only concern is with himself.* He observed his fine clothing and soft hands. *He probably has inherited his wealth and never worked a day in his life. Now all he can think of is living forever . . . probably because living has been so easy for him. Let's splash a little reality on him. Perhaps it might wake him up. He obviously has learned how to flatter in order to get what he wants.*

"Why do you call me good? No one is good but God alone." He let this sink in and then continued," You know the commandments, keep them." The man replied, "Teacher, I have kept all these since my youth." When he said this with such earnestness Joshua felt a wave of caring concern for the man. He stared into the man's eyes, determining how best to respond to his appeal. *He really believes he has kept the Law, and he probably has . . . at least the letter of the Law. Still, it's obvious that he has missed the point and has never understood or fulfilled the spirit underlying the Law. He is the best dressed and (noticing his girth) the best fed of anyone I have seen in this village. Yet, there is no companion with him and I doubt he knows the names of most of these people. He has used his wealth to isolate and insulate himself from others.* Finally he arrived at his decision. *If he truly is serious about his soul I could help him. He needs to learn life the hard way though.* With this, he responded, "You lack one thing: Go, sell all that you possess, give it to the poor and follow me." All this time he continued to gaze into the man's eyes, searching his soul for some sign of genuine concern.

The man remained kneeling. Even from a distance those watching could see the anguish on his face as he wrestled with his decision. *Come on, fellow,* thought Joshua. *I can see there is good in you. You've just never given it a chance to show.*

The man finally stood upright, still gazing back at Joshua. His hands were trembling as he raised them toward Joshua in a gesture of hopelessness. His words were barely audible: "I cannot," he whispered hoarsely . . . "I cannot," he repeated as his shoulders sagged. He turned and as one who has just lost a battle . . . he walked away, his once proud head bent in defeat.

Joshua anguished within as he watched him leave. He silently mused, *There will be so many like you, my lost friend. They will want and they will wish, but they will never quite find whatever they are lacking to make this pilgrimage of the soul. They will remain where it is safe and comfortable - - - in their homes and in their minds.* He turned to his disciples: "It is easier for a rope to pass through the eye of a needle than for a rich man to enter the kingdom." *1

Simon reacted defensively to what Joshua said, possibly because he knew that by Capernaum standards he, himself, was considered to be wealthy. "Look!" he practically shouted, "We have left everything to follow you."

Joshua raised his hand as though to calm him and replied in a slow, soft voice: "Anyone who has left home and family for the sake of the Good News will receive more now, and —in the end — eternal life." Even as he said this, some inner part of him was feeling distress: *Why is it they still worry about what is in it for them? Have they traveled with me so far and learned so little on the way?*

They had picked up more followers on their way. There were many who felt the need to be near him and to learn from him. They were disciples, students, as well. They were not, however, a part of the inner circle: The Twelve. Whenever they camped, these followers camped nearby, but never near enough to intrude

---

*1 Although the translations continue to use the term *camel*, there is a belief among many scholars that the original term, spelled much like the word for camel, meant *rope*. This makes more sense and does not have Jesus mixing metaphors.

on the privacy that bound the Twelve with Joshua. Now that they were approaching Jerusalem they felt excitement, but also some fear. They had heard the gossip about Joshua being a "Wanted Man" for his violations of the Mosaic Law, and the Romans' fear that he might be planning an armed revolt. They also had heard that he had said something about being arrested and executed, so although they wished to be near him, they did not want to be too near.

As Joshua and the Twelve set forth again to Jerusalem, he announced rather casually, as though to give a reminder of why they were going to the City of David at this time, "The Son of Man will be handed over to the authorities, mocked, spit upon, flogged and crucified, but will rise again on the third day."

Hearing this, James and John began whispering to one another: "I tell you this whole thing is going to be over before we know it and the new Kingdom will arise and our cousin, Joshua, will be the King" said James. Then he added: "The question is who will be his assistants when that happens?"

John nodded passively. He never was one to worry about being in charge, since James had been telling him what to do for most of his life. Still, he had to agree with James on this. Simon, whom Joshua keeps calling *Rock*, was close to Joshua. Then there were Thomas, whom Joshua also seemed to like for his forthrightness., and Judas who had wormed his way close to Joshua and was more sophisticated than the rest.

"Let's settle this now, Brother", demanded James. " Now, before the others start asking special favors. We are his cousins. We have a right."

With that, he grabbed John's arm and began moving rapidly up to the front where Joshua was walking with Simon and Mary.

When they came even with the three, Mary sensed they wished to speak with Joshua in private so she took Simon's arm and slowed their pace so that they quickly fell a few paces behind.

"Teacher," said James when he felt they had all the privacy they would be able to attain, "We would like you to do whatever we ask you now."

"What would that be?" responded Joshua feeling somewhat leery of what would follow.

"Grant us to sit at your right hand and left hand when you come into your glory," blurted James, who was being pushed along by his passion.

Joshua looked over at John who was looking somewhat embarrassed, but eager for an answer. "You do not know what you ask," he replied, thinking *What do I have to say – to do – to get them to understand?* Then he looked at the two of them and continued, "Are you able to drink from the cup that I drink or be baptized with the baptism that I am baptized with?" Even as he spoke the words he realized the impression given to them would be quite different from his meaning. Yet he felt compelled to speak metaphorically since he believed that would create pictures in their minds they might remember later on, after . . . well . . . after . . . .

Without hesitation both responded almost in unison "Oh yes, we are able."

Joshua looked at them and said simply, "Yes, you will drink from my cup and share my baptism, but to sit at one of my sides is not mine to grant."

Needless to say that when the Ten heard of what James and John had asked they became angry with the brothers.

"Who do they think they are?" "What right have they to expect more?" "That was a selfish thing to ask." "Some nerve!"

Joshua heard all this and more from the Ten, so he decided to put a stop to it before it further divided the group he had worked so hard to develop as a family,

"Listen to me," He shouted above the murmuring. "You know that among the Gentiles those regarded as rulers lord it over the people. They act like their position gives them special privileges. That is not the way it is in the Kingdom. Those who wish to become great must first become servants. Those who wish to be the very first must become the servant of everyone. The Son of Man did not come to be served but to serve."

I hope that brought some sense into their heads, he thought as he finished.

CHAPTER FIFTY-THREE

BLIND SIGHTED

As they were leaving Jericho, a blind beggar, named Bartimaeus, the son of Timaeus was sitting by the roadside, plying his trade of begging. When he heard that Joshua of Nazareth was passing by, he began to call out, "Joshua, Son of David, have mercy on me." Those standing near him told him to be quiet, but he persisted and cried out more loudly. Joshua stopped and called to Bartimaeus to come to him. Immediately those by him changed from denigrating him to encouraging him, saying "Take heart. He is calling you," So he went to Joshua, being guided by his voice.

As he approached, Joshua thought, I wonder what he wants. *It could be that he thinks I have money, since we are noted for being charitable. I hope, however, he has enough faith to ask for what he really needs.*

"What can I do for you?" he inquired as Bartimaeus came before him.

His sightless eyes seemed to be staring directly at Joshua as he replied simply: "Teacher, let me see again."

A smile of satisfaction spread across Joshua's face as he said, "Go. Your faith has made you well."

Bartimaeus smiled and nodded, and as he did so the cloud that sat upon his eyes faded from view. He blinked once, then, this time he actually was looking at Joshua. He gave a quick gasp, and saw Joshua nodding and smiling. For a moment he turned to go back to the people he knew. Then abruptly he turned back to

Joshua, and noting the crowd that was following him, walked over and found a place among them. *I wish the others over there could see as well as Bartimaeus,* thought Joshua as he motioned to his followers to move on.

CHAPTER FIFTY-FOUR

A HIGH AND A LOW

As they entered the village of Bethany, just outside of Jerusalem, Joshua was mulling over how he might enter Jerusalem in a manner that made a strong statement to the Jews but that would be overlooked by the Romans. He recalled that the Sanhedrin had once conducted a long debate in their attempt to resolve the issue of Sabbath Law in such a way as to allow some degree of normal family activity. Over the years the Law had become increasingly oppressive, not even allowing families to gather for the observance. The definition of *work* had been applied to the simple act of walking. If one walked too far then, by definition, they had *worked*. In doing so they had violated the Law. A family member who lived at one end of the city could not visit the rest of the family who lived at the other end. Even the more rigid members of the Sanhedrin agreed that this was unreasonable, and would not be required by God. Finally they had agreed that one could walk to the city's edge from anywhere in the city walls and be within the demands of the Law. Someone then raised a pertinent question: "Which walls?" the person asked. "The present walls or the walls of David's city?" Like any vital, long-established city, the old sections had been abandoned and the city stretched in new directions. The original city of David had been just outside of Bethany, and some family members of Jerusalem's residents still resided there. After considerable discussion, one of the leaders said, "David's City! As far as Bethany!" The others agreed and the matter was settled.

The prophet Zechariah had proclaimed, Rejoice greatly, O daughter of Zion! Shout ahead, O daughter of Jerusalem! Lo, your king comes to you; triumphant and victorious is he, humble and riding on a donkey, on a colt, the foal of a donkey." [*1] *A warrior comes on a horse. A Jewish king coming in peace would ride a donkey.* He thought about this for a while and then decided: *That is what I will do. I will enter David's city, riding a donkey. That should tell the people that I come as a peaceful anointed one.*

"Bartholomew! Philip! Come here, I need you to run an errand." The two rushed to him and Joshua continued, "Go to that village over there and you will find a donkey's colt tied by a house. Untie it and bring it to me. If anyone asks what you are doing just say, 'The Lord has need of it,' and he will let you have it."

Bartholomew and Philip nodded, turned and ran to the next village. Everything happened as Joshua had said it would: They saw the colt and untied it, and a man stepped out of the house and asked what they were doing. They gave the prescribed response, the man smiled and indicated for them to take the colt. They returned and as they gave the tethering rope to Joshua they cautioned, "The owner said the colt had never been ridden, so you had better be careful."

"Don't worry," Joshua responded. "I think this little fellow and I will get along well." The colt was standing still, but obviously quite nervous. Joshua began patting the colt to calm him, then he bent over and began whispering soothingly into the animal's ear. As he did so the colt quieted and began breathing slowly.

When they saw this, both Bartholomew and Philip took off their outer tunics and spread them on the colt's back for Joshua to sit on. Joshua smiled at their thoughtfulness and then easily, as though he had ridden all his life, he lifted one leg over the colt's back and slid onto the makeshift saddle.

[*1] Zechariah 9:9

"It is time to move on to Jerusalem," he said with an air of joyful anticipation.

The Twelve plus all the other disciples rushed ahead of him and began spreading their garments and leafy green branches in front of him as he proceeded along the road, down the Mount of Olives and up toward the gates of Jerusalem. Spontaneously, sensing what was occurring, some of them began shouting, "Blessed is he who comes in the name of the Lord! Blessed is the kingdom of David that is coming!" Others simply began shouting with tones that soon took on the character of a musical chant: "Hosanna! Hosanna in the highest!"

People near the open city gates saw the approaching parade and heard their shouting and began rushing to them to join in whatever celebration was taking place. A few, noting Joshua on the colt, rushed to others who were within sight and sound of the gate, shouting "Come see! Come see! There is some important person coming on a donkey's colt!"

The word spread quickly through that section of the city and people began lining the streets to see what was happening.

As the people recognized Joshua, their excitement grew and they began passing the word along with a sense of glee: "It's that Galilean rabbi and healer who is riding from Bethany on a donkey's colt!"

"From Bethany?" someone asked.

"Yes! From Bethany!" another replied. "You know what that mean's don't you?"

After a brief pause a light went on in the person's eyes and he practically shouted: "Yes! Yes! He is entering through the gates of David's city." Then he added with obvious delight, "And the stupid Romans won't even begin to suspect."

"How clever! How clever!", others shouted when hearing this.

The word continued to spread and the excitement grew greater and greater, as Joshua rode, waving from time to time at those who were shouting praise and words of support to him.

I hope they understand the donkey part of this, Joshua mused as he continued to smile, nod and wave to the crowd.

He rode up to the Temple. Then he dismounted his donkey, gave him a gentle pat, and slipped a piece of fruit into its mouth. "Thanks for the ride, little fellow," he said. Then he strode into the Temple and looked around.

Just as I remember it, Joshua thought disgustedly. *Money changers and merchants taking advantage of the pilgrims' piety. The priests surreptitiously lining their own pockets while ostensibly serving Yahweh. Well, Jeremiah, I guess you have your answer,* he thought angrily [*2] He continued watching for another minute. Then he turned and left, walking with a sense of determination as he did so.

"We need to leave the city," he told his followers. "We will return to Bethany for the night."

[*2] 7:11 Jeremiah asks, "Has this house, which is called by my name, become a den of robbers in your eyes?"

CHAPTER FIFTY-FIVE

DECISION TIME

That night as they gathered together for the evening meal, Joshua looked at the fish, bread and lightly cooked vegetables which the women had prepared. Their aroma was compelling as always, but this time he felt no desire to partake of them.

"Your dinner looks delicious, ladies," he offered. "However, I believe I would just prefer to stroll off by myself. I have much to think about this evening."

Everyone nodded differentially. They had learned to expect his change of moods. Normally Joshua was cheerful, even playful at times. However there were times when a heaviness seemed to weigh upon him and he needed to have time alone to work through whatever was bothering him. Those times were few and far between, and he always returned from his brief solitary sojourns.

I can no longer stand by and watch my father's house being desecrated by these self-seeking so called servants of the Temple. It evolved so slowly that no one seemed to notice when it crossed the line. There is no sense of worship there. It reeks the stench of a slaughter house! The pious pilgrims may leave with a sense of satisfaction in having done their duty, but they cannot leave with a sense of having stood in the Presence of Yahweh in all his splendor. There is no sense of awe or feeling that one has been — in any way — changed by the experience. He paused and replayed the scene in his mind. *The only change is that their purses are lighter than when they entered The Temple of the Lord,* he concluded with a note of sarcasm.

He strolled back toward the Mount of Olives and gazed out toward Jerusalem where the lights from the Temple were burning brightly as lines of pilgrims sought to offer their sacrifices to their God.

This is where I make the stand, he thought. *Here in my father's house.* Joshua felt a surge of diverse feeling move through him at the thought. It was a mixture of excitement, sorrow and deep devotion blended together. For a moment he turned his thoughts from inward to upward: *Father, I love you with all my heart. I am certain you know that. I know what you want of me, and I will be true to your will. It just hits me so hard to realize — to accept — that this now is the time and that your house is the place. I cannot put it off. I cannot let the priests and merchants make a mockery of your Temple any longer.*

I ask now only for the strength to complete my work. He turned and began to find his way through the darkness to where his disciples had settled in for the night.

CHAPTER FIFTY-SIX

SHOWDOWN TIME

The next morning, Joshua arose early, but instead of finding a quiet place for prayer he called out in a harsh voice: "Everybody up! We have things to do today. Women, get some food ready. Men, pack up all the things you and the women will need for the day. Take what you will not need to some of the nearby houses and tell the people there to watch them until our return this evening."

"What's gotten into him," Levi said more as a complaint than a question."

"I don't know, but I think we want to stay out of his way today," responded Judas.

The others quickly picked up his mood and the morning meal was a quiet one. The disciples alternated between looking questioningly at one another and glancing at Joshua when they thought he was not watching them.

Joshua sat unmoving for most of the meal. He ate little, but when he had taken the last bite, and before he even had finished chewing it, Joshua rose up and ordered: "That's enough. Let us head back to the city."

As they walked back toward the city Joshua saw a small fig tree in the near distance. It was not the season for figs, but Joshua decided he would like a taste of the sweet fruit, *to get the bad taste of last night out of my mouth,* he thought. Abruptly, he raised his hand to halt the group while he veered over to where the fig tree was.

"What's he doing?" John quietly asked James. "There are no figs on that tree."

"Do you want to tell him that?" responded James with not so much as a look at either John or Joshua who now was almost to the tree.

All the disciples just stood and watched Joshua as he stood by the tree searching its branches for fruit.

As Joshua searched for some sign of a fig he suddenly realized how foolish he must appear to those watching. *This seething anger of mine has caused me – a good Galilean boy – to behave like some stupid city boy. I should have realized there would be no figs on any tree at this time of the year. Well I suppose I might just as well go back and let them laugh at me. Rock or James will probably have something to say. Before I go, however, I better get rid of some of this anger before I hurt the wrong people.*

He looked directly at the tree and shouted, "May no one ever eat figs from your tree again!" and he snapped his fingers as he did so.

"What was that about?" asked Bartholomew of no one in particular, as he watched Joshua turn from the tree and head back to the group.

"Don't even ask" a voice responded quietly.

Joshua stepped back in front of the disciples with a look that echoed the unknown voices' sentiments, and they proceeded on their way in strained silence.

When they arrived at the Temple, Joshua almost rushed into the outer yard and began driving the merchants away from their booths and tables, shouting: "Is it not written that my house shall be called a house of prayer for all the nations, [1] but you have made it a den of thieves!" [2]

He came at them so unexpectedly and with such a violence of movement and voice that the merchants never attempted to stop

---

[1] Isaiah 56:7
[2] Jeremiah 7:11

or confront him. They jumped out of his way and fled from the courtyard as though their very lives were in peril.

Once outside the courtyard they did not stop, however. They went immediately to the palace of the high priest. "This man is a threat to our Temple – to the work that feeds us - to our entire way of life," they pleaded. "You must put a stop to him."

Joseph Caiaphas, the high priest, did not hesitate. He instantly saw the danger. He, himself, received a percentage of whatever any priest collected for refunding the proper coins or gave approval to questionable sacrificial animals. Further, he had heard the word about Joshua's clever entrance and feared that his presence might incite a riot that would quickly become a bloodbath. It was with a mixture of greed and public safety that he nodded his head in agreement and assured the merchants, "Do not worry, my friends. I will take care of this Galilean before the Festival of Unleavened Bread takes place."

With this assurance the merchants turned and left. However, they did not return to the Temple, but found other, more suitable ways to pass the day.

As soon as they had left, the high priest called to one of the chief priests and ordered, "Aaron, find Isaac the Pharisee. You know the one I mean: The pompous one, who came here months ago complaining about the Galilean heretic. I need to speak with him as soon as possible about an important matter."

"I know the one you mean. I will find him," the priest replied. Then he left the high priest pondering, *What is the best way to handle this threat? I must come up with an answer quickly.*

CHAPTER FIFTY-SEVEN

THE PLOT

When Isaac heard that he was being called to speak with the high priest he was elated. At *last, they are ready to listen to me,* he thought. *When I heard of his grand entrance and then his tearing up the Temple I assumed they would come running.* He smiled at the idea. *Now I am the one they need to turn to . . . and I have an excellent idea, of course.* Again, he smiled with self-satisfaction at being the one in control.

He turned to the chief priest who had delivered the message and said, "Tell Joseph I shall be with him shortly. There is some pressing business I must attend to. When it is completed I shall come to him as quickly as I can."

Aaron was startled by Isaac's response. First, to call him by his given name, Joseph, was a breach of etiquette. Second, when the high priest bids one to come it is assumed that whoever is called will stop whatever he is doing and respond immediately. He hesitated, unsure of how to respond. He felt he should chastise Isaac for his behavior and demand he come immediately. Still, he hated confrontations. He had managed to rise to his position by compromising and obeying. He knew he was not a strong person and had come to terms with that. Also, he had sensed a note of urgency in Caiaphas' request that suggested he needed Isaac's cooperation or support. He stood confused and dismayed, trying to decide what to do next.

Isaac noted the discomfort of the priest: *Perhaps I pushed things a bit far. It was enough just to be able to say what I did. I probably should not risk irritating Caiaphas. He could be dangerous.* Having decided this in the instant that the priest hesitated, Isaac smiled, stood up and offered: "But, if the high priest requires my services I suppose I can delay the other matter for the moment."

Aaron breathed a sigh of relief. *Thank the Lord,* he thought *It would have been very difficult for me to confront this strong Pharisee, particularly when I was unsure of whether I should even attempt to do so.* "Very well, he responded simply. Follow me please."

When they arrived at his palace, Caiaphas arose and greeted Isaac warmly while quietly indicating to Aaron that he should leave them alone. He brought him to a place near the balcony where a collection of posh pillows was strewn about. He selected one for himself and indicated that Isaac should do the same. Then he clapped his hands and told the servant who appeared to serve "some of our finer wines for my guest."

They both waited until the wine had been poured and they had tasted it, with Isaac's eyes giving appropriate approval. "Now please tell me what prompts my appearance here today," Isaac said. Then he leaned into his pillow and waited for Caiaphas to respond.

"This troublesome Galilean whom you told us about a few months ago has come to our city and is creating problems. I fear he might set off a riot that could cause many of our citizens to be wounded or slain." Having said that he paused, leaned toward Isaac and asked in a conspiratorial voice, "You have met the man and have been able to appraise him and his followers. Do you have any suggestions of how we might go about handling this?"

Isaac held back a smile. Instead he caused his face to appear as though he was deeply disturbed and considering the matter carefully. *The old fool finally is ready – no needing – to listen to me now. No more harmless heretic safely off in Galilee. Well I've been thinking about this for months. I know I have a plan that will work and will rid us all of this false prophet/messiah. For a* moment he envisioned the gratitude Caiaphas would have for him and even imagined himself being lauded in the Temple by the priest. He sighed and set aside his reverie. "Caiaphas, I believe I have come up with an idea that will solve your problems."

"What is it, Isaac . . . my friend?" he added while thinking: *I hope this pompous snob actually has a worthy idea.*

"While I was in Galilee I recognized one of Joshua's followers as a man who grew up in Jerusalem. His name is Judas, Judas Iscariot. I remember him as an earnest young man who had some desire to become a scribe. He was a good student, but he did not have the patience to study as he must to become a scribe. Nor did he have the proper breeding either," Isaac added with obvious disdain. "I am sure some of your priests would remember him."

"Go on", Caiaphas urged, being eager for Isaac to get to the point.

"A priest who remembers him shall invite him here for a private talk. Once here, you will appear and address him, as you addressed me. This should impress him as to the importance of the meeting. You then will tell Judas of your fears for the city and for Joshua himself."

"Yes, yes. Continue," urged Caiaphas, beginning to sense Isaac's plot.

"I was about to," Isaac responded with a condescending smile. "You next will explain that Joshua is wanted by the authorities because of his heretical teachings. That, as he probably realized, is the reason for Joshua to have led them to Caesarea Philippi: A place of refuge. Explain to him that you fear arresting him in public because that might set off the riot. Assure him that your only wish is to keep Joshua out of public sight until the end of Passover and the visitors have left the city. It is a form of protecting him as well as the city. Also, as an extra incentive, tell Judas that there is a reward for turning in wanted criminals. You can give him thirty pieces of silver which he is free to use as he desires. If he wishes to add it to the group's treasury — I know that he serves as the treasurer — he can do that. Tell him to think of all the good that money can do."

As he listened to Isaac's plot unfolding, Caiaphas felt an increasing sense of pleasure and excitement. He leaned forward and asked in a confidential tone, "If this works as you say it will, what do you suggest we do with your Galilean friend when we have him?"

Ah, now I have you ensnared, as well, thought Isaac with a sense of gratification. *You want me to make the suggestion, but I shall put that entirely in your hands . . . knowing full well what you will do with my "Galilean friend."* He smiled back slyly at Caiaphas: "That, my dear Caiaphas is entirely up to you."

The two sat staring into one another's eyes for a long moment, each savoring the scent of victory.

WHO IS THIS MAN?

The next morning, as Joshua and his band of followers were walking back to Jerusalem, Bartholomew looked over to where the barren fig tree was standing. *I still don't understand what Joshua thought he was doing,* he mused. As he did so, he noticed that the tree appeared to be a bit limp, and even more barren of leaves than it had appeared to be yesterday. He nudged Philip and gestured toward the tree. "I'll be . . ." Philip muttered quietly. Then he turned back and motioned for some of those behind to look over at the tree. As they did so, each one turned back with a look of consternation and confusion on his face. *What is going on here?* Thomas questioned. *Maybe my idea of a God's messiah is a bit short of what it actually is. Yet, I get the impression that things are about to go bad for him. I need to know more – to understand better.* Without realizing it he had slowed his pace while mulling this over. Quickly he picked up his pace and settled back into the group . . . still turning his head to take another look at what appeared to be a withered fig tree. Finally he could take it no more. He quickened his pace and soon was walking beside Joshua. He pointed back toward the fig tree: "Look, Master, the tree you cursed has withered." Joshua glanced back over his shoulder and saw that the tree, indeed, now looked dead.

Without breaking stride he responded loudly enough for all to hear him, "Have faith in God. You can move mountains and perform other unimaginable acts if you trust in God's power and call upon it in your lives."

I did not plan to use that poor fig tree as a teaching tool when I cursed it, he reflected. *Perhaps, however, this made a stronger impression upon them than some of the healings. They need to learn and they need to learn quickly how powerful God's spirit is when called upon and used wisely . . . wiser than my killing that poor tree . . .* he added somewhat ruefully.

When they arrived back in the Temple grounds some of the priests, scribes and elders came out to confront him. They had met earlier in the day to plot how they might discredit him before the crowds that inevitably followed him.

"By what authority do you do and say the things you do" they demanded. They hoped he would either hesitate or make some outlandish claim such as saying, "Yahweh gave me this authority." Either reply, they thought, would discredit him: The first too hesitant; the second, too bold.

Instead, Joshua stepped toward them and responded, "I will answer your question if you will answer mine: Was the baptism of John's from heaven or did it have only human origin?"

The group stepped away as though by command. There was no opportunity to discuss it privately. The eyes of the crowd had shifted from Joshua to them. Some of the crowd looked expectant. Others were beginning to smile and even chuckle. Joshua had them in a dilemma. In spite of that, they briefly turned toward one another and expressed their thoughts. "If we say from heaven, he'll ask why we don't believe him," one muttered. "True", said another, "but if we say it was human this crowd could become nasty." They looked to their spokesman for guidance. He decided that ignorance was the safest response: "We do not know," he replied.

Joshua, smiled at them and said in a manner that dismissed them: "Neither will I tell you by what authority I do what I do." He turned away and began walking further into the Temple grounds as he said this.

Nicodemus has been watching the exchange from a distance. He turned to his friend, Joseph of Arimathea, and said, "I knew it! I was certain of it, when I heard of him. Now I am more certain than ever. That is the young boy who challenged me – and the entire Sanhedrin – during Passover about twenty years ago. He has that same look in his eyes: intelligent and piercing, as though he was looking into your mind. He speaks with the same authority that caused me to feel a bit intimidated – when he was just a lad." He signaled for Joseph to follow him. "Let us stay close and listen to him some more."

Joseph was still staring at Joshua. He had been confronted by more than a dozen of the religious leaders in Jerusalem, and had made them appear to be ignorant weaklings. "I am as eager to do so as you are, my friend," he responded as he began walking. "Thank you for inviting me to join you today."

"I did not want you to miss seeing and hearing this man," Nicodemus replied. "Unlike so many of our colleagues, you not only possess a fine quality mind, but that mind is open to new ideas – to learning new truths. We need more like you in this city."

Joseph felt a tinge of gratitude and pride at Nicodemus' words. He had come to Jerusalem less than ten years ago, having made a fortune as a trader. All his life he had studied the Torah and the writings of the prophets. It had been his dream to one day retire and live near the Temple where he could converse with the wise religious leaders from sun up to sun down if he so desired. His wealth had opened doors immediately, and soon he was invited to be a part of the Sanhedrin. He and Nicodemus had become friends rather quickly. They shared the same perspectives on the

Scriptures, and also on some of the outdated interpretations which seemed oppressive and non essential.

Together, Joseph and Nicodemus trailed behind Joshua and his followers for most of the day. They listened to him tell parables which, if properly understood, were criticizing the priests and elders. He did so with apparent impunity because of the loyal and large crowds which were constantly present.

When the day had ended, Nicodemus returned with Joseph to his villa on the edge of the city, where they enjoyed a fine dinner, fine wine and stimulating conversation.

"If that man is not the long-awaited Messiah," Joseph declared, "then I have misread the Scriptures."

Chapter Fifty-Nine

The Setup

The next day, as Joshua and The Twelve started toward Jerusalem, Joshua said to them: "Today, I want you to go about the city on your own. There is no need to remain with me. The crowds of followers are so plentiful that I will be safe enough without you. Enjoy yourselves. See the market places. Spend the day as you choose. When the sun begins to settle in the West, assemble near the gate and remain until we all are together."

The mood seemed lighter after that. There would be no tense encounters to endure. They would not have to be on constant alert to look for signs of approaching soldiers.

At the city gates they began separating into groups of two, three and four. Most had never visited Jerusalem until then and were eager to visit the markets, to stroll the streets just soaking up the atmosphere of the city.

Judas went off by himself to roam through some of the old, familiar places where he had grown into young adulthood. He was nearing his childhood home when one of the chief priests, who had stationed himself in that area, saw him and approached him.

"Aren't you Judas Iscariot?" he inquired as he neared him.

Judas looked over to the speaker, startled and suspicious, but the moment he recognized the priestly garments he relaxed. "Yes, I am. I once lived near here and wanted to see my boyhood home again," he responded rather cheerfully, feeling somewhat flattered to have been remembered by someone of priestly status.

"I thought I recognized you," the priest responded. "I remember you as an intelligent young man with a genuine interest in the matters of our faith."

Again, Judas felt uplifted by the priest's flattery, never suspecting that his words were part of a ruse to create a sense of trust. *I must have made a greater impression than I realized, he thought. Perhaps I should have – no! I had no chance to become a priest. A scribe, perhaps. But I had no blood ties with the priesthood.* "Thank you for your kind words, he replied simply.

"Why don't you visit your old home later, and come with me to the Temple," the priest offered by way of invitation.

Having nothing to do, and realizing that the priest might be going into some of the private areas where he could meet with other priests, the offer was too good to resist.

"I would enjoy that," he responded eagerly. So the two began to wend their way through the winding streets of the city toward the Temple, which could be seen at a distance.

Aaron was bored just standing at the entrance to the men's courtyard, waiting to see if any of the various priests had located Judas. Caiaphas had ordered more than a dozen of the priests to scatter through the city in search of Judas. There were only a few days left until the beginning of Passover. If the plan was to work they had to find him at least two days before then. *Look at the pilgrims lining up with their sacrifices, he thought. Every year it is the same routine. They begin coming early. Even though it is an open yard the sheer number of these unwashed Galileans creates an unpleasant stench that reaches up to the Temple entrance. Then you blend that with the odor of blood – with all the animals screaming as their throats are slit, and I am more than delighted to be one of Caiaphas' special aides.*

Even though he was bored and a bit offended by the smell Aaron felt a glow of pride and satisfaction in having obtained a special place in Caiaphas' priestly hierarchy. *For a person without noteworthy abilities I have done well for myself*, he reflected.

Just as he was congratulating himself he spied one of the priests approaching the courtyard in the company of a Galilean. *Perhaps we have Judas coming now*, he thought. He saw the priest smiling his way and breathed a sigh of relief. *Caiaphas will have his man, today. And I can move away from this confusion of stench and sound.*

"Aaron, I want to introduce you to a man who should have studied to be a scribe," the priest called out as they approached the gateway. "He used to live in the city, but moved to Galilee to inherit some property, I believe. His name," he added carefully, "is Judas Iscariot."

"Not Judas Iscariot, who is a close aide to Joshua of Nazareth?" Aaron asked as they had agreed.

Judas was both a bit startled and flattered to be recognized by his name and his relationship to Joshua. "Well, yes, I am the treasurer for his group of disciples," he acknowledged with a sense of pride in his position. He was too caught up in the flattery to be suspicious.

"What luck!" exclaimed Aaron. "Caiaphas, our high priest, was just telling me he would like to speak with you if I ran across you. I do not know what he wants, but he seemed pleased when someone told him you were back in the city."

This sent Judas' head spinning. *Me?* he thought incredulously. *I did not think anyone would remember me – never the high priest. I must have been talked about by some of the other priests who remembered my skills.* By this time Judas was completely disarmed and ensnared by the compliments. Aaron took his arm and easily led him away to the high priest's estate . . . as easily as the many pilgrims were leading their sheep into the Temple for slaughter.

Aaron entered Caiaphas' room with Judas by his side. There was a sense of triumph in his manner as he introduced his companion: "Here is the man you were inquiring about, my lord. I found him by the Temple gates. I knew you were eager to see him so I brought him directly here."

Caiaphas rose with a look of delight on his face: "Judas Iscariot! I have heard of you from some of my high priests. It seems you made quite a lasting impression on them when you were here in Jerusalem. I would like to see if it is true that you have the grasp on the Law that some say you have. Aaron, please bring some of our finer wine and serve it to our guest." With that Caiaphas led Judas over to some seats by a large window where he could overlook the city . . . and be properly impressed.

"It is a beautiful city, is it not?" Caiaphas said casually as they seated themselves.

"Yes, indeed. It is beyond beauty," replied Judas, who for the first time saw Jerusalem laid out beneath him, with the Temple reflecting the rays of the sun, gleaming like gold.

"It would be tragic if it was destroyed," commented Caiaphas with a slightly ominous tone. He paused to see Judas' response. But Judas was so enthralled with the view and with the moment that he missed any sense of impending doom that Caiaphas wished to communicate. He merely replied off-handedly, "Yes it would be tragic," as he seated himself and turned to Caiaphas with a smile.

I suppose I shall have to be a bit more direct, thought Caiaphas. *It would appear that I totally disarmed him and there is not a hint of suspicion left in him.* He took heart at this thought and proceeded more aggressively than he originally planned.

"This is one reason I wanted to meet with you, Judas. Not only did I wish to talk with this young man who was remembered as a promising scholar, but I have a concern for what might happen to this sacred city and to your leader, Joshua of Nazareth if the crowd becomes too enamored with him during this Passover."

Judas had difficulty processing the high priest's words at first. He had been expecting a congenial afternoon of exchanging pleasantries and theological insights. Now there seemed to be some hint of danger as well. Before he could gather his thoughts, Caiaphas continued, looking directly into Judas' eyes as he did so.

"I hear rumors of a uprising, Judas." He lifted his hand to quell any response from Judas, and continued: "I know your Joshua has done nothing wrong, and I believe he has no intention of creating a disturbance. Still . . . there are those who only know of him, who believe he might be this long-awaited Son of David who is to come and drive out the Romans. The crowds who hailed his entrance last Sunday are spreading that word," he lied.

Judas sat silently waiting for the high priest to continue before making any appraisal of the situation. So Caiaphas continued: "You understand that there is a warrant for his arrest as a heretic." Again, he lifted his hand and smiled warmly to stop any response. "Oh I know he is not guilty of that, but charges have been made. He at least suspects that, which is why he took you all to Caesarea Philippi where you would be free from any legal pursuit."

Judas nodded his understanding, and Caiaphas continued: "What I would like to do in order to avoid any possibility of a bloody riot is to place your leader in some safe place until the visitors leave the city and Jerusalem returns to normal." He leaned toward Judas in a gesture of intimacy and said: "You understand the city, Judas. You understand how many can be swayed – even incited – by a few words. You probably saw it happen a few times while you were here."

At this he stopped to give Judas time to process what he had said. All the while he watched Judas' face closely to see if he might require more prompting.

Judas sat quietly mulling over what the high priest had said. *It is true. I told Joshua that the city is different, but he did not seem to appreciate what I said as a warning. Now he came riding that donkey as a king . . . and the people may have thought he was giving them a signal to prepare to revolt.* He agonized at the thought. *Oh, Joshua, why didn't you show more caution? You are not a fighter! You are a Galilean. Brilliant, inspiring – yes! I have never met the likes of you . . . but you are a naïve Galilean in spite of that. You could get us all killed . . . and destroy the city as well.*

His mind seemed to go blank at that thought and he just sat as though in a daze.

Caiaphas carefully scrutinized Judas' face during this inter-lude. *He is taking this seriously. I see no trace of suspicion in him. I shall just let him play this out in his mind. Soon enough he will ask what he can do.* He leaned back and sipped his wine, still carefully watching his prey swallowing the bait.

Slowly, Judas began to think his way through the situation. It never occurred to him to question Caiaphas' motives. He simply accepted what the high priest had told him, and proceeded from there. *We are in trouble! Joshua's life is in peril. If the Romans even suspect that he plans to start an uprising they will kill him without hesi-tation. I know I cannot get Joshua to believe that.* A thought occurred to him – *Oh my God! Joshua did say something about being crucified and rising. Does he have some idea that he is immortal?* He panicked at this possibility. *He could get everyone killed. Everyone!* Again, his mind seemed to go blank at the idea and he just sat, absolutely still . . . totally stunned.

As Caiaphas continued to observe the emotions surging though Judas he relaxed and continued to patiently sip his wine. *He is mine.* The thought pleased him immensely.

Judas' mind was racing now, exploring every possibility of ac-tion. But every path led nowhere. Finally – defeated and desperate – he looked at the high priest and asked simply, "What can I do?"

Caiaphas donned a sympathetic expression. "You can help us protect him and the city if you care to", he said reassuringly, soothingly.

Judas' eyes brightened and he nodded for Caiaphas to continue.

Careful now, Caiaphas thought as he felt Judas becoming secure in his net. *Don't try to pull him in too fast.* "We fear that if we attempt to pretend to arrest him in order to take him to a safe place the crowds would begin the very riot we wish to avoid. If you really care to help, you could tell us where we could find him alone, in the darkness of night."

Judas continued to nod eagerly and Caiaphas continued to lay out his carefully devised plan.

When he had finished he reached inside his tunic and pulled out a small, finely crafted leather pouch. "There is a reward, you realize, for assisting in capturing a wanted person. I shall give you thirty pieces of silver. This should ease your leader's indignation at what he will believe to be your betrayal when we free him." He handed Judas the pouch and patted his hand as he did so.

"You can trust me to let you know. It should be within two days", he promised.

"Oh yes," the high priest responded. "We can trust one another in this matter. It is for the good of everyone."

PRELUDE TO CHAPTER SIXTY

There are two opposing witnesses to the character of Jesus' Last supper: The synoptic Gospels call it the Passover. The gospel of John, however, says it was two days prior to the Passover. This would make it a kiddush. A kiddush was held weekly on the eve of the Sabbath, or on the eve of any other holy day. The day prior to Passover was the Day of Preparation: a holy day. John even observes that Jesus could not be allowed to remain on the cross on such a holy day (John 19:31). His body had to be removed before sundown, for sundown was the beginning of the Day of Preparation.

As pleasant and tradition-bound as it may be to think of the Last Supper as a Passover meal, John's case is far superior to the Synoptics. Unfortunately, Mark's account is filled with contradictions which one cannot be aware of unless they read Greek and have some formal training in New Testament studies.

Mark's first error or contradiction is found in Mark 14:1. It says "It was two days before the Passover and the Festival of Unleavened Bread. The story then is interrupted and not resumed until 14:12 when it says, "On the first day of Unleavened Bread, when the Passover lamb is sacrificed . . ." The festival is clearly identified as the *Festival of Unleavened Bread*. However at the celebration of that meal the bread served is clearly identified as *leavened* bread (Mark 14:22). Unless one reads it in the Greek, however, one would never know, for the translations all simply define it as *bread*.

This writer believes that the original account of Mark was interrupted at this point in order to allow it to configure with a growing popular idea of the meal having been the Passover. Whoever did this, however, overlooked the need to make the bread into *azumos* (unleavened bread) rather than *artos* (leavened bread). He also obviously was unaware of the Jewish cycle of the day and its implications for his version of the event.

The second error in Mark's account is that he – or someone – overlooked the difference in the Jewish day cycle and the Roman or western day cycle. The Jewish day begins at sundown, as indicated in John 19:31. Therefore if the Last Supper had been the Passover then Jesus was crucified on that same day since it did not end until the following sundown. The thought of Jesus having been allowed to be crucified on the holiest of days, when his body was not even allowed to remain on the cross on the day of Preparation is unthinkable.

In this next chapter I blend John's version of the meal with Mark's. I do not see them as opposing but supplementary. John was aware of Mark's story, but he wished to tell more. He bypassed Mark and added the portion of the foot washing because it made an important statement.

All this, dear reader, is merely my explanation for why the event unfolds as it does. I offer it in advance so that these details do not cause you to struggle through the chapter.

CHAPTER SIXTY

IN REMEMBRANCE OF ME

The Passover would be in two days, but Joshua sensed that he did not have two days remaining, so he had asked the men to prepare a simple kiddush meal, made up primarily of figs, olives, nuts, leavened bread, honey – and wine, of course. The kiddush cup was an essential part of the meal. It was the custom for the men of a village to gather on the eve of a holy day to eat lightly and prepare themselves for the day that was to come. The next day would be the Day of Preparation for the Passover. A kiddush was in order. It was also appropriate, for that night would prove to be anything but a time for feasting.

A new follower had offered the upper room in his house for the meal. The men began to gather there at sundown: the beginning of the day. They waited outside until Joshua arrived. Then they followed him into the upper room. Joshua invited Judas to sit by him at the table. He had felt Judas' emotional withdrawal since the day he went to the Temple by himself. *Something has taken hold of him. He no longer is able to look me squarely in the eye, as he did the night we talked on the hillside. I can see guilt and uncertainty crawling around inside him. This can mean but one thing: Judas plans to betray me. There are enough trumped up charges to arrest me. I know that. However they do not even attempt to do that because they fear the crowds that constantly surround me. Still, if they could catch me apart from those crowds . . .* He let the thought fade away. There was no reason to pursue it, for he had already worked his way through that possibility. It was one reason he selected this room from someone barely associated with him for this probably-last-supper with the Twelve.

When Simon Rock entered he saw that Judas was seated in the place he usually occupied, and that Joshua was engaged in conversation with him. In a fit of petty anger he immediately strode to the far end of the table and seated himself in the position of lowest rank.

Joshua noted this from the corner of his eye. *Rock has to learn to control his emotions much better if he is to assume any significant position of leadership in this group. Yet, if not Rock, then who?* He glanced about at the others and mentally shrugged them off, and quickly returned his attention to Judas. "What is the mood of the city, my friend?"

Judas winced at the words. *You will not think me a friend for long, I fear.* "The great surge of admiration and expectation from Sunday has faded, Master. The Pharisees have been spreading lies about you and warning the people that you may cause trouble."

"And you, my friend? What is your mood at this moment?" He said the words kindly. Still, they caused Judas to recoil slightly and to lower his eyes. *No doubt about it. Judas will betray me. I do not know if it will be while we eat – or later when I go to pray.* He felt a wave of sadness sweep through his being. Finally he forced a smile, waiting for Judas to gather his composure enough to reply.

"I? Er, ah, I am just happy to be with you, Master. Why would I have any other mood but of love and loyalty?" Even as the words left his mouth he could feel the bitterness of their after-taste. *Oh, God! What if I am wrong? If I am doing something foolish?* Quickly he reassured himself. *No! The priests can be trusted. They will keep him safe until the city is back to normal. Then we can all return to Galilee and live safe, productive lives, caring for the people there.*

Joshua looked over to see Simon, still sulking at the place he had chosen. *It is time to teach you another lesson, Rock,* he reasoned.

Time to teach you all a lesson, I believe. You are still too wrapped up in yourselves – too concerned with what you will receive as my disciples.

Joshua rose abruptly and walked directly to the entrance where he picked up a pitcher of water that lay on a small table. He selected a towel and girded it about his waist.

All conversation ceased immediately. Someone gasped. Most held their breath. This was a private feast. The home owner was not present as a host. There had been no servant to wash their feet as they entered. Not a single one of them had thought to serve that role. Instead they had sought out a seat they thought appropriate for their status in the group and then began to talk with one another.

It was too late to do anything now. Joshua obviously had assumed the role of the servant and was about to wash their feet.

Joshua looked about and went directly to John. He knelt at his feet and tenderly began to wash away the dirt and dust. John sat quietly – awkwardly so – vainly attempting to look as though this was a normal thing to happen. Then Joshua proceeded to the next disciple, Andrew, who at first made some gesture of resistance, then quietly – obediently – watched uneasily as Joshua repeated his cleansing ritual. By the time he arrived at Simon's place the tension permeated the room. Simon had sat silently watching Joshua move toward him.

This was my role, Simon thought. *I lost my temper and intentionally selected the lowest position . . . thinking, "I'll show him," I suppose. Well Simon as the self-appointed person of lowest rank the foot washing was your task.*

As Joshua knelt before him and reached for his foot, Simon pulled his foot away and blurted out, "Lord, you will never wash my feet!"

Joshua gazed steadily into Simon's eyes and replied, "Simon, unless I wash your feet you will have no share in me."

Simon raised his hands and replied, "Then also my hands and my head, please!"

But Joshua shook his head as he reached for Simon's foot and said, "Your feet are enough, Rock." and he proceeded to wash Simon's feet, wiping them carefully with his towel when he was through.

He finished by washing Judas' feet. Then he walked back and placed the pitcher and towel on the table. As he returned to his place he said, "If you would be a master you must first be a servant. We come to serve not to be served."

As he sat, Joshua placed his hand on Judas' shoulder and addressed to the still-subdued disciples: "Truly I say to you, one of you will betray me: One who is eating with me." He spoke this simply, not as an accusation but more as a matter of information.

The men stopped what they were doing and stared at Joshua in disbelief. John, who was seated on the other side of Joshua, was stunned: *Did I hear him correctly? His tone was as though he was simply telling us what would be served tonight. But his words – I'm sure I heard the words – were that one of us would betray him!* He shuddered and looked about at the others. *They look as shocked as I do. Not a one of them looks guilty. I can't see Judas, but he has become so close to the master of late; it could not be him.*

As he was processing these thoughts, Joshua added, "It is one of the Twelve, one who is dipping bread into the dish with me." John saw a hand pull back quickly from the dish in front of Joshua. *That has to be Judas. Something is wrong here. Joshua must be testing us in some new way. Not Judas. Not any one of us would ever betray the master.*

Then Joshua added another thought: "The Son of Man will go as it is written of him, but woe to the one who betrays him; it would be better for that man if he had never been born." As he finished speaking, John heard a stirring, and saw Judas departing.

"That which you must do, do quickly," Joshua half-whispered to Judas as he hastily disappeared through the doorway. John assumed that Joshua had dispatched Judas on some errand, as did the others who noticed Judas' hurried departure.

This evening the kiddush was lacking its normal vitality. There was no theological give and take, no planning for the week ahead. Joshua's words about betrayal had dulled even their appetites. Each person ate in silence. They realized that the Pharisees had made false charges against Joshua. The only reason he had not been arrested was the authorities' fear of the crowds. However, in the evenings there were no crowds, which is why they usually left the city and returned to Bethany where the village people would hide and protect them. Tonight, however, Joshua had specifically stated his desire to remain in Jerusalem.

Something is happening that I can not understand, muttered Simon to himself. A wave of fear blended with sadness swept through him as he thought this. He looked about at the others. Each was somber and lost in thought. *I have never felt so close to anyone in my life as I have to these companions. Even Andrew and I have formed a bond that is much tighter than we have ever known. This man we call master has changed our lives. He has transformed the way we even think about life. Now it is all coming to an end.* Another chill rushed through his being, and a profound sense of sorrow began to claim his soul. He absentmindedly reached for a fig, stuck it in his mouth and began chewing on it.

John was still trying to piece together the things Joshua said with the action of Judas to make some sense of what was happening. *Joshua would not send him off to betray him. He would have kept him here if he thought Judas posed a threat. Yet he said it was the one dipping in the dish with him, and that was Judas' hand that I saw.* He sat mulling this over in his mind. *I just do not understand, so there is nothing to do but wait and watch to see how this plays itself out?* He gathered a handful of nuts and popped them in his mouth. Then he lay back, closed his eyes and began to munch on them.

Joshua watched the silent dramas unfolding in each of those at the table. *They are afraid. I can see it in their eyes. I did not wish to upset them. Yet I had to tell them what was happening so that they might better understand what still is to happen.* He breathed a long sigh. Then he sat perfectly still, trying to determine what to do with the moment. Slowly, deliberately, he reached for an untouched loaf of dark, leavened bread made from the heavy grains brought up from Galilee. His action caught the attention of the men and they fastened their eyes upon him. For a long moment he merely held the loaf outward and at eye level, as though he were a priest offering a gift upon the altar. Then ever so slowly he began to tear the loaf in two.

"This is my body given for you." He gazed into the eyes of each of his followers, and then added. "Do this in remembrance of me." With that, he tore a small piece from one of the halves and passed each half along. One he handed to John on his right and the other to Thomas on his left. Each man silently tore a piece from the loaf and, following Joshua's cue, held it, waiting for the next instruction. Carefully, with a sense of reverence, Joshua placed the piece in his mouth and began to chew upon it – again with the same sense of reverence.

The others followed his example and also began to chew slowly, quietly . . .. Some obviously were confused and merely chewed dutifully. Others had caught the mood and slipped deeply into themselves. James felt as though he was kneeling before a gigantic white wall, overwhelmed by a silent force he could not grasp. Philip felt himself engulfed by an invisible presence of peace and certitude. Levi felt as though he was being bathed in a soft light that soothed every fiber of his being. Bartholomew felt safely nestled in a soft whitish light.

Each of those who had grasped the mood of the moment felt that he had in some mysterious manner slipped into another realm of being and that they had become intimately bound to one another.

Slowly they opened their eyes and looked again toward Joshua, who seemed to be gazing at each one of them simultaneously.

He tore off another piece of bread and dipped it into the dish, scraping up the mixture of fruit and honey and placing it delicately in his mouth. The others took his cue and continued with their eating. *Life goes on. They must realize that. It will go on even more fully for them after tonight. They must learn to relish all they will experience.* With this thought he slipped back into dealing with his own concerns for what he now knew was about to occur.

I do not really want to experience the events that shall happen this day. No one in their right mind would want to. Still, I am increasingly certain this is what Yahweh wants for me. I try to find another way to end this mission he has laid upon me, but none seems to work. He looked about and observed that the men had effectively finished the kiddush. With a sigh of resignation he reached for a cup, filled it afresh with wine. This time he rose, instantly demanding the attention of all.

"This is my blood of the new covenant, poured out for you and for many."[1] With that, he lifted the cup to his lips and drank

---

[1] Only the Gospel of Matthew (26:28) adds "For the forgiveness of sins." Luke follows Mark in omitting that phrase. The early Christian writing known as *The Didache* (the Teachings [of the apostles].) calls the meal the Eucharist (Giving of Thanks) and makes no mention of it as a sacrifice. This addition in Matthew reflects a growing understanding among some of the Western Christians that Jesus' death was a sacrifice. This, however, is not the view of the Eastern Church, as well as many Western Christians. As a matter of fact, *there is no official doctrine of atonement accepted by any of the Church councils.* It developed more as a matter of preferred interpretations by those who think of God as a harsh judge and not the loving father depicted by Jesus in his life and actions – and particularly in his story of the Prodigal Son.

deeply from it. Then slowly, deliberately, he handed the cup to John and nodded, indicating that he, too, should take the cup and drink from it. Each, in turn, took the cup and drank deeply from it. Then they waited for Joshua to explain the meaning of what he had done. This was a common practice with him. He often performed some unusual act; then, after letting them ponder on it for a while, he would explain it. He was a great teacher in this regard: First create the question in their minds; then teach into their curiosity and confusion. This time, however, he merely took the cup when Thomas handed it to him, sat it on the table, and said, in a matter-of-fact manner, "I shall not drink of the fruit of the vine again, until I drink it anew in the Kingdom of Yahweh." Then he motioned for them to follow him out into the night.

CHAPTER SIXTY-ONE

GETHSEMANE

They quietly followed Joshua as he moved through the back streets of the city, until he came to a gate that exited Jerusalem. "Ah ha, he does plan to return to Bethany, after all," Simon whispered to Andrew. "We have been worrying all night for no reason. Judas probably went ahead to prepare a room for us." Andrew grinned and nodded, while silently breathing a sigh of relief. John elbowed his brother and nodded toward Bethany, sitting just across the valley. Silently, they weaved their way through the many trees on the Mt. of Olives as they descended to the place known as Gethsemane: The Olive Press. A giant flat rock, placed there by some act of nature centuries ago, served as the foundation for a huge round stone that was used to press the oil from the batches of olives which were brought there. The oil was far more valuable than the olives which held it, and the owner of the press lived quite well from this happenstance of geology.

At a certain place, Joshua halted the group. "You will all become deserters this night. When I am raised up, however, I shall go before you to Galilee, and you are to follow me there." Simon rushed forward and protested," Even if every one else becomes a deserter, I will not!" Joshua looked at Simon, shook his head and said, "Simon, my Rock, this very night, before the cock crows two times, you will deny me three times." With tears of passion dripping down his face, Simon almost shouted his response: "Even though I must die with you I will not deny you!" Everyone else quickly joined in with the same sentiment. Joshua looked at each in turn. His love for each was obvious, yet each averted his glance as he seemed to be gazing into their souls. He smiled, then indicated that they should wait for him while he went to pray. Only Simon, James and John should accompany him. Some felt slighted by this, but had long-since learned to accept it. As with any of them, Joshua had bonded more closely with a few. They happened to be James and John, his cousins, and Simon the one Joshua called "Rock." Bartholomew volunteered to go back toward the gate to keep watch for them. The others settled themselves into whatever seemed to be a comfortable space to begin their wait.

When Joshua spied The Olive Press he held up his hand to stop the others. He turned and faced them. They had never seen him looking as he did at that moment. He was not their strong, confident leader. He looked distressed and vulnerable. When he spoke it was with a degree of passion they had never heard from his lips: "I am deeply grieved, even to death," he said in what was little more than a whisper. "Remain here and stay awake." Even though it was spoken kindly, they heard it more as an order than a request. Immediately the three of them found some comfortable looking piece of ground and placed themselves on it. They did not attempt to locate a place where the three of them could be together. They sensed the occasion did not call for speaking. Their task was simply to wait in silence while Joshua did what he came to do. Still, this sudden turn of events – this detour from Bethany – this sudden expression of deep emotion disturbed them. They were alone and vulnerable. The night was dark. Soldiers could come upon them unseen . . . if someone had told them where to find them. Simon felt another shudder of generalized fear ripple though his body. *Here we are: Alone; unprotected. Our leader looks on the verge of collapse, and not even one of us has any idea what to do if he does.* He sat, fighting off a chill that was not caused by the night air.

Joshua had arrived at the huge flat rock which formed the base of the press. He threw himself on the ground feeling pressed by unseen forces, much as the countless number of olives that had preceded him to that place. "Abba - Father, for you all things are possible, so I implore you to remove this cup from me." He paused, gathered himself, then he continued: "Yet, not what I want, but what you want." He lay quietly for a long moment, waiting – hoping for some sign. *A lamb like the one given to Abraham when he was ready to sacrifice Isaac, would be nice*, he thought wryly. Then, still caught in the struggle of whether to cross over to Bethany and put off the inevitable for another day, or to remain and let Judas' betrayal run its course, he sat up, peered across the valley where he could dimly see some lights still shining in the homes of his Bethany friends. He rose, stretched himself and roamed over to where he had left his three companions.

Each one is asleep. Sound asleep! He shook his head sadly, looking about at each of them scrunched up against the trees. *I cannot say that I blame them. They really do not want to be here. There is nothing they can do but wait. Helplessly waiting is a terrible agony. Since I told them to stay I suppose this is their only way to escape the sense of helplessness. Still, I need them to remain awake.* He walked over to where Simon was sleeping and said rather gruffly: "Simon, are you sleeping? Could you not stay awake for me for an hour? Pray that you never come to this hour of testing, for the spirit may be willing, but the flesh is weak." Simon roused from his slumber and looked sheepishly at Joshua, but before he could gather his wits to offer an apology, Joshua had turned away and began walking back to Gethsemane. He looked toward James and John who had been awakened by Joshua's voice. For a moment each sat upright, and looked about as though keeping watch. However, their eyes began to cloud over: The result of the wine combined with their feeling of utter helplessness.

Joshua again positioned himself flat and outstretched on the rock. This time his mind drifted to the possible events of the day. Abandoned by everyone he called "friend." *The women, though — they might remain,* he thought. *They would be considered harmless. Mary would know that. Still, if Judas is correct, the very people who seemed to admire me would be the ones screaming for my blood.* He paused to allow this thought to soak in. *Then what good did all this do?* He lifted his head skyward. *What did my life accomplish, Father?*

What will my death accomplish? Even if you raise me as I am convinced you shall, what lasting effect will it have? Will it just be the topic for men to discuss over a cup of wine and the women to speculate about at the wells and market places? Then forgotten — as I soon shall be forgotten? As though in response, a series of past events flashed through his mind: The child he raised from the dead; the lepers to whom he had given new life; the many sightless persons who had been given sight; the changes in the villages simply because he had spoken or visited there: They had become more communal — more caring for one another. These were not figments of his imagination. In many ways Yahweh had given new life to his children — and Joshua had been the instrument. *Father, I can only believe you will use this death of mine in some way that sees beyond my ability to fathom. 'Still I say again, please remove this cup from me'. Find some other way for me to fulfill this mission you have given me. The thought of crucifixion causes me to tremble deep within my soul . . . . Still, my father, it is your will — not mine — that I must follow.*

Slowly, almost plaintively, he repeated his now-familiar mantra: *Wherever you lead; whatever you ask; I will be faithful. Make my way clear, is all I ask.*

He paused again, waiting — hoping — that some sign — any sign — might be given to spare him the shame and agony of the cross. He looked down at his hands, clasped together as in prayer, but white-knuckled and perspiring from unconscious straining.

He shook them free of one another; then he used them to raise himself up from the rock. One more time he turned his head toward the lights of Bethany. "Bethany, Bethany," he whispered longingly. "How uncommonly attractive you are to me at this moment." He allowed himself to remember a few nights ago when he was seated with the Twelve – Judas was at the table with the rest. The lamb was wonderfully seasoned. The wine was perfect: not too dry; not too sweet. There was much laughter . . . as in – *Was it just last week?* He smiled in wonderment. *Yes, it was just last week that life was so simple – so good – so very good. We had not yet come to Jerusalem* The smile quickly faded and was replaced by a look of sadness which was uncommon to him. He straightened himself, and then strode over to where Simon, James and John were waiting.

Once again he found them asleep. There was some part of him that was sympathetic and understanding, but there was another who felt they already were abandoning him. He walked over to each and shook them rather forcefully. Without a word he returned to Gethsemane, lowered himself on the rock and continued to pray. It took a moment for any of the three to gain enough sensibility to respond and by that time Joshua had disappeared into the darkness. Sheepishly they looked at one another and lifted their hands in some form of supplication. Then they quickly turned away from one another in mutual embarrassment.

Now his petition included new concerns: *Father, I do not want to die alone. Too many people die alone – even when surrounded by family and friends. Simon, James and John are already abandoning me. They have no tolerance for my pain so they separate themselves from me. The women may be there, but will not dare to be too close. All the others will be shouting as I have heard them shout at other victims of the Romans' cruelty. There is some vile quality that resides in far too many people that erupts whenever a defenseless victim appears. They jeer and they cheer.*

They are terrified by pain and death, but they also are fascinated by it. Like children shouting insults from the safety of their windows, these people will put forth their false bravado once I am safely nailed to the cross. He shivered in revulsion at the thought. *Please, father, at least spare me this: Do not let me die alone!* Although his eyes remained dry throughout this silent outburst of emotions, he felt the tears gushing forth from his heart.

For what seemed an eternity he lay there stretched out on the stone . . . waiting for some word of reprieve or at least assurance that this one request would be granted. Finally, hearing none, he rose wearily and walked back to where the three were waiting. When he saw them sleeping, he clutched his hands together in despair. This time he spoke loudly – loudly enough for those who were left farther behind to hear his voice. "Are you still sleeping? Enough of this! The hour has come when the Son of Man is betrayed into the hands of sinners. Get up!" He practically shouted: "Come let us go. See the one who betrays me is here."

Still trying to recover their senses, Simon, James and John looked about them and saw Judas leading a mob from the Temple armed with swords and clubs. Judas had agreed upon a sign to identify Joshua because the priests did not want to arrest all his disciples. It would be enough to capture the leader. "The one I kiss will be the man we want. Arrest him and lead him away under guard."

The mob with Judas had no focus and had begun to mill around, and the other disciples, hearing the sounds, had begun to gather. Judas rushed toward Joshua, embraced him and began to kiss him fervently.*1 Even as he did so, his mind was crying out, *Forgive me, my master! This is the safest way for you. Really! You may never understand – and may wish to be rid of me, but I am doing this to save you and to preserve the peace in Jerusalem.* The men with Judas rushed up behind him and clutched Joshua. One of those standing near Joshua pulled a sword and cut off the ear of the high priest's servant. Joshua raised his hand as though to tell his disciples to not resist. Then he called out, "Have you come out with swords and clubs as if I were a bandit? I was with you, teaching in the Temple every day, and you never arrested me."

Without attempting an answer, the mob from the Temple led him away. His disciples stood by and watched helplessly.

*1 *Kataphilesen* is the term used to denote this kiss. It literally means *fervently kissed*. Translators tend to overlook this quality and merely say *kissed*. This gives the impression that the kiss was a mere signal: A perfunctory, dispassionate peck on the cheek. This writer believes it reveals a genuine, passionate affection for Joshua as Judas seemingly betrays him. The kiss, as I understand it, is Judas' last attempt to display his devotion as he turns him over to the authorities for what he believes to be a noble reason.

Note: I credit this interpretation of Judas' betrayal to Clarence Jordan, translator of *The Cotton Patch* Version of Scripture. It is the only interpretation that makes sense in all of its aspects: Throwing the coins back at the priests, the suicide of remorse, the kiss of passion.

CHAPTER SIXTY-TWO

THE TRIAL

They took Joshua to Caiaphas, the high priest, where he was gathered with the chief priest, elders and scribes. Simon had followed the mob until they went into the courtyard. Then he found a place by the fire where he could warm himself until someone would reappear with Joshua.

Within the room where Joshua had been taken the high priest sat appraising the man who had been brought before him. *So this is Joshua of Nazareth: The miracle worker and teacher of heresies. He looks rather ordinary to me. He dresses more like a peasant than a rabbi or healer: homemade tunic and sandals.* He continued to study him, now looking more at the man than his garb. *Intelligent eyes. Even as a prisoner he carries himself like a ruler. I see why Isaac had trouble with him. Well we shall see soon enough what he has in him.* He turned to the group and asked, "What are the charges against this man?"

A stream of accusations gushed forth from a dozen or more of the crowd. Their voices produced a cacophony of meaningless noise.

"Wait!" the high priest demanded in a voice just below a scream. "Raise your hands and I will let you speak, but for no more than a minute. We want to move forward on this." He pointed at the first speaker.

"This man claimed he would destroy our Temple and rebuild it in three days without using his hands. He is a threat and a maniac."

The next designated speaker said, "He claims to be a king."

The next said with a sneer, "He claims he is the Messiah." To which the entire gathering began muttering and scoffing at Joshua.

All the while Joshua was observing as though he was an uninvolved spectator. *These men are the leaders we are told to respect and obey?* he asked himself. *They act more like angry children, and their words are foolish. Can they really be so ignorant of what I was saying? - - - what I was doing? Why they are wasting time, I do not understand. They mean to kill me. That is obvious, so why not just turn me over to Pilate and demand my death?*

The high priest raised his hand to indicate that the statements of charges had come to an end. "Are you the Messiah?" he asked Joshua; looking directly into his eyes.

"I am," responded Joshua in a matter of fact manner. "And you will see the Son of Man seated at the right hand of Power and coming with the clouds of heaven."

Hearing this, the high priest tore has own garments as a sign of lamentation. With a sorrowful voice he addressed the gathering: "You have heard his blasphemy. What is your decision?"

Once again they all began shouting, but even though their sentences were unintelligible, the word *death* was clearly heard time and time again throughout the din of noise. Some of the elders and scribes began spitting on him and cursing him. All the while Joshua continued to watch impassively. *Finally, these overgrown children have voiced the decision they had made before they even ordered my arrest.* He breathed a sigh of relief, *Now we can get on with it. I just want this to end soon,* he thought as some inner portion began to anticipate the painful ordeal that lay ahead.

Simon remained in the courtyard, uncertain of what he could or should do. Still, there was something within him demanding that he remain as close as possible to his master in this dreadful hour. He kept his eyes on the entrance where he had last seen

Joshua. As he was warming his hands over the fire a servant girl of the high priest came by and glanced at him as she was passing. She stopped abruptly and took a long second look at him. *I have seen him before,* she thought. *Yes, it was at the market, earlier this week. He was with the man I saw who was just hauled before my master.* She took a step toward Simon: "You were with this Joshua of Nazareth!" she said in an accusatory voice.

Simon lowered his head and looked away from her. "No! You have mistaken me for someone else," he responded. Even as he did so he was aware that his thick Galilean accent clearly identified his place of residence. In the momentary silence that followed, a cock crowed in the distance. The girl turned to those nearby and pointed at Simon saying, "This man is one of *them.*" Again Simon denied it, wincing in agony as he realized that everyone had to recognize his accent. *Oh why, why did I stay here?* he cried to himself. *There is nothing I can do against the mob that has Joshua.* Some of the bystanders now stepped toward him: "You are one of them, for you are Galilean," one said sternly. "No! No I am not," Simon shouted in response. By this time he was terrified, desperately attempting to control the panic that had seized him. "I may be Galilean, but I do not know the man you speak of. I never even heard of him until now." Before anyone had the opportunity to react, Simon rose quickly and walked hastily away from the courtyard. As he did so, he heard a cock crow a second time. He did not look back, but attempted to look as though it was anger and not fear that was driving him. Once outside of the courtyard Simon slowed his pace, but continued to walked steadily until he had passed safely though the city gates. When he felt himself to be out of sight, he fell to his knees, buried his face into his hands and with his entire body trembling . . . wept uncontrollably.

While Simon was having his time of trial in the courtyard, two of the guards had taken Joshua into an inner room, tied him securely, wrapping a rope around him beneath his armpits. Then they lowered him into the cistern where he spent the night hanging in the dank darkness.

CHAPTER SIXTY-THREE

BEFORE PILATE

In the morning, the two guards returned and laboriously hauled Joshua out of the cistern. For a moment Joshua stood motionless, blinking his eyes and breathing the fresh air into his lungs. *I had not planned on that,* he thought. *I wonder what else is going to occur that I had not planned on.*

Before he had the opportunity to speculate along those lines, one of the guards poked him with the point of his sword. "Get moving, you filthy heretic. You have an appointment with the Roman Prefect." With this he added an additional shove with his hand. It came so unexpectedly that Joshua almost stumbled and fell as he was taking a first step.

Why is it that some people need to have someone they can bully and boss? He asked himself as he walked along a descending path. *Is it that this is the only way they know to relate, or is it that they have been so constantly abused and debased that they feel some uncontrollable urge to hurt others? I suppose there will be a few more like this fellow who will take advantage of the situation today. Might just as well brace myself for it,* he thought as he continued to descent toward Pontius Pilate's palace.

Meanwhile Pilate was pacing nervously in his reception room. He had received word from his informants that a heretical self-pro-claimed Jewish Messiah was going to be handed over to him, and that the Jewish religious authorities wanted him to be crucified.

Why can't these people at least live in harmony among themselves? he questioned as he paced. *I have enough trouble trying to keep the peace and keep Caesar happy with sufficient taxes and tributes,* he thought. *If this Galilean is another one of their sword swinging Second Davids then we probably are best rid of him. Still, I have heard nothing about him being a threat to the peace. It's probably just one of those petty things these Jews always seem to be worrying about: Someone violating the Sabbath or not following some of their purity regulations. This one must have blown things out of proportion, however, if they want to kill him.*

He stopped and gazed out the window, surveying the scene below. The streets were jammed with nonresidents who had come for their annual Passover festival. *At least the commerce will be good this year, and I can gather more taxes for Caesar.* "Hail Caesar," he muttered sarcastically. *How much longer is he going to keep me in this miserable place? My wife hungers for the ambiance of the Roman courts.*

His thoughts were interrupted by a soldier who stepped in and announced that the Galilean had arrived.

Well let's get this over with as quickly and painlessly as possible, thought Pilate, as he indicated for the soldier to bring him in.

The solder exited and quickly returned with Joshua, hands still bound.

Pilate, quietly appraised Joshua as he entered the room and approached the place where he sat. *He doesn't look the worse for wear. No cuts or bruises I can see. His tunic is a bit dirty and his feet are filthy, but he carries himself well . . . almost a bit of a swagger even though he looks weary.*

"Are you the king of the Jews?" he asked abruptly. No niceties or casual preliminaries: Straight and to the point.

"You say so." Joshua responded in a quiet monotone.

"The chief priest has accused you of many things. How do you answer those charges?"

An awkward silence ensued. As Pilate sat, waiting for some response, he mused, *What is this fellow doing? He knows I can release him or order his death. He just stands there staring at me as though I was a meaningless stranger inquiring into his private business.*

For a long moment Pilate sat, staring at Joshua and patiently waiting for some reply. He began to feel awkward, as though he was in a staring contest like a couple of school boys . . . and he was losing. He rose from his cushioned seat and strode over to a distant window that overlooked the courtyard below. A crowd had begun to gather. He remembered that a custom at their Passover holiday was to have him release one of the prisoners whom they would choose. *It has something to do with their once having been enslaved and set free, he vaguely recalled.*

Well, here is my chance to get rid of this fellow and get on with the business of the day. Pilate felt a wave of relief as he realized this. Quickly he formed a plan: *I have this murderer, Barabbas, who was arrested in the last insurrection. They will not want that renegade running free in the streets,* he reasoned. *I will make him the other choice, then let this Joshua go back home to Galilee. My guess is that it is pure jealousy that has him in this situation.* He stepped out on the balcony and addressed the crowd: "This year I offer you a choice between Joshua the healing prophet from Galilee or Barabbas, the man who committed murder and is sentenced to die. Whom will you choose to set free?"

To his surprise the voices began to chant, "We want Barabbas. We want Barabbas. Give us Barabbas." Unknown to Pilate it had been the priests who had assembled the crowd and encouraged them to free "our freedom fighter, Barabbas."

What is happening? asked Pilate to himself. *I do not want to free this murderer; neither should they. The man could stir up a riot that would lead to a slaughter.*

"Then what should I do with this man that many of you call The King of the Jews?" he pleaded, hoping this would bring at least some of the crowd to their senses.

Pilate had been outmaneuvered, however. The chief priests also had stirred up the crowd to call for Joshua's death, calling him a dangerous trouble maker who would destroy the Law of Moses.

"Crucify him! Crucify him!" was their angry response.

Pilate hesitated. He was in a dilemma of his own making. He did not wish to kill this harmless Galilean, but even more importantly he did not wish to free a dangerous anti-Roman murderer.

As he stood in his indecision the sound of the crowd grew louder and more agitated.

Calls of "Free Barabbas! Free Barabbas!" blended together with demands to "Crucify him! Crucify him!"

Finally Pilate turned to Joshua, stared briefly into his eyes, then he turned to the soldier and said, "You have heard the crowd. Take this man below and prepare him for crucifixion and tell one of the others to go to the prison and release Barabbas."

The soldier stood still for a brief moment, then stepped over to Joshua, grabbed him firmly by his arm and led him away.

CHAPTER SIXTY-FOUR

THE GAME OF KINGS

The soldier could barely contain his pleasure and excitement as he led Joshua into the courtyard. "Attention, all of you. This man claims to be *King* of the Jews!" he shouted. Instantly the soldiers realized the implications. Garrison soldiers often broke the tedium of dull duty by playing a game known as "The Game of Kings." The design for the game was carved in the stone of the courtyard. It was played with dice, with penalties and rewards for certain combinations. It was a cruel game, but the officers allowed it. Some even encouraged it because it allowed the soldiers to vent any pent up anger against authority on the condemned prisoner. They put a robe and fake crown on him, mocked him, spit on him, and abused him, all the while hailing him as king. Some of the rougher soldiers might even kick him and smash their fist into his face . . . all the while pretending to be bowing to him as king.

The winner won the right to slay the king with his sword.

"Good for the men's morale," claimed many of the officers.

"Good for us, too" thought many of the officers. *"It vents their anger on others than us."*

Quickly some of the soldiers had gathered the paraphernalia they kept stored nearby. One placed a purple cloak on Joshua's shoulders. Another pushed a crow of thorns tightly down on his head, causing blood to pour out in three or four areas. Many began to bow down in front of him or to salute him mockingly One grabbed a long, heavy reed and began to pummel his head.

Another spat upon him. All the while each in turn stooped down and rolled the dice, moving his token appropriately after he saw the results.

They are going to crucify him, so what does the winner get?" asked one of the soldiers as he knelt to take his turn with the dice.

"Let him have the prisoner's tunic" replied another. They paused, looked at the tunic and at one another. "Good enough. It's the playing that counts," agreed the dice thrower.

So that's what I am to them, thought Joshua. A game. A way to pass the time. Nothing more. His eyes lifted skyward. *Father, is this what you had in mind when you created us?* The idea seemed to cause more pain than that which the soldiers were inflicting. *How do we humans ever sink to such low levels?* The question seemed to absorb his attention and for the moment he was inured to the punishment the soldiers were meting out.

One of the soldiers disappeared then reappeared with a scourging whip in his hand. It was a terrible looking instrument, with barbs on the ends of the many leather straps. He tore back the robe and began beating Joshua mercilessly until one of the officers stepped forward. "Wait a minute, Alieus," the officer demanded. "We need this man healthy enough to carry his cross."

Reluctantly, the soldier, who obviously had been drinking too much wine that day, dropped the whip. Without a word he walked over to a bench and sat, pouting like an angry schoolboy who had just lost a favorite toy.

Joshua watched this interchange, his head bent drooping from the burning agony of the whip. He could feel the blood dripping down his back. Although he had barely moved a muscle during the ordeal he felt exhausted and wished very dearly that he could just lie down and rest for a moment or so. Even as this desire was expressing itself wordlessly the centurion stepped forward and declared. "Enough of the game, men. We need to move on to

Golgotha. It already is late in the morning. We shall have to force our way through the market area and it will take some time before we are able to get where we need to go." "Emil," he shouted, calling to one of the men standing by the game, waiting his turn with the dice. "Pick up the cross beam for his cross and lift it onto the prisoner's shoulders. The custom is that he must carry it."

Emil walked over to where a few large wooden beams were piled. He grabbed the first he saw and took it to Joshua. "Hold onto this and do not drop it. Someone will whip you if you do," he warned.

Joshua nodded his understanding. He steadied himself for a moment, testing the weight and balance of the beam. Then he fell behind one of the soldiers and began walking into the city.

He had not gone more than a mile before he realized the entire ordeal: dangling over the cistern for the night, unable to sleep, the beating and whipping had drained him of his usual energy. He was stumbling. He was a bloody mess. His feet slipped over any wet spot. People in the crowded street bumped against the wooden beam and caused him to loose his balance.

The centurion turned back observed Joshua's condition. *We must get to Golgotha in good time. I do not want the reputation of not being able to deliver on schedule*, he thought. He looked into the crowd and spotted a fairly sturdy looking man. "You there!" he commanded.

Simon of Cyrene had come to the city for the Passover. His wife was tending to purchasing the food they would need while there. He was merely passing the time by roaming through the market stalls and admiring the craftsmanship of the artists. He was lost in thought when he heard a commanding voice directed his way. He looked up and saw a Roman centurion pointing at him. "Me?" he asked incredulously.

"Yes, you. Come here", the centurion answered with an obvious air of impatience. "You are to take this prisoner's cross beam and carry it for him. I will tell you when you may let go if it and return here."

Simon was a stranger, but he knew enough to not even question a centurion when ordered to do something. The law was that any Roman soldier could order any Jew to carry a burden for one mile. *If he wants me carry this all day, I suppose I must do it,* Simon philosophized as he lifted the beam off of Joshua's shoulders and placed it on his own.

Although Simon did not turn his head to look at the prisoner by his side he sensed his presence – a powerful presence. *His body may be weary,* Simon thought, *but this man's spirit is strong. I wonder what he has done that the Romans want to kill him.* They walked along together, neither of them speaking to the other, but Simon silently growing in his admiration for this stranger by his side. *I do not understand this, I sense no fear in him, no weariness of soul. I even feel a certain serenity just walking by his side. I wonder if he could be this prophet from Galilee that I have been hearing about. Many believe he is the messiah, the anointed one of God. Not as another King David, though. No sword. No bloodshed. They say he proclaims a peaceful kingdom, so why should the Romans want him dead? It makes no sense. But if he is a king – even of a different kind – I shall do my best to let him be seen as a king by these dirty Romans.*

Having made this decision, Simon began offering words of encouragement to Joshua as they walked.

CHAPTER SIXTY-FIVE

BETRAYED!

Judas had spent the night outside of Caiaphas' villa waiting for the dawn. He trusted the high priest. Still, he had an uneasy feeling now that the plan actually was in motion. He assumed Caiaphas would have Joshua confined to a room in the villa, treating him as more of a guest than a prisoner. At least that is the impression the high priest had given him. However, the manner in which the guards had handled him once he had been placed under arrest suggested that they did not understand what actually was happening. That made sense, of course. There was no reason for them to know. *He could have told them to treat Joshua kindly,* Judas reasoned. *There was no need for drawn swords or for shoving him.*

Something just did not feel right about the evening. As he waited he reviewed in his mind the conversation between himself and Caiaphas. *I know what he said about the danger was true. Joshua did take us to Caesarea Philippi, and there could only be one reason for that. I must just be feeling jittery because it is out of my hands now. I've done my part. I can only wait.* He relaxed and leaned back against a tree and closed his eyes for a brief nap.

Judas was startled from his nap by the sound of men stomping down the path toward the city. They were muttering and making far too much noise to be merely taking a morning walk into town. He peered around the tree and saw Joshua, hands bound in front of him, and being led with a short rope like an animal.

His mind tried to grasp what he was seeing. *This is not what we planned.* He started to scream for them to stop, but realized that would be futile. No one in that crowd knew of what he and the high priest had discussed. Some instinct told him that if he interfered he, too, might be bound and led down the path toward Pilate's palace.

He ducked his head behind the tree and held his breath until they all had passed beyond his sight. Then, surreptitiously, he began to follow.

When he arrived at Pilate's palace he stationed himself in a distant corner in the courtyard as a crowd began to gather. He noticed that the people in the crowd were being led – herded actually – into the yard by some of the priests.

For a long time they merely waited while the priests walked among them, obviously stirring them up, but Judas could not hear their words.

Finally, Pilate appeared at his balcony and began shouting to them. He said something about offering them a choice. *What is it he is saying?"* thought Judas: *"King of the Jews" I can make that out. Barabbas? Who is this Barabbas?*

Pilate shouted even louder and this time Judas heard the choice clearly: "Joshua or Barabbas?"

This must be what Caiaphas planned, Judas thought with a flood of relief. He has planned that the crowd should demand his release. We can go back to Galilee now. Today! He laughed aloud as he realized the cleverness of the high priest's plan. The Romans, themselves, will release him. The people will cheer and we can go home.

Even as he was celebrating this, some portion of his mind was contradicting him: "Barabbas! Give us Barabbas!" is what the crowd was shouting.

Judas listened carefully now as Pilate demanded, "Then what should I do with Joshua?"

"Crucify him! Crucify him!" they shouted back almost in unison.

Judas' mind was reeling. He steadied himself by placing a hand on the wall beside him. He was too stunned to even try to reason what had happened. All he knew was that his master was about to die . . . and he . . . he, Judas Iscariot, had caused this to happen.

Tears flowing from his eyes he literally staggered to the courtyard entrance and weaved through the crowd toward the street that would lead to Golgotha.

Once there, he again found a secluded corner where he could see the street clearly. After what seemed to him to be a lifetime he heard the soldiers approaching with three prisoners stripped almost naked and carrying the cross bar upon which they would be nailed. Joshua, however, was not carrying a bar. Another man was, and as he walked along he appeared to be speaking to Joshua from the corner of his mouth.

Blood is dripping down his face from that terrible crown of thorns they have placed there. His eyes are tired. His moth is swollen and bleeding where some coward hit him, he thought angrily. *His entire back is covered with blood. Oh my God what have I done?* He practically screamed. Judas stood, transfixed, wanting to look away, but finding it impossible to do so.

Joshua was almost at a point even with Judas, when his head suddenly swung to the right and for a brief moment he looked directly into Judas' eyes. Weary and beaten as he was, his eyes seemed to penetrate into Judas' soul: no recrimination; no anger. Only a sad acknowledgement that tacitly declared, "I understand and I forgive." Then he turned his head forward and continued on his way.

The dam burst within Judas. He slumped to the ground and gathered himself in a fetal position . . . blubbering like a broken-hearted child.

By the time his sobbing had calmed the throng had moved far beyond where he lay. Slowly he arose, his head still spinning, and he began to grope his way back to the Temple.

I recognized some of the priests in Pilate's courtyard. They are always at the Temple! Judas thought angrily. *Dirty, cheating priests, prying on people's piety to line their own pockets. I should have known better than to trust any of them! Caiaphas: The high liar! The worst of the lot!* He began to weep again, "My God! My God! What have I done?"

He continued staggering through the streets picking his way through the crowd that seemed to have returned to their shopping, glad the disturbance was over and they could continue searching for bargains.

When he arrived at the Temple he rushed through the outer courtyards and right up to the Temple's entrance. There he saw the priest who had lured him to Caiaphas' villa standing beside the one who had pretended to befriend him.

"You thieving, lying murderers!" he screamed, so loudly that the pilgrims in line looked his way.

Seeing them, Judas shouted louder: "These pious priests who are slaughtering your gifts for their own gain are nothing but criminals. Criminals dressed in priestly garb!"

He turned again to the two he knew who now were standing, frightened and unsure of what Judas was planning to do.

Judas reached inside his tunic and pulled out the fine leather pouch Caiaphas had given him. He untied the draw string, lifted the pouch over his head and began to swing it wildly, scattering some of the silver coins as he did so. Then he stopped, reached his hand inside the pouch and threw a handful of the coins directly at the two priests. As they ducked to avoid being hit, Judas threw the bag at them as well. "Here, take this also," he shouted at them. "You can use it for transporting the coins from the Temple to the money changers!"

Those in the courtyard stood as still as statues during all of this. As Judas spun around and began striding out of the yard a few pilgrims in the line began cheering. Judas, however, was oblivious to their cheers. He walked toward the far city gates, not even acknowledging the guards' greetings as he passed through.

Once outside – on the opposite side of where Joshua now was hanging on a cross, he pulled a knife from beneath his tunic and thrust it deeply into his stomach. As he lay dying in the barren field his hand began to stretch out . . . toward Golgotha.

CHAPTER SIXTY-SIX

GOLGOTHA

Joshua felt as though they had been trudging their way through seemingly endless streets of Jerusalem forever. The insults no longer were anything but blurs of distant speech. The faces of those who watched also had become blurred, fading into the backgrounds of the many market stalls and continual walls.

He was only dimly aware of passing through the thick city gates where he now felt an openness of space and the absence of crowds. Simon continued to speak words of encouragement to him, but they no longer really mattered. *Let this come to an end. I want no more of it*, were his only thoughts . . . if they could be called "thoughts." It was more of a vague longing of the soul than a clear message of his dimming mind.

"Take heart, my friend. We are almost there." Simon whispered in his ear.

Joshua raised his head and through squinted eyes saw a rocky hill in the form of a skull directly ahead of them.

"Just a few more steps and we shall be there," whispered Simon. "You can make it. Do not let the Romans see you stagger."

With these words, Joshua straightened himself as best he could and lifted his head. He reached down for something deep within and, for the moment, he regained something of the old familiar stride that had been admired by so many. Not as some beaten slave but more like a king, Joshua ascended the hill with his servant, Simon, bearing the instrument of his execution for him. He approached the place where the vertical post had been planted in the ground, looking directly into the eyes of those men awaiting him with a hammer and nails in hand. Then he stopped and motioned to Simon to relinquish his burden as though it was his right to direct his own demise.

The centurion almost gasped in amazement to see the sudden resurgence of this man who had been so cruelly scourged. *Look at him: bloody, and badly beaten!* he thought. *Yet this man who should either be dead or whimpering in the street from the scourging stands there like the one who is in command.* Then, as though suddenly remembering that he was the one in command, the centurion stepped forward and began giving the orders:

"You!" he said, pointing at one of the soldiers, "Lay him down and nail his wrists to the crossbar." He pointed at two of the largest soldiers. "When he is finished you two lift the bar and place it on the post. Then," he pointed back to one who held the hammer: "You nail his feet to the post." He then turned to Joshua and inquired, "Would you like some wine mixed with myrrh? It will lessen your pain."

Joshua hesitated for just a moment. *I will not give these men the satisfaction of thinking I cannot bear the pain.* "No," he said, as though declining an offer from a servant. "That will not be necessary." Then he added, "But thank you."

The centurion stood for a moment, still foolishly holding the cup toward Joshua as though he expected him to drink from it. "As you wish," he said with a touch of respect in his voice. Then he turned again to his men and said in the most commanding tone he could muster, "Well do not just stand there. Get on with the crucifixions. When you have finished with this man, place that one." He pointed to one of the other prisoners, "over on that post, and then the other one over on that one," he gestured toward a post on the other side of Joshua.

With that, he turned and stationed himself at the outer edge of the scene. He folded his arms and looked about: First at the crowd and then back at his men and Joshua in a manner he hoped would convey the impression that he was the commander.

Joshua felt a rush of pain as the soldier nailed his wrists to the wooden beam. It passed quickly, however, as it blended in with the searing pain that now seemed to have taken up residence in his body. As they hammered the nails into his feet he watched with an almost detached curiosity. *I thought the nails were in the legs, but of course the bone is thick. That would create a problem. The feet make more sense.* Even as these thoughts moved through his mind he almost laughed at the absurdity of them.

Now I wait . . . just hang here until the last bit of life has drained out of my body.

I wonder how long that will take . . . I hope not too long, he thought as he became increasingly aware of the ever-present agony that burned everywhere within him.

He attempted to diminish the pain by focusing upon his surroundings. On his right he saw one of the prisoners – a petty thief who had made the fatal mistake of attempting to steal from the wife of a Roman diplomat. The man was quietly weeping and muttering to himself, oblivious to the crowd that had gathered closer now that the three of them were safely nailed to their crosses. Joshua looked at the small crowd that had focused upon this poor thief and thought he could see the husband of the woman the man had tried to rob. He was well dressed – obviously a Roman. He showed no emotion, but simply stared at the man with a sense of distain and satisfaction, watching his aguish.

He looked over to the prisoner on the other side who seemed to be sneering back at the crowd, not wishing to give them the satisfaction of seeing his fear or his pain. The man had not been scourged. Joshua made a quick calculation: *He is young and muscular. It will take some hours before the pain weakens him enough to tear his façade. By that time most of the onlookers will have gone away. He just may be able to hold out . . . but then . . . he may be too healthy and it will take days for him to die. The crowd will be back . . . and they will see him in all his weakness and all of his pain.*

What is it, he thought, *that causes people to be so attracted to watching death? They fear it for themselves but are drawn to it when it happens to others.* He pondered this for some time. *They simply do not understand it, is my guess. They have no grasp of Yahweh's great plan for all his people. They see death as the end of everything, so they fear it . . . yet are fascinated by its mystery.*

His thoughts were interrupted as another surge of pain raged through his body. For a long while he just hung there, inert, not unconscious but only vaguely aware of even his own existence. No thoughts occurred. The continual stream of insults hurled by some cowardly bystanders was no more than indistinct, distant roars, like the sound of waves splashing themselves on a beach.

Finally the pain had dulled to the point where he was, once again, aware of where he was and what was happening to him.

His head was bent down so he first became aware of the soldiers playing a game of dice beneath him. *The Game of Kings goes on*, he thought. *The winner doesn't get to kill me, so they are playing for my robe. How pathetic! What happened to them that they have no feeling for other people? They do not realize* it, *but they are captives more than the people they believe they control. They are imprisoned within themselves — unable to become free and to live in a caring community.*

He quickly turned away from them, partly in disgust, partly in despair for them.

He began to listen to the voices in the crowd, distracting himself by trying to guess their motives for being there.

"You up there!" some shouted. "You who destroy the Temple and rebuild it in three days." Joshua turned his head to see who the speaker was. It was one of the Pharisees, shouting and shaking his fist at him. "Yes, you!" the priest said now that he had Joshua's attention. "Well, miracle worker, come on down off of that cross and save yourself!" he taunted, and looked about with satisfaction at those near to him. Joshua looked carefully at the speaker. The sun was glaring into his eyes, but he recognized the speaker's voice. It was Isaac, the Pharisee who had questioned him back in Galilee. *I had embarrassed him then,* Joshua thought. *This is his petty little way of getting back at me.*

Joshua ignored the taunt and looked away as though Isaac had never spoken. Words no longer mattered to him. Words were only . . . well . . . only words. They had no substance. He was dealing directly with reality. *Pain, thirst, death. These are my realities now. Your words cannot and will not affect me,* he thought. *Put on your mighty display for others if you must. But I no longer listen . . . or even care what you say.*

I am finding it difficult to breathe. It is as though my lungs are being squeezed.

For a long time Joshua was content to just hang on the cross in silence, trying to quiet the storm that raged through his body.

Some of the priests and scribes joined in the mocking.

"Let this self-appointed messiah come down from the cross so that we also may believe in him." someone shouted, and this was followed by roars of laughter.

Once again Joshua ignored them. *Words. Only words,* he thought.

After a while Joshua focused again on the crowd. This time he peered farther back, wondering if any of those who had been his disciples were among them. His eye caught three women huddled together, watching intently but apparently trying to be un-

noticed. *Mary Magdalene! Salome! . . . and Mary, Clopas' wife!
Why am I not surprised? Your loyalty has always been extraordinary.
The men have all the power and authority in this society of ours, but you
women are possessed of a strength and courage that puts so many of us to
shame.* He nodded ever so slightly in their direction, so as not to
draw any attention to them. Mary raised her hand as though she
was straightening her garment . . . but Joshua understood that she
was signaling acknowledgment of his awareness of them.

The late morning sun was relentlessly beating down upon his
bare skin. Sweat was dripping from his hair into his eyes. He
looked away from the crowd, turning his face as far northward as
possible to avoid the glare in his eyes. The sky there was black.
What appeared to be an endless stream of dark clouds were rolling
toward Jerusalem. He felt a twinge of relief as he gazed at the
approaching clouds. *Well at least I will not fry to death,* he mused
wryly.

He watched the clouds with a sense of detachment. They were
approaching rapidly, as if being blown along by some unseen,
powerful force. Within minutes they had arrived and shrouded
the entire area in darkness. The air cooled and the earth itself
seemed to become calm and silent.

Somewhere from a deep well that still flowed within him, a
feeling of warmth and love seeped throughout his being and, for
the moment at least, he felt no pain – no discomfort.

He lay still, holding on to that precious moment until the
pain crawled back into his consciousness. Then he began to force
pleasant memories into his awareness. He conjured up early recollections of his days with Joseph. His father had seemed so tall
and strong and wise in their early days together. There came the
day when he invited Joshua to "Come to work with me and I will
show you how to build things that will last." He had eagerly held
out his hand to receive his lunch as Mary always prepared one for

Joseph. Then they went off to the city of Sepphoris where Joseph was constructing a house. The family for whom he was working was obviously wealthy. The plans called for a combination of wood and stones. The stones were to be shaped so that they fit together snugly and would not require much filling. Joseph carefully demonstrated his technique for shaping the stones with a piece of metal he called a chisel. He also taught Joshua what to look for in selecting a tree for its wood. Most of all Joshua remembered the banter between them as they walked or worked. Joseph had a different way of looking at life than most of the men of the village. He saw beneath the surface – things that required an insightful inner eye. As a result he not only imparted wisdom but humor during their time together. At this remembrance, some part of him wondered briefly if he would see Joseph again . . . anytime soon.

Before he could linger over that thought he lifted his body to take a deep breath, and a surge of scorching pain swept through him and erased everything from his mind except the terrible awareness of burning agony. The words of David came pouring out of his mouth: "My God! My God, why have you forsaken me?" [1] The soldiers interrupted their game and looked up when they heard him shouting. Isaac, watching from afar, grinned openly as the words reached his ears. When Nicodemus heard his cry he winced inside, sensing the horrible pain that would have required Joshua to cry out in that manner. He looked over at Joseph of Arimathea, who nodded back sadly.

I must not let that happen again, Joshua thought. *When there is nothing you can do but die, then how you die is important.* Quickly his mind rushed to a passage further along in the psalm: *For dominion belongs to the Lord and he rules over the nations. Yes, to Him shall all the proud of the earth bow down, before him shall bow all who go down*

[1] Psalm 22:1

to the dust, and he who cannot keep himself alive. Posterity shall serve him; men shall tell of the Lord to the coming generation, and proclaim his deliverance to a people yet unborn that he has wrought it. [*2]

One of soldiers who apparently had dropped from the game came running to Joshua. He had a sponge stuck on a long pole offering him some of the drugged wine that had been offered to him earlier. As he did so, he said to those nearby, "Let's see if Elijah will come and take him down." Joshua ignored his words, and drank the wine gratefully.

He immediately slipped into a quiet stupor – no longer looking about – no longer hearing the words. Everything had become blurred.

For a long time he merely hung passively, almost oblivious to his surroundings. He vaguely felt the weakness overtaking his weary frame . . . the life draining from his body. He desperately needed to breathe, but that required more effort than he wanted to give . . . and more pain than he wished to endure.

Darkness . . . silence . . .

Dim thoughts began to drift by, and Joshua watched them as though observing a pantomime drama.

Then he felt a stirring as he saw himself walking into a house he vaguely recognized. It was Rachel's, and she was in the kitchen, preparing a meal. She turned and smiled as he entered. Next to her, sitting on the table was a lovely little girl about three years of age. For some reason he could not understand, he knew her name and called to her: "Rebecca, my little darling," he heard himself saying as he lifted her to him and kissed her on her forehead. On the floor beside them, a baby boy was playing, and Joshua knelt down and lifted him up. "Little Joseph," he whispered. "I missed you today." Then Rachel stepped toward him and for a brief moment he felt

---

[*2] Psalm 22:29-31

her warm body next to his in a loving embrace . . . Then a torrential flood of pain surged through his being, and Rachel and what-might-have-been Rebecca and Joseph disappeared from his vision.

The rupturing pain in his heart overrode that which was in his body. He screamed aloud with a cry of despair that startled the bystanders and seemed to echo across the land.

Then . . . slowly he felt himself sinking deeper into the darkness that engulfed him. Deeper and deeper he sank. All awareness of pain diminished and finally vanished.

There was only quietness – peace.

The crowd sensed what was happening. Some wept. Some yelled out their final insults. But Joshua no longer could hear them. His body sagged on the cross, but he already had gone far beyond the place of the skull, far away from the walls of Jerusalem.

> *. . . slowly, as though rising from the depths of a bottom-less ocean,*
> *Joshua became aware – of being – of his being - of his awareness of his being.*

Then, as he felt himself rising, he noticed a distant light began to glow through the darkness. Joshua felt himself drawn closer and closer as the light glowed brighter and brighter. The light soon began to surround and embrace him – *Yes*, he thought – *This light actually is embracing me. I cannot feel it . . . yet I do feel it somewhere deep within some portion of my being.* He did not question it or wonder. He merely accepted and gave way to its soothing softness and warmth. A sense of peace such as he had never experienced seemed to reside everywhere within him. He heard – no, not *heard*; rather he *understood* unspoken words whispering into his soul: "Welcome home, my son."

CHAPTER SIXTY-SEVEN

THE BURIAL

When the centurion, who had stood facing Joshua throughout the entire ordeal, realized that Joshua had breathed his last, he looked out at the crowd and declared solemnly: "Surely this man was a son of a god." [*1].

The soldier who was leading in the game, picked up Joshua's tunic, stood up, laughed and said, "He died just at the right time. I had just gone ahead." Another responded in disgust: "Stubborn Jews! Even when you kill them they have a way of beating you."

Salome and her two companions stood silently weeping for a long moment, then they turned away and went back toward the city gate. "What will happen to his body?" Salome asked aloud. "Let us stay by the gate to see," Mary Magdalene suggested. The others nodded and so they sat down against the wall and waited.

Joseph of Arimathea went immediately to Pilate's palace and requested permission to bury Joshua's body. Pilate was surprised to learn that Joshua had died so quickly, so he told Joseph to wait until he received verification that Joshua actually had died. He summoned the centurion and began pacing nervously while waiting for him to arrive. *Is this some sort of trick?* he asked himself. *Normally it takes a few days for a man to die in this manner. That is one reason we use crucifixion against these pesky Jews. It strikes fear into*

[*1] The Greek reads: "*Alethos outos 'o anthropos uios theou en.*" This literally means: Truly this the man a son of a god was." In order for it to say "*the* son of *the* God" both *uios* and *theou* would have had to be preceded by *'o* as *anthropos* was. In the Greek whenever *theous* is meant to designate the Christian deity, it is always preceded by the definite article *'o* (pronounced *huh*).

their hearts when they walk along the road and see one of their own twisting in agony on a cross. But then, he remembered, *the man did receive a terrible scourging. That alone might have killed many men.* With that thought, he relaxed, seated himself by a window and ordered a guard to pour him a glass of wine.

He had barely begun sipping the wine when the centurion appeared and gave assurance that Joshua actually had died. "On your way out," he said, "tell that well-dressed Jew who will be sitting in the outer room that he has my permission to bury his friend." With that, he relaxed, turned to look out the window with a sense of satisfaction and took a deep drink of his wine, savoring its flavor in his mouth before swallowing.

Joseph returned to Golgotha where he met with Nicodemus who had already arranged for Joshua's removal from the cross and had recruited two acquaintances to assist with carrying the body to Joseph's tomb. Joseph was a strong believer in the coming Kingdom of God and had purchased a plot of land just outside of the city wall. There was a long-standing belief that any future resurrection would begin in Jerusalem, so those who could afford it, had their burial place near the city in order to be among the first. At this time Nicodemus was pleased that his friend had such foresight. It meant a short exertion at worst.

The four men carried Joshua's body to the tomb. Joseph unfolded the linen cloth he had brought along and with great care and tenderness – as though dressing a delicate child – they wrapped his body in the cloth and they lowered it slowly to the ground in the place provided for it.

When the three women had seen Joseph returning to Golgotha, they followed at a distance and continued on until they saw where the men had laid Joshua's body. "When the Sabbath is over," Mary said, "we shall return to prepare his body properly." I have already purchased spices so that we may properly anoint him," offered

Salome. As she said this, she turned and gazed toward the tomb that now held her nephew's body. *Oh Joshua! Joshua! My beloved boy! I could not have loved you more if you had been mine and not my sister's.* Brushing an unashamed tear from her eye, she said, "Let us meet here before dawn so as not to attract unwanted attention."

CHAPTER SIXTY-EIGHT

THE EMPTY TOMB

When the Sabbath had ended the three women met where they had last watched the tomb. "I have the spices," said Salome. "And I brought a fresh cloth . . . with a fresh odor," added Mary Magdalene in such a way that no explanation was needed.

"Ready?" asked the other Mary. Without waiting for a response she continued, "Then let's go."

The three walked across the open space until they could dimly see the tomb carved into the side of the low-lying cliff. Suddenly Salome recalled seeing the four men roll a huge wheel-shaped rock along a slot until it completely sealed off the tomb entrance.

"Who will roll away the stone?" she asked. The other women stopped as though they had walked into a tree. "I never thought of that!" Mary Magdalene said half in disgust, thinking that their careful planning had completely overlooked the obvious.

"Well the three of us can try, and if we cannot do it, we can go and ask James and John," said Salome. "I know I can get them to do it for us," she added with a trace of a chuckle.

With that assurance they continued walking until they could see the tomb clearly in the dusky light.

"Wait!" Mary exclaimed in a whispering voice. "Someone already has rolled the stone away. The entrance is open."

A wave of fear flowed through the trio as they stood staring at the open tomb. Still they proceeded, a bit more carefully, to the open entrance way. As they entered they saw a young man, dressed in a white robe,*1 sitting on the right side. "Do not be alarmed, he said. "You are looking for Joshua of Nazareth who was crucified. He has been raised; he is not here. Look," he said, pointing at the place where Joshua had been laid. "There is the place where they laid him. Go tell his disciples – and Rock – he added with emphasis – that he is going ahead of you to Galilee. There you will see him just as he told you."

They turned and fled from the tomb, saying nothing to anyone – even to each other. What they had just experienced was beyond their comprehension. It terrified them. In confused alarm and fright they huddled together and walked away as quickly as they could.

---

*1 Mark, the earliest of the gospel accounts says, "young man" where Matthew and Luke speak of either one or two "angels". The term angel (Greek angelos) actually means *messenger*. Time and circumstances transformed the term to its present day meaning, but at the time of Mark's writing *angelos* designated a messenger.

INTERLUDE

This is the original ending to Mark's account. For this writer, the ending serves as a proof for the resurrection. It is more convincing than many of the tales of post-resurrection sightings. The reason is this: I believe the acceptance of Jesus' resurrection was so widespread that there was no need to go beyond this ending when the account was written. The appearances were added with the passage of time, when there were many who had never heard of - or had difficulty believing in – the resurrection. At this time, later copyists began to add the tales they had heard in order to give more credibility to Mark's account.

Eventually these additions became known as the longer ending.

This writer has taken the liberty of adding a third ending. I do this primarily because my personal faith does not rest on a physical resurrection. Paul only encountered the resurrected Christ – not the physically resurrected Jesus. We, today, will not encounter a physically resurrected Jesus, but it is my firm belief that we *can* and *do* encounter the Risen Christ as surely as did Paul on the road to Damascus. The purpose of our Christian faith is not to learn *about* Jesus, and to be able to quote ancient Scripture *about* him. The quest for today's Christian is to find a vital, redemptive relationship *with* the Risen Christ. In this living relationship we are able to live and to act in the fellowship and knowledge of the Living God.

It is this understanding that I offer my completely non-Biblical, non-traditional ending.

CHAPTER SIXTY-NINE

VISITATIONS

James lay sleeping in the house he shared with his mother, Mary, and his brothers and sisters. He was far removed from Jerusalem and had no knowledge of what had happened to his brother, Joshua. He was roused into a foggy awareness that something was different in the house. He lay quietly for a moment, listening to ascertain if there was someone awake and moving. As he lay there his eyes began to survey what might be in the room, for he felt a presence, as he did whenever someone whose presence he was unaware of actually was somewhere nearby.

"Anyone there?" he inquired rather foggily, still trying to pull himself from his once-peaceful slumber.

"James," a familiar voice whispered. "James" the voice repeated. "Say nothing. Just listen," the voice ordered, quietly but firmly. "You know who I am. There is much you soon will learn Wait until others tell you about me and what has happened. Then go to Capernaum and find your cousins and Simon. There will be a few others with them, but go first to those three and tell them this: 'Joshua has told me to join you. Simon you will know this is true when I ask you about a cock crowing.' Call him Rock. He likes that and needs to hear it from you. Then say to James and John, "You will know this is true when I tell you that you are not to sit on either side, but you *are* to drink his cup.' Can you remember that? Just nod if you can. I can see you clearly." James nodded and waited for his brother to continue.

"James, I need you to take charge of these disciples of mine. Don't ask why. You will learn soon enough," he added hastily. "Simon Rock has great possibilities, but he is not yet ready to take the lead. James and John are good men but their task will not be to lead. That is why I need you, James. You know me and you know my thinking. Be true to that. When you learn what has happened I think you will believe the things I have tried to teach you. Now close your eyes and return to your rest. In three days you will hear the word from Jerusalem that will tell you it is time to act."

There was a long pause. Then the voice whispered, "I love you my brother. Remember that, and tell the whole family: Mary, Elizabeth, Joanne. Simon, Joseph and Judas. Tell each of them that. Address them by name when you do."

James nodded his agreement and waited to see if Joshua would tell him more. When there had been nothing said for a minute or so, he whispered, "Joshua, are you still there?" There was no sound in response. James lay quietly for a moment, attempting to digest what he had just experienced. *There had been no sound of movement. Yet he came and he left.* He asked himself, *Did I actually see him? There appeared to be a dim figure in the corner where I heard his voice. But I don't believe I really saw him . . . or anyone,* he added to himself. Eventually James felt sleepy and so he rolled over and closed his eyes. But throughout the remainder of the night, he slept only fitfully.

Simon had found a place outside of the wall where he felt reasonable safe. There was a patch of olive trees that gave some shield against the wind. He had wrapped himself in a spare robe he had brought along to ward off the chilly nights that were the rule in Jerusalem in the spring of the year. His sleep was constantly interrupted by brief flashes of images of Joshua hanging on a cross. He had watched the entire episode through a small window in a house by the wall. He had seen him staggering toward the hill and then straighten, and with the bearing of a king ascend to the place where he was to die. He had watched and winced while the soldiers nailed his wrists and his feet to the cross. He had agonized throughout the six hours he watched his master die, all the while mentally flagellating himself for his cowardliness. Now in the early hours, as dawn was approaching, weariness had finally won the battle for sleep. His breathing was slow, even with a trace of a snore as he lay motionless on the ground.

A quiet voice began to break into that peacefulness: "Rock. Rock," it repeated. "Rock, do you hear me?" Not quite awake but able to give some response, Rock mumbled, "No, I am not awake. Let me sle- - - " Suddenly his mind had grasped whose voice he was hearing. Before he could move, however, the voice said, "Stay still, Rock. Just lie still and listen. I told you that I would rise again, and I have. Don't move!" he commanded. "Just lie there and listen to me. You need to understand and remember what I am going to tell you. Mary Magdalene will confirm this. I *have* risen. Yahweh means for our lives to continue beyond this earthly existence. We are to use this time for preparation for that life as well as to enjoy this one and live in a way to help all others. I want you to go to the place in Galilee where we first crossed over to the Decapolis. Do you remember where that was? Nod if you do." Simon, thought for a moment then nodded. "Good. My brother James will meet you later in Capernaum. Remain in the area until he arrives. He is to take my place. Do you understand? Nod again if you do." Again, Simon nodded. "Good. You will finally take that place, Rock, but you have much to learn before you will be ready. I want Mary to go to Galilee with the others. Find someone from our number to replace Judas before you go. When I leave, get up. You will not be able to sleep after this anyway," the voice said with a laugh.

Simon wiped his eyes and waited for more instructions, but none were forthcoming. He looked around to see if there was any sign of Joshua. There had been no sound of footsteps, but he was gone.

Simon waited for a moment for his head to clear. Then he rose and went to find the others.

Mary Magdalene had returned to her room, alone and still shaking from the experience. Her room had but one narrow window, designed to let some air circulate but not large enough for any invasion of her privacy. The darkness of the night still clung to the walls. She was content to sit alone in that darkness, sorting through the extraordinary events of the morning. *I know we saw the open entrance, the young man and the empty tomb. But what does that mean? I saw Joshua die! I know he is dead, and the dead do not rise.* She hesitated . . . *but he did say that the Son of Man would rise in three days. We did not know what he was talking about at the time. He so often talked in riddles.*

As she worked with that thought she heard a voice from behind her, "Do not turn around, Mary. Just listen."

Mary froze when she heard the voice. *It's Joshua. I would know that voice anywhere,* she thought.

"What you saw this morning is real," the voice continued. "I have risen and you are to tell the others, particularly Rock, that I will meet them in Galilee. I have told Rock, but he will need your assurance. You are to go there with them. It is there that I shall meet with all of you and tell you what you are to do. For the moment it is best that you all leave Jerusalem."

Mary waited, wanting to turn to see him but half afraid to do so, and dutiful enough not to.

Finally, the voice spoke once more: "Mary, your task will be very difficult. The men, even some of our own, will not want to listen to a woman. They will attempt to defame you and silence you so that your understanding of my respect for women is lost or forgotten. Still, I ask you to be true to what you have learned from me. Eventually . . . some day . . . we men may wake up to what you women have to offer in wisdom and strength."

The voice stopped there, and Mary almost turned, but held herself in check. *He is right, but he is right that I must try to be heard,* she thought, silently vowing to be true to his wishes.

"Go to Galilee, Mary. I will see you there."

There was no other sound. No footsteps. No opening or closing of her door. Yet she knew he had gone. Mary Magdalene sat for a long moment, trying to hold on to what had just occurred. Then she bent over, placed her head in her hands and the tears that had been held back so valiantly began to flow.

- -

James continued to work, waiting as he did so for whatever word was to come. He said nothing to anyone about the visit – or dream – or vision - - - whatever it was! There had been some implied understanding that he was to wait for the message before telling anyone. Still, the days dragged on and it was difficult for him to remain focused upon the many tasks he had to fulfill.

On the third day, in the evening as James was standing outside his home waiting for the women to announce that the meal was ready, he looked up to see his neighbor, David, approaching with his donkey pulling an empty cart. *It must have been a good week for him,* thought James. *His goods are gone so he must have money in his pockets. His wife will be happy.*

As David approached, he called out: "James, I have something sad but marvelous to tell you."

Instantly, with heart pounding, James rushed to meet David as he continued to approach his house.

The moment they were close enough to talk in a normal voice, David began telling what he had heard about Joshua on his travels. As James listened to David telling his remarkable story – his eyes began to sparkle with excitement. *David, my neighbor, is the messenger I was told to wait for, he thought elatedly.* The moment David concluded his tale, patted his donkey and continued on his way home, James turned and began walking rapidly. Then he started trotting – finally he was running as fast as he could toward his house. He burst through the door shouting, "Mother! Elizabeth! - - All of you, listen!!

I have wonderful news to tell you!

Made in the USA
San Bernardino, CA
19 November 2017